THE ACHIEVEMENT OF SHERWOOD ANDERSON

Essays in Criticism

The Achievement of

Edited
with an Introduction

The University of
North Carolina Press,
Chapel Hill

SHERWOOD ANDERSON

Essays in Criticism

by RAY LEWIS WHITE

The University of North Carolina Press and the editor wish to express their gratitude to the following persons and institutions for permission to reprint copyrighted material:

To Mr. Waldo Frank for his "Emerging Greatness," *Seven Arts,* I (November, 1916), 73–78.

To Mrs. Signe Toksvig for Francis Hackett, "To American Workingmen," *New Republic,* XII (September 29, 1917), 249–50.

To Twayne Publishers, Inc., for Rex Burbank, "The Populist Temper," *Sherwood Anderson* (New York, 1964), pp. 48–60.

To The Michigan State University Press for Bernard Duffey, *The Chicago Renaissance in American Letters* (Lansing, 1954), pp. 194–209.

To *The New Republic* for "M. A.," "A Country Town," *New Republic,* XIX (June 25, 1919), 257–60.

To The Duke University Press for William L. Phillips, "How Sherwood Anderson Wrote *Winesburg, Ohio,*" *American Literature,* XXIII (March, 1951), 7–30.

To William Sloane Associates for Irving Howe, "The Book of the Grotesque," *Sherwood Anderson* (New York, 1951), pp. 91–109. Copyright 1951 by William Sloane Associates, Inc.

To The Purdue Research Association for Edwin Fussell, "*Winesburg, Ohio:* Art and Isolation," *Modern Fiction Studies,* VI (Summer, 1960), 106–14.

To Mr. Waldo Frank for his "*Winesburg, Ohio* after Twenty Years," *Story,* XIX (September–October, 1941), 29–33.

To Mr. Joseph Wood Krutch for his "Vagabonds," *Nation,* CXXI (December 2, 1925), 626–27.

To *The Georgia Review* for Walter B. Rideout, "Why Sherwood Anderson Employed Buck Fever," *Georgia Review,* XIII (Spring, 1959), 76–85.

To Mr. James Schevill for his "The Glitter of Communism," *Sherwood Anderson* (Denver, 1951), pp. 275–94.

To Mr. Charles Child Walcutt for his "Sherwood Anderson: Impressionism and the Buried Life," *American Literary Naturalism: A Divided Stream* (Minneapolis, 1956), pp. 222–39.

To The Louisiana State University Press for Frederick J. Hoffman, *Freudianism and the Literary Mind* (Baton Rouge, 1957), pp. 229–50.

To Harold Ober Associates, Inc., for William Faulkner, "Sherwood Anderson: An Appreciation," *Atlantic,* CXCI (June, 1953), 27–29. Copyright © 1953 by The Atlantic Monthly Company.

To *The University of Chicago Magazine* for William L. Phillips, "Sherwood Anderson's Two Prize Pupils," *University of Chicago Magazine*, XLVII (January, 1955), 9–12.

To The Viking Press, Inc., for Lionel Trilling, "Sherwood Anderson," *The Liberal Imagination* (New York, 1950), pp. 24–33. Copyright 1941, 1947 by Lionel Trilling. Reprinted by permission of The Viking Press, Inc.

To The Viking Press, Inc., for Malcolm Cowley, "Anderson's Lost Days of Innocence," *New Republic*, CXLII (February 15, 1960), 16–18. From *Winesburg, Ohio*, by Sherwood Anderson, Introduction by Malcolm Cowley. Copyright © by The Viking Press, Inc. Reprinted by permission of The Viking Press, Inc.

To *Shenandoah* for Frederick J. Hoffman, "The Voices of Sherwood Anderson," *Shenandoah*, XIII (Spring, 1962), 5–19.

To *The Midwest Quarterly* for David D. Anderson, "Sherwood Anderson after 20 Years," *Midwest Quarterly*, III (January, 1962), 119–32.

In Honor Of

Eleanor Copenhaver Anderson

ACKNOWLEDGMENTS

I wish to express my appreciation to Dr. H. B. Rouse and Dr. E. L. Rudolph of the University of Arkansas for guiding my early study of Sherwood Anderson; to the staff of The University of Arkansas Library for help in the compilation of these critiques; to The Newberry Library for a grant-in-aid to enable me to work with the Sherwood Anderson Papers; to Dr. Claude W. Faulkner and Mr. Rex Perkins of Fayetteville, Arkansas, who know the debt I owe them; to my colleagues in the Department of English of North Carolina State University for tolerating my frequent dissertations on Sherwood Anderson; and to the many critics and scholars who have answered my questions and allowed me to reprint their essays in this volume.

On behalf of scholars interested in the life and work of Sherwood Anderson, I wish especially to thank Mrs. Eleanor Copenhaver Anderson for kindly encouraging all students of her husband's literary career.

RLW

North Carolina State University
at Raleigh

CONTENTS

THE ACHIEVEMENT OF SHERWOOD ANDERSON

Essays in Criticism

INTRODUCTION

Ray Lewis White

1.

Sherwood Anderson (1876–1941) occupies a distinctive position in the history of American letters. He was the first American novelist of consequence to break firmly away from the tradition of gentility that had dominated the writing of fiction in the United States. He was a leader in the movement to revitalize the stream of literary naturalism by demonstrating a concern with inward, psychological reality rather than the journalistic, documentary recording of outward experience. He was among the first American writers to become aware of the implications in the work of Sigmund Freud, D. H. Lawrence, James Joyce, and Gertrude Stein. He influenced the development of the American short story more strongly than anyone except, possibly, Edgar Allan Poe; the contemporary short story has become a major form of literature through Anderson's achievement. His dramatic rejection of the business ethic in order to pursue literary endeavor has become part of the folklore of American literature. His writing strongly influenced the work of such diverse authors as Hart Crane, William Faulkner, Erskine Caldwell, Katherine Anne Porter, Ernest Hemingway, Henry Miller, James T. Farrell, and Nathanael West; indeed, Anderson was instrumental in helping Faulkner and Hemingway publish their first books. Moreover, no other writer has so thoroughly understood and so well expressed the peculiar status of the serious writer in the United States. His published works include eight novels, four collections of short stories, three books of poems and plays, more than three hundred articles, reviews, and essays, and three volumes of autobiography. He left eleven hundred manuscripts, including unpublished fiction and journals, and over twelve thousand letters written to and by most of the artistic and intellectual leaders of the twentieth century.

By the time of his death in 1941, Sherwood Anderson had seemingly won ample fame for this large volume of work. He had seen his name become common knowledge across the United States and Europe. Younger writers had paid tribute to his example and inspiration, and *Winesburg, Ohio* (1919) had been firmly established as an American classic. Among the critics and authors who had praised Anderson's writing were the following: Henry Seidel Canby, Waldo Frank, Malcolm Cowley, Hart Crane, Theodore Dreiser, Clifton Fadiman, William Faulkner, Howard Mumford Jones, Sinclair Lewis, Ludwig Lewisohn, Henry Miller, Gertrude Stein, Mark Van Doren, Edmund Wilson, and Thomas Wolfe.

And yet, in spite of this recognition, Sherwood Anderson's reputation in American letters has never been secure. At the time of his death in 1941 and with the publication of the unfinished *Memoirs* in 1942, writers and critics examined Anderson's career in order to find the measure of his achievement. His novels and essays were called "a study in non-discipline," [1] and it was said that his work lacked "the mark of high distinction that is needed to set off his undoubted originality." [2] Lionel Trilling spoke for those younger critics who found that Anderson's later works "were all too clearly an attempt to catch up with the world, but the world had moved too fast." [3] Maxwell Geismar issued the famous statement that "Sherwood Anderson had the ill luck, as was T. S. Eliot's, to become an ancestor before he became mature," [4] and Max Gissen declared that "by 1926 he had had his full say; from then on there was no development, only a sensuous, nostalgic surrender to inner confusion." [5] Harry Hartwick called him "Dreiser with the

1. Margaret Marshall, "Notes by the Way," *Nation,* CLIX (May 16, 1942), 574.

2. J. K. Paulding, "Sherwood Anderson's Memoirs," *Commonweal,* XXXVI (April 24, 1942), 20.

3. "Sherwood Anderson," *Kenyon Review,* III (Summer, 1941), 293.

4. "Babbit on Pegasus," *Yale Review,* N.S. XXXII (Autumn, 1942), 183. Geismar somewhat modified this view in *The Last of the Provincials* (Cambridge, 1947), pp. 223–84, and in his Introduction to *Sherwood Anderson: Short Stories* (New York, 1962).

5. "Back to Winesburg," *New Republic,* CVI (April 20, 1942), 548.

backbone removed. With his advent naturalism changed from muscles to nerves. . . . "[6] Finally, Alfred Kazin expressed sympathy for Sherwood Anderson's heroic struggle to overcome the limitations of the minor artist: "If he had not sought so much, he could not have been humiliated so deeply. It was always the measure of his reach that gave others the measure of his failure."[7]

If these and other literary obituaries had been accurate estimations of his achievement, Sherwood Anderson's name would soon have been forgotten by all except specialists in American literature. However, the decade after Anderson's death saw a revival of interest in his life and writing. Fortunately, the main cause of this renewed interest in Sherwood Anderson can be discovered. In 1947, Eleanor Copenhaver Anderson presented her husband's papers to the Newberry Library in Chicago.[8] The opening of this collection to scholars resulted in several outstanding publications. Paul Rosenfeld, who had edited the *Memoirs* for posthumous publication in 1942, compiled a fine collection of Anderson's stories and essays, *The Sherwood Anderson Reader* (1947). This was soon followed by *The Portable Sherwood Anderson* (1949), edited by Horace Gregory. While these volumes did not serve Anderson's reputation so well as Malcolm Cowley's *The Portable Faulkner* (1946) did for that then neglected writer, these two anthologies pointed the need for more intensive study of Anderson and his place in American letters.

Two lengthy biographical studies of Anderson soon appeared. The first, written by James Schevill,[9] the son of a close friend of the writer, was a competent account of Anderson's life but a rather inadequate critique of his works. Schevill sought to provide for Sherwood Anderson "a record of his bitter and often unconscious struggle to penetrate a materialistic world with the rays of the great images, both the dangerous rays and the healing rays."[10] If this study failed to account for Anderson's literary successes and failures, Irving Howe's *Sherwood Anderson*[11] was written with the preconception that Anderson was a distinctly minor writer. Howe considered Sherwood Anderson interesting as an example of the writer who must suffer because

---

6. *The Foreground of American Fiction* (New York, 1943), p. 112.

7. *On Native Grounds* (New York, 1942), p. 217.

8. See "The Sherwood Anderson Papers," *Newberry Library Bulletin*, 2d Ser., No. 2 (December, 1948), 64–70.

9. *Sherwood Anderson* (Denver, 1951). See "The Glitter of Communism," reprinted herein.

10. *Ibid.*, p. xiv.

11. New York, 1951. See "The Book of the Grotesque," reprinted herein.

America has not learned properly to appreciate gifted minor authors. These biographies, supplemented by two doctoral dissertations (sadly not yet published), remain the foundation for all serious study of Sherwood Anderson. William A. Sutton, in his "Sherwood Anderson's Formative Years (1876–1913)," [12] compiled the first accurate account of Anderson's life before he became a literary figure, revealing the fantasies which the author developed as part of his "legend." Working with the manuscripts in the Newberry Library, William L. Phillips reconstructed the occasion and method attending the composition of Anderson's masterpiece, *Winesburg, Ohio*, in his "Sherwood Anderson's *Winesburg, Ohio*: Its Origins, Composition, Technique, and Reception." [13] Also from the Newberry's Anderson Collection, Howard Mumford Jones and Walter B. Rideout compiled and edited a highly selective collection of Anderson's letters, published in 1953.[14]

Shortly after the appearance of these studies of Anderson, two of the foremost American authors publicly stated their indebtedness to Sherwood Anderson. William Faulkner, who owed the publication of *Soldiers' Pay* in 1926 to Anderson's influence with the publisher Horace Liveright, recalled his first meeting with the author: "I knew that I had seen, was looking at, a giant in an earth populated to a great —too great—extent by pygmies, even if he did make but the two or three gestures commensurate with gianthood." [15] And James T. Farrell wrote of the "singular humaneness of his characters" and added: "Sherwood Anderson influenced me, perhaps more profoundly than any other writer." [16] In addition, there appeared studies that attempted to relate Anderson to the literary movements of his era. Charles C. Walcutt discussed Anderson's particular adaptations of the traditions of naturalism,[17] and Frederick J. Hoffman republished his earlier discussion of

12. Ohio State University, 1943. Parts of this study are published in *Northwest Ohio Quarterly*, XIX–XXII (1947–1950).

13. University of Chicago, 1950. Summarized in Phillips' "How Sherwood Anderson Wrote *Winesburg, Ohio*," *American Literature*, XXIII (March, 1951), 7–30, and reprinted herein.

14. *Letters of Sherwood Anderson* (Boston, 1953).

15. "Sherwood Anderson: An Appreciation," *Atlantic*, CXCI (June, 1953), 29. See William L. Phillips, "Sherwood Anderson's Two Prize Pupils," *University of Chicago Magazine*, XLVII (January, 1955), 9–12. Both essays reprinted herein.

16. "A Memoir on Sherwood Anderson," *Perspective*, VII (Summer, 1954), 83, 87.

17. "Sherwood Anderson: Impressionism and the Buried Life," *Sewanee Review*, LX (Winter, 1952), 28–47. Reprinted, with minor revisions, in his *American Literary Naturalism: A Divided Stream* (Minneapolis, 1956), pp. 222–39, and in this volume.

the role of Freudian theory in Anderson's fiction.[18] An invaluable bibliography, while not nearly exhaustive and complete only through 1959, was compiled by Eugene P. Sheehy and Kenneth A. Lohf.[19] More importantly, *Winesburg, Ohio* was reissued in a scholarly-sound edition by Malcolm Cowley;[20] the success of this reprint motivated Maxwell Geismar to collect the finest of the short fiction for publication in *Sherwood Anderson: Short Stories*.[21]

The popular and scholarly interest in Sherwood Anderson at the present time is demonstrated by three recent publications. The literary magazine of Washington and Lee University, *Shenandoah*, devoted its spring, 1962, issue to Sherwood Anderson. Among the valuable articles included are discussions of Anderson's achievement by Frederick J. Hoffman, Walter B. Rideout, James K. Feibleman, and others.[22] In 1964, Rex Burbank published his *Sherwood Anderson* in Twayne Publishers' United States Authors Series. This study contributed little of value to the complex questions of Anderson's place in the tradition of American letters, but Burbank occasionally showed an illuminating understanding of the novels and stories.[23] Also in 1964, Brom Weber provided a useful but rather superficial survey of Anderson's career in his *Sherwood Anderson*, written for the University of Minnesota Pamphlets on American Writers.

These volumes and the large number of articles on Sherwood Anderson that now appear frequently in popular and learned journals seem to disprove the wisdom of those critics who apparently wrote Anderson's literary epitaph in the early 1940's. Why did these leaders in literary affairs fail to foresee the coming renaissance of interest in Sherwood Anderson, and, more importantly, what is the extent and significance of this renaissance? To answer these questions with any degree of accuracy, it is necessary to examine Sherwood Anderson's literary career—the criticism of his work and his reactions to that criticism—from the publication of the first novel in 1916 until the writer's death in 1941.

18. "Anderson—Psychologist by Default," *Freudianism and the Literary Mind* (Baton Rouge, 1945), pp. 230–55; slightly revised 1957, pp. 229–50, and reprinted in this volume.

19. Los Gatos, California: The Talisman Press, 1960.

20. New York, 1958.

21. New York, 1962.

22. Hoffman's "The Voices of Sherwood Anderson," pp. 5–19, is reprinted herein.

23. See especially Burbank's "The Populist Temper," pp. 48–60, reprinted herein.

2.

In the first years of any new movement in literature, when intellectual leaders, literary critics, and writers themselves are demanding complete acceptance of the products of the new movement, literary criticism can seldom be objectively fair and aesthetically balanced. Masterpieces can be blindly overlooked while lavish praise is spread upon books destined for early oblivion. Critics naturally laud the works that further the literary programs that they personally favor. Thus Sherwood Anderson's first two novels—*Windy McPherson's Son* (1916) and *Marching Men* (1917)—were championed by proponents of the new, raw masterpieces that mid-western America had long been expected to produce. Both of these apprentice novels, deeply flawed as they are, were never neglected by reviewers, although they were by no means profitable to Anderson or to his publisher.

Windy McPherson's Son, Sherwood Anderson's chronicle of the poor boy who finds unlimited income and quite limited satisfaction in big business, was called by H. W. Boynton "perhaps the most remarkable" book of the year 1916,[24] "an extraordinary book . . . of a constructive realism, in contrast with the destructive naturalism of a Dostoevsky or a Dreiser." [25] Francis Hackett predicted that "Mr. Sherwood Anderson's name is likely to become familiar to readers of American fiction. Out of the slag-heap, as the romancers see it, he has extracted a veracious novel." [26] The relationship of Sherwood Anderson's work to Edgar Lee Masters' *Spoon River Anthology* (1915), more obvious in the later *Winesburg, Ohio* (1919), was noticed by a reviewer who wrote for *The Nation*: "Caxton [Iowa] is as real as Spoon River, and its author portrays it without idealization; but, fortunately lacking Mr. Masters' keen scent and relish for evil, he has given us a truer and sounder picture." [27] William Lyon Phelps was jarred by the "crudity" of *Windy McPherson's Son,* but he admired the force, the "raw vitality" enough to predict of Anderson: "Some day his decided gifts will ripen; he will not only see things in their proportion; he will be able to draw them according to scale. . . ." [28] By far the soundest review of *Windy McPherson's Son* was written by Waldo Frank, who remained a trusted

24. "Some Outstanding Novels of the Year," *Nation,* CIII (November 30, 1916), 508.
25. "Some Stories of the Month," *Bookman,* LIV (December, 1916), 393.
26. "A New Novelist," *New Republic,* IX (January 20, 1917), 336.
27. "Current Fiction," CIV (January 11, 1917), 50.
28. "Three Not of a Kind," *Dial,* LXI (September 21, 1916), 196–97.

admirer of Anderson's work until the writer's death. In his "Emerging
Greatness," Frank recognized the essential merit of Sherwood Anderson's immature novel: "Puerile, fumbling stuff it is—its efficiency of
presentment about on a level with McPherson's method of gaining the
light. Yet through it all is a radiant glow of the truth." [29] Frank stated
that *Windy McPherson's Son* "is Mr. Anderson's first book, and . . . a
succession of them are already written and will appear in their
turn." [30]

Fortunately, Sherwood Anderson did not publish, if he really had
already written, the succession of novels mentioned by Frank. While he
was writing the stories that constitute *Winesburg, Ohio,* however,
Anderson let one other apprentice novel be published.[31] *Marching Men*
(1917), like *Windy McPherson's Son,* was more the product of a
scribbling manufacturer than of a liberated soul of the Chicago
Renaissance, but this second novel is vastly different from the first one,
and it appealed to critics for a perhaps unexpected reason: *Marching
Men* is a prolabor work that champions the martial, disciplined force of
massed men. H. W. Boynton saw this somewhat mystical, somewhat
naturalistic work as "a sort of parable or prophecy. . . . Its prophet is a
prophet of the masses, of mankind, the toiler finding his place in the
sun." [32] To a more perceptive critic, however, the work was a "paean to
order and . . . a naked and somewhat febrile celebration of force," and
its author seemed occupied with force in "a slightly pathological
fascination." [33] Aside from curiously foreshadowing Nazi Germany,
Marching Men is important in Anderson's career for what Francis
Hackett called the writer's view of "the rawest American people, brutal
in their callous acceptance of their own ugly and shoddy material
condition, flaccid in their personal tastes and futile in their spurts to
escape from banality. . . ." [34] Already Anderson was classed in the
school of naturalism, a classification that he was never to accept.

Sherwood Anderson's next book, *Mid-American Chants* (1918), was
a scarcely noticed collection of free-verse poems on aspects of mid-
America, derivative in style and content from Walt Whitman and Carl

29. *The Seven Arts,* I (November, 1916), 75. Reprinted herein.
30. *Ibid.,* p. 78.
31. See Phillips, "How Sherwood Anderson Wrote *Winesburg, Ohio.*"
32. "A Stroll Through the Fair of Fiction," *Bookman,* XLVI (November,
1917), 338.
33. George B. Donlin, "Discipline," *Dial,* LXIII (September 27, 1917), 274.
34. "To American Workingmen," *New Republic,* XII (September 29, 1917),
249. Reprinted herein.

Sandburg and merely indicative that Anderson could imitate his literary associates in Chicago.[35] To someone who knew only these poems and the first two novels, the appearance of *Winesburg, Ohio* in 1919 must have been astounding. Some of the Winesburg stories had been separately published in "little magazines," but the collected edition slowly brought to Anderson the sound critical approval that he wanted and needed.

Inevitably, Anderson's masterpiece was compared with the work of Edgar Lee Masters: " 'Winesburg, Ohio' is a prose Spoon River Anthology. Acridly written, these interrelated studies of half-articulate people who do not know what they want deal more often than not with the pathological, but they deal understandingly and honestly." [36] The beauty of Anderson's sketches of the helplessly lonely people in a fictional Ohio town was not immediately noted; instead critics praised the tales as a new form of fiction: "As a challenge to the snappy short story form, with its planned proportions of flippant philosophy, epigrammatic conversation, and sex danger, nothing better has come out of America than *Winesburg, Ohio*." [37] Even those critics who understood Anderson's method and purpose could not appreciate his achievement: "Some of his sketches which are all impressionistic, have an underlying significance and real beauty of feeling, but more of them are descriptions somewhat boldly naked, of the commonplace, without a spark of life or creative feeling." [38] *Winesburg, Ohio* was never a best-selling book; only gradually did it become famous and profitable to Anderson. The author was branded immoral, perverted, and blind to the happier aspects of the American small town. One critic who saw great merit in the book in 1919, H. W. Boynton, praised Sherwood Anderson for avoiding "the spiritual grossness of the Russian naturalists and their imitators," while he worried over the apparent psychoanalytical doctrine that with Anderson "sex is wellnigh the mainspring of human action." [39] Boynton came close to later evaluations of Sherwood Anderson's purpose when he wrote: ". . . always he seems to be after the true morality that governs men and women when they are at odds

35. See the "gift-book" selection from *Mid-American Chants, 6 Mid-American Chants by Sherwood Anderson/11 Midwest Photographs by Art Sinsabaugh*, introduction by Edward Dahlberg (Highlands, N.C., 1964).
36. "Books of the Fortnight," *Dial*, LXVI (June 28, 1919), 666.
37. M. A., "A Country Town," *New Republic*, XIX (June 25, 1919), 257. Reprinted herein.
38. *Springfield Republican*, July 20, 1919, p. 15.
39. "All Over the Lot," *Bookman*, XLIX (August, 1919), 729–30.

with, or merely conforming to, conventional morality." [40] Anderson later wrote of the reception of *Winesburg*: "[It] amazed and confounded me. The book was widely condemned, called nasty and dirty by most of its critics. It was more than two years selling its first five thousand." [41]

In a terse summary of his own career, Sherwood Anderson wrote that "if *Winesburg, Ohio* tried to tell the story of the defeated figures of an American individualistic small town life, then my later books have been but an attempt to carry these same people forward into the new American life, into the whirl and roar of modern machines." [42] Anderson tried in *Poor White* (1920) to use the main character as a representative of the inventor who corrupts an older society in the name of progress. Critics were sympathetic to this theme, but they noted what became standard criticism of Anderson's novels: ". . . the definiteness of characters and events is blunted by structural looseness and a diction that alternates between the pretentious and the mean." [43] Robert Morss Lovett criticized Anderson's failure at structure in long fiction: "It is in lack of emphasis that Mr. Anderson's novel falls below the effect of his short stories. Poor White does not end—it merely stops." [44]

As though he recognized this criticism of his novel as valid, Anderson's next two books were collections of short stories—*The Triumph of the Egg* (1921) and *Horses and Men* (1923). These stories, at least the best of them, remain with *Winesburg, Ohio* the most highly praised work of Sherwood Anderson. *The Triumph of the Egg* won the first *Dial* award of two thousand dollars for contributing to American writing, and such stories as "I Want to Know Why," "The Egg," and "I'm a Fool" are frequently reprinted in anthologies of outstanding short fiction. Writing of this book, Robert Morss Lovett praised Anderson's ability to demonstrate "the terror of life before its vast unknowability and the pathos of its trivial futility." [45] Lawrence Gilman tried to analyze the appeal of these tales by Anderson: "He is a naturalist doubled by a mystic: he is both seer and poet; and oft of the drab, pitiful, terrible subject matter of his tales—tales of trivial, gross, stunted, frustrated, joyless, ugly and twisted human lives—he is able to disclose . . . the infinite pitifulness of these souls who are our-

40. *Ibid.*, p. 730.
41. *Sherwood Anderson's Memoirs* (New York, 1942), p. 294.
42. *Ibid.*, p. 290.
43. "The Epic of Dulness," *Nation*, CXI (November 10, 1920), 597.
44. "Mr. Sherwood Anderson's America," *Dial*, LXX (January, 1921), 79.
45. "Elemental Things," *New Republic*, XXVIII (November 23, 1921), 384.

selves." [46] Commenting on *Horses and Men*, Newton Arvin recognized the place which Anderson would seek in American life: "Mr. Anderson is attempting—more or less unconsciously, no doubt—to fill the role of bardic poet: to put into simple and beautiful forms the vague and troubling pains of a bewildered people, to personalize a rather mechanical life, to give new values to a world that has discarded its old ones as invalid." [47]

In his personal search for these new values, Anderson seized upon the Freudian theory that was fascinating American intellectuals in the 1920's. In two novels, *Many Marriages* (1923) and *Dark Laughter* (1925), Anderson wrote of sexual fulfillment as the most desirable value of what was to be the new society. *Many Marriages*, a strong declaration of sexual freedom, remained Anderson's favorite among his books. In 1935 he wrote: "It was a book written to bring flesh, the feel of flesh, as far as I could go with it, into prose." [48] This novel was attacked and banned in many places, and it was called "a pretentious tract upon a trite theme, the slavery of the marriage bond." [49] Ludwig Lewisohn saw it as the herald of a new freedom in American literature: "He raises a prophetic and passionate cry against the sloth of our hearts, the atrophy of our senses, the cowardice of our thoughts." [50] And Edmund Wilson, while protesting the pale characterization in *Many Marriages*, wrote beautifully of Anderson: "Here, as elsewhere, we are at once disturbed and soothed by the feeling of hands thrust down among the bowels of life—hands delicate and clean but still pitiless in their exploration." [51]

Dark Laughter was quite successful financially for Sherwood Anderson, for it was the only one of his works to become a best-seller at its publication. Profits from it enabled him to leave permanently the literary society of New York, as he had earlier left the business society of Ohio, to live in rural Southwest Virginia. *Dark Laughter* contrasts the "white laughter," civilized laughter of sterile society, with the spontaneous, carefree "dark laughter" of the Negro in the South. To Henry Seidel Canby, Anderson saw uncannily "the half lights of subterranean passions which unmake us if we do not use them." [52] Significantly, Canby

46. "The Book of the Month: An American Masterpiece," *North American Review*, CCXV (March, 1922), 414.
47. "Mr. Anderson's New Stories," *Freeman*, VIII (December 5, 1923), 308.
48. *Letters*, p. 338.
49. H. W. Boynton, "Man the Blunderer," *Independent*, CX (March 31, 1923), 232.
50. "Novelist and Prophet," *Nation*, CXVI (March 28, 1923), 368.
51. " 'Many Marriages,' " *Dial*, LXXIV (April, 1923), 400.
52. "The Woman Takes Dark Laughter," *Saturday Review of Literature*, II (October 10, 1925), 191.

announced that " 'Dark Laughter' proves that Anderson can plan and carry through the organism of a novel, a point which has been in doubt." [53] Herschel Brickell agreed: "Sherwood Anderson proves in 'Dark Laughter' that he has sufficient technical resources to encompass the writing of a well integrated, skillfully done novel, which for all of its resemblance to a symphonic composition is held tightly together by a definite, clearly revealed theme. There can no longer be any doubt of his ability to make sustained flights; for several years few have denied him a high place among living short story writers." [54] Perhaps unfortunately, Anderson tried to emulate the achievement of *Ulysses:* "I think as a matter of prose experiment you will sense what Mr. Joyce was driving at when you read *Dark Laughter.*" [55] The fragmentary prose of the novel left Anderson open to charges of confusion, muddlement, and puzzlement—terms that were applied to his work for the rest of his life. *Dark Laughter* is, indeed, the only substantially satisfying novel by Sherwood Anderson, but it must be read carefully. As Joseph Wood Krutch remarked, "Anderson is not a deep thinker, and it is one of the absurd results of the conventional thought-patterns of our age that he is taken as a critic of society; but he is, nevertheless, a poet who feels things deeply in his own particular way." [56]

It is quite easy to forget that Sherwood Anderson began his creative life only when he was nearly forty years old. By 1926, therefore, when he was fifty, Anderson felt ready to examine his own life and accomplishments. In two semi-autobiographical books, *A Story Teller's Story* (1924) and *Tar* (1926), the author related a highly subjective, often historically inaccurate version of his youth in Ohio. This period of self-assessment apparently led critics to examine Anderson's achievement for themselves. Generally, they found much to admire, but little of it was in the later work. Reviewing *Tar*, Clifton Fadiman wrote: ". . . it is always a little embarrassing to read a new novel by Sherwood Anderson. It is like being present at a birth. . . . In novel after novel, Mr. Anderson continues to render, with a disturbing effectiveness, his mental and emotional birthpangs, but somehow we never see the baby." [57] Joseph Collins charged Anderson with a vision of life "fragmentary, incomplete, unbalanced," and obsessed with ugliness, gloom, and sensuality.[58]

Other writers now had little sympathy for Anderson. William

53. *Ibid.*
54. "An Armful of Fiction," *Bookman*, LXII (November, 1925), 338.
55. *Letters*, p. 148.
56. "Vagabonds," *Nation*, CXXI (December 2, 1925), 627. Reprinted herein.
57. "Endless Adolescence," *Nation*, CXXIV (February 2, 1927), 121.
58. *Taking the Literary Pulse* (New York, 1924), p. 47.

Faulkner and Ernest Hemingway deserted him to carve out their own
careers apart from Anderson's fatherly but embarrassing influence.
Upton Sinclair found no merit in his work: ". . . take the thirteen
volumes of Sherwood Anderson and analyze the characters: men and
women who cannot make love, cannot consummate love, cannot
restrain love, cannot keep from being suspected of perversity. . . . saying the same thing over and over, a dozen times on a single page." [59]
Similarly, Lawrence Morris declared that Anderson had "reached [his]
critical point. And there he stuck. . . . The author of 'Winesburg,
Ohio' is dying before our eyes." [60] As though to augment these
obituaries, two lengthy studies of Anderson appeared in 1927, by N. B.
Fagin [61] and Cleveland Chase. [62] Fagin had great praise only for
Sherwood Anderson's achievement with short fiction; Chase's thesis was
that the author skirted "the edges of great writing only to slip back with
a regularity that becomes monotonous into the second-rate." [63]

Amid such discouraging estimates of his work, Sherwood Anderson
found that he no longer commanded a faithful audience of readers.
After *Dark Laughter,* none of his books sold well or occasioned soundly
admiring reviews. *Sherwood Anderson's Notebook* (1926) and *A New
Testament* (1927) were collections of essays and "thoughts" which
probably should not have issued as books. *Hello Towns!* (1929), a
collection of articles from Anderson's two country newspapers, has
consistently been neglected, although Anderson remains the only
important writer in American literary history to abandon writing
professionally for editing and publishing obscure rural weekly newspapers. Quarrels with Faulkner and Hemingway, combined with what
Anderson felt was neglect of his work by the public, deeply hurt the
Anderson ego, famous for its sensitivity. To combat the charge that he
had nothing new to say, Anderson tried to bring Winesburg into the
twentieth century by expressing his sympathy for the labor-socialist
movement of the early 1930's. *Beyond Desire* (1932), like most of our
Marxist fiction, neglects method for message. Reviewers who praised
the doctrine of the novel ignored the really poor technique. In his "Red
Pilgrimage," Granville Hicks spoke of "the awakening of a people
[that] may be foreshadowed in this awakening of a writer who has

59. *Money Talks* (New York, 1927), p. 122.
60. "Sherwood Anderson: Sick of Words," *New Republic,* LI (August 3,
1927), 278–79.
61. *The Phenomenon of Sherwood Anderson* (Baltimore: Rossi-Bryn).
62. *Sherwood Anderson* (New York: R. M. McBride).
63. *Ibid.,* p. 5.

always been close to them." [64] Two critics who did comment on the style of *Beyond Desire* echoed the earlier adverse judgments of Anderson's novels. T. K. Whipple stated: "Questioning and bewilderment, of course, have always been as conspicuous in the author as in his people, but in his better works, for all his perplexity, he was able as writer and artist to deal with his material. That ability seems to have deserted him." [65] And Clifton Fadiman agreed: ". . . the dismal fact persists after almost a score of years: he is not by nature a novelist. Not one of his long fictions has stood the weathering of time." [66]

In one more novel, *Kit Brandon* (1936), Anderson tried to recapture his early fame, but this "reminiscence" of rumrunners in the Appalachians was scarcely noticed by the public. To Mark Van Doren, *Kit Brandon* showed Anderson's "greater and greater liking year in and year out for a way of writing that is more like the way a baby reaches for something than the way a man writes when he has something to say or maybe a story to tell." [67] And to Geoffrey Stone, *Kit Brandon* was just "one more addition to the *corpus* of Andersonian bewilderment." [68]

In only one case were the critics of Anderson's later work seriously wrong in their judgment. *Death in the Woods* (1933), Anderson's last collection of short stories, contains works that are among our finest short fiction—"Brother Death," "Like a Queen," and "Death in the Woods." Perhaps because these were stories and not extended writing, Anderson recaptured the tender charm of *Winesburg, Ohio*, *The Triumph of the Egg*, and *Horses and Men*. However, reviewers accustomed to knocking Anderson's work missed this proof that he had not completely lost the ability to tell great stories well. John Chamberlain called the stories in *Death in the Woods* "all variations on this eternal theme of wonder," but he added: "Mr. Anderson remains incapable of irony, of satire, of any studied view of the human comedy." [69] And T. S. Matthews wrote of being "so used to Anderson now, to his puzzled confidences, his groping repetitions, his occasional stumblings into real inspiration that perhaps we tend to underrate him as an American phenomenon. Or perhaps we no longer overrate him." [70]

64. *New Republic*, LXXIII (December 21, 1932), 169.
65. "Sherwood Anderson," *Saturday Review of Literature*, IX (December 10, 1932), 305.
66. "Still Groping," *Nation*, CXXXV (November 2, 1932), 342.
67. "Still Groping," *Nation*, CXLIII (October 17, 1936), 252.
68. "Rather Bewildered," *Commonweal*, XXV (November 20, 1936), 110.
69. "A Story Teller Returns," *Saturday Review of Literature*, IX (April 29, 1933), 561.
70. "Novels, Stories and Prophecies," *New Republic*, LXXV (June 7, 1933), 105.

Fortunately, for all of his tremendous ego, Sherwood Anderson came to accept gracefully the decline of his reputation in his later years. In 1930 he could write: "I have been writing for a good many years and have had some success. On the whole, my success has been what I suppose I might call an artistic success, rather than financial. However, I have had no special reason to quarrel with my fate in that direction. . . ." [71] Comparing himself with Herman Melville, who suffered a similar fate of obscurity in his old age, Anderson commented: "I used to look with horror, for example, upon the fate of Melville. There were years of his life when he was an old man, as I will presently be, and when he had nothing. . . . Why, it does not seem any more such a sad fate. I should be able to gather up remembrances on which I can feed. I think of that often in the night." [72] Sherwood Anderson did gather up his memories; in the process, he realized that his career had been "fortunate despite the fact that I cannot rank myself among the heroes. There has been something of struggle but little enough of the heroic in my life. For all my egotism I know I am but a minor figure." [73] Yet surely no minor figure has occasioned so much debate over his contribution to American letters.

Traditionally, the decline in quality and appeal of Sherwood Anderson's work has been accounted for by blaming his failures on the influence of the literary movements in which he took part. Thus it would seem that Anderson's association in the Chicago Renaissance led to his best work—*Winesburg, Ohio* and the early short stories. Then the writer was adopted and advised by the "intellectuals," who taught him about Freud, Lawrence, and Marx. Supposedly, the examples and theories of these men corrupted some natural genius in Anderson, who had been heralded as the untutored spokesman for small-town America. Trying to please his educated friends, Anderson wrote as they advised but not so well as they expected, causing them to desert him for the more appealing figures of Hemingway, Faulkner, and Wolfe.

There is some basis for this view of Anderson's career. Feeling uneducated and slightly pitied by those intellectuals who liked his work and who offered their praise and advice, Sherwood Anderson expanded his role-playing, a constant factor in his personality, to include the roles of prophetic midwestern bard, Freudian and Lawrencian philosopher, and socialist tractarian. However, such an explanation ignores the rather obvious impossibility of an author's remaining forever at an early stage of his career, no matter how successful that period may be. As

71. *Letters*, p. 210.
72. *Ibid.*, p. 241.
73. *Memoirs*, p. 3.

great as *Winesburg, Ohio* is, one cannot imagine Anderson's writing ten volumes of Winesburg stories. A writer must respond more to his genius than to his critics, and Sherwood Anderson's creative spirit demanded that he write novels, poetry, and plays, as well as short stories. There is almost no evidence that Anderson seriously listened to sound literary advice, although his tremendous ego was cut by every word of harsh criticism directed toward him.

What can now be said of the apparent renaissance of interest in Sherwood Anderson? First, the present intensive investigation of Anderson's life and writing is a part of the attempt of American scholars to trace the literary traditions of their country. Because of the nature of literature, serious scholarly study must usually remain several decades behind current writing, and only now are the outstanding authors of the period 1900–1940 coming in for exhaustive treatment. The large number of recently published studies of such figures as Dreiser, Hemingway, O'Neill, Fitzgerald, and Wolfe has naturally led to an awareness of Sherwood Anderson's rather prominent place in the era when these writers flourished. The author's extreme sensitivity to, or at least his voluminous comment on, the literary movements of his time makes a knowledge of Sherwood Anderson's career necessary to any student of modern American letters.

Secondly, the study of Sherwood Anderson is highly rewarding in itself. Few American writers have lived as colorfully and as spontaneously as Sherwood Anderson, and few authors have committed as much of themselves to the public gaze, consciously playing various roles to establish a "legend." The complexity of Anderson's character, the unusual circumstances of his becoming a writer, and the movement of his career can never be reduced to any simple analysis. Similarly, Sherwood Anderson's writings defy any definitive study; as much as students of Anderson may wish for the "final word" on his accomplishment, it is doubtful that such a study could be written or, if written, that it would long remain the standard comment on the writer who accepted for himself the term "minor."

3.

So extensive is the published discussion on Sherwood Anderson that there could be many shelves of collected criticism such as this. Yet the reviews, impressions, appreciations, and scholarly studies in this book are (after, of course, Anderson's own books) the essential starting point for appreciating Sherwood Anderson and his writing. Each essay, the outstanding study of its type, has been included for the particularly valuable comment that it makes on Sherwood Anderson. Thus the reviews of Anderson's first books by Waldo Frank, Francis Hackett, and "M. A." show the early high expectations for the writer's career, while that of Joseph Wood Krutch treats Anderson at the height of his popular esteem and intimates the impending decline of his critical reputation. The discussions of *Winesburg, Ohio* include William L. Phillips' masterful investigation of the book's composition, Edwin Fussell's examination of Anderson's theme of isolation, Irving Howe's treatment of Anderson's idea of the "grotesque," and Waldo Frank's evaluation of Anderson's masterpiece twenty years after its publication. Two discussions of Anderson's political inclinations, "The Populist Temper" by Rex Burbank and "The Glitter of Communism" by James Schevill, reveal the writer's concern with social issues, while Walter B. Rideout provides the only close study published on Anderson's unique career as a country newspaper editor. To place Sherwood Anderson in the various literary movements that engaged him, Bernard Duffey discusses Anderson and the Chicago Renaissance, Charles Child Walcutt treats Anderson in the tradition of naturalism, and Frederick J. Hoffman analyzes the influence of Freud on Anderson's work. After William Faulkner's appreciation of Anderson, the fascinating but ambiguous relationship of Anderson with William Faulkner and Ernest Hemingway is dealt with by William L. Phillips. Then four eminent scholars, after long study of Sherwood Anderson and his place in American letters, provide their final evaluations of the writer's achievement: Lionel Trilling finds Anderson almost irrelevant now; Malcolm Cowley and Frederick Hoffman find a small but important place for Anderson's work in our national literature; and, finally, David D. Anderson closes the present discussion with his appraisal of Sherwood Anderson two decades after the writer's death.

I trust that this outline of the contents of *The Achievement of Sherwood Anderson* will demonstrate my desire to present the very best criticism of Sherwood Anderson and my concern that this criticism be in balance between favorable and unfavorable comment. The scholars represented herein are to be commended for their objective study of Sherwood Anderson and the interesting presentation of their ideas and conclusions. The place of original publication for each essay is given in the notice of copyright, and the brief introductory prefaces are intended to make the contents into a unified survey of Anderson's career and to indicate why each essay seems to me valuable to Anderson scholarship.

In conclusion, it is my hope that this book will contribute to each reader a deeper understanding of the achievement of Sherwood Anderson.

WALDO FRANK

claims the honor of being the first critic to find the promise of greatness in Sherwood Anderson. When Frank was an editor of The Seven Arts in 1916, he discovered the newly published Windy McPherson's Son and recognized in this first, "apprentice" novel a power that had appeared before in American literature only in the work of Theodore Dreiser. Frank felt, however, that Sherwood Anderson had escaped the slavery to "the cult of the American fact" which had captured Dreiser, while he would never succumb to the frightened withdrawal from American life which is exemplified by Henry James.

In "Emerging Greatness," which appeared in the November, 1916, issue of The Seven Arts, Frank recognizes the unsatisfactory ending of Windy McPherson's Son, a sentimental flaw that Anderson tried to correct in the 1922 edition of the novel. Frank's expectation that Sherwood Anderson's future work would be both better and different from this first novel found fulfillment in Winesburg, Ohio, published three years after this prophecy of "Emerging Greatness."

EMERGING GREATNESS

Waldo Frank

We do not expect an Apocalypse, here in America. Out of our terrifying welter of steel and scarlet, a design must come. But it will come haltingly, laboriously. It will be warped by the steel, clotted with the scarlet. There have been pure and delicate visions among us. In art, there has been Whistler; and Henry James took it into his head to write novels. But the clear subtlety of these men was achieved by a rigorous avoidance of native stuff and native issues. Literally, they escaped America; and their followers have done the same, though in a more figurative meaning. Artist-senses have gone out, felt the raw of us, been repulsed by it, and so withdrawn to a magnificent introversion. So, when we found vision in America, we have found mostly an abstract art —an art that remained pure by remaining neuter. What would have happened to these artists, had they grappled with their country, is an academic question. But I suspect that the true reason for their *ivory tower* was lack of strength to venture forth and not be overwhelmed. This much is sure, however—and true particularly of the novel—that our artists have been of two extremes: those who gained an almost unbelievable purity of expression by the very violence of their self-isolation, and those who, plunging into the American maëlstrom, were submerged in it, lost their vision altogether, and gave forth a gross chronicle and a blind cult of the American Fact.

The significance of Sherwood Anderson whose first novel, "Windy

McPherson's Son," has recently appeared (published by The John Lane Company), is simply that he has escaped these two extremes, that he suggests at last a presentation of life shot through with the searching color of truth, which is a signal for a native culture.

Mr. Anderson is no accident. The appearance of his book is a gesture of logic. Indeed, commentators of tomorrow might gauge the station at which America has arrived today by a study of the impulses—conscious and unconscious—which compose this novel. But it is not a prophetic work. Its author is simply a man who has felt the moving passions of his people, yet sustained himself against them just enough in a crude way to set them forth.

His story has its beginning in an Iowa town. His hero, with a naive unswervingness from type, is a newsboy. His passion is money and power. He goes to Chicago. He becomes rich. He marries the daughter of his employer. And then, he becomes powerful. There is nothing new in this; although the way of telling it is fresh and sensitive. This is the romance of inchoate America. Like the Greek fables, it is a generic wishfulfillment to be garbed by each poet in his own dress. It has been done in a folk way by Horatio Alger; with a classic might by Theodore Dreiser. But so far, it has been the entire story. With Mr. Anderson, it is only the story's introduction.

When Sam McPherson, by a succession of clumsy assaults, charges to the control of the Arms Trust of America, he does not find there, like his novelistic brothers, a romantic and sentimental and overweening satisfaction. He finds a great disgust, a great emptiness. And he becomes interested in his soul! He learns that what he has done is spiritually nothing; that it has left him as helpless before the commands of life, as in the old days when he amassed pennies in Caxton, Iowa. It dawns on him, that if man is a measurer of truth, he has paralyzed competition, enslaved wealth, disposed of power without really growing at all. So Sam McPherson puts aside his gains; and pilgrimages forth, searching for truth.

This is the second part of the novel; and in it lies the book's importance. McPherson's quest of the grail is an awkward Odyssey indeed. It has the improbability of certain passages of Dostoëvski—the improbability of truth poorly or clumsily materialized. Moreover, in it we find an unleashed and unsophisticated power that we have all along awaited in the American novel. The resemblance to the Russian is, I am convinced, a consequence of a like quality in the two men. It is a temperamental, not a literary thing.

The abdicated millionaire works as a bartender in Ohio, as a builder

in Illinois; he joins a threshing crew in the West and a mining camp in
the South. He knows prostitutes and working-girls. He tries to help and
seeks truth. He learns that labor-unions are more concerned over the
use of scab machinery than by the prospect of losing a righteous strike;
that the men are more interested in a raise of wages than in preventing
a private band of grafters from stealing the town's water-works. He
becomes very miserable over the lot of the street-walkers. He asks the
drinkers in the saloon where he is employed why they get drunk, and is
discharged with an oath. Puerile, fumbling stuff it is—its efficiency of
presentment about on a level with McPherson's method of gaining the
light. Yet through it all, is a radiant glow of the truth. Read the
newspapers and the Congressional reports; read the platitudes of
investigating commissions, of charity organizations, of revivalists and
mushroom mysticisms—and you have the same helpless thing in
extension. Sam McPherson, bewildered with his affluence and power,
seeking the truth in the fair plains and the cancerous cities, ignorant
and awkward and eager—is America today. And Sam McPherson, the
boy, arrogant and keen and certain, hiding from himself his emptiness
with the extent and occupation of the materials that his land floods
upon him, is the America of our fathers.

For a feel of the America of tomorrow, do not look to this book. I am
sure that Mr. Anderson will conduct himself better in subsequent
works than he has in the conclusion of "Windy McPherson's Son." As
we find the faint footprints of Horatio Alger at the book's beginning, so
at the end is the smirch of Robert W. Chambers. (But after all, Balzac
could not so wholeheartedly have swallowed France, had he not taken
Pixérécourt and Madame Scudéry along.) When Sam marries Sue
Rainey, it is with the understanding that they are to have children and
that they are to live gloriously for them. For a while, the magnate's
money-madness slackens. But the pact fails, for the children can not
come. Coolness between the two, with the goal of their creed denied
them:—and at length, when Sam sacrifices his wife's father in his
grapple toward dominion, she flees to New York. The man over whose
fat body he has stepped to power shoots himself. And, sick of his
tawdry, superficial kingdom, McPherson wanders off.

He gains nothing from his experiments, and this is well enough. He
hunts in Africa, leisures in Paris, canoes in Canada and sentimentalizes
in New York. All this we forgive him. But one day, he finds himself in
St. Louis. He encounters a drunken mother, buys her three children,
packs them into a train and drops them at the feet of his wife who, like
some diluted Penelope, has been awaiting his return in a villa on the

Hudson. "Not our children, but just *some* children is our need," he pronounces. And so, walks "across the lighted room to sit again with Sue at his own table, and try to force himself back into the ranks of life." This is the last sentence of the book; the one episode that is *made* and insincere. I hope Mr. Anderson is ashamed of it. I hope he does not really believe that all man has to do, to find God, is to increase and multiply more helpless creatures like himself. This pretty surcease to trouble that comes from transferring the problems of life to the next generation is a biological fact. But it is not art. For with it is dimmed all the voluptuous speculation which flushes the novel as a sunrise transfigures a plain. Let life be happy, if it can. The sacred duty of art is to remain sorrowful, when it has challenged a consciousness of sorrow; to abide in the uncertain search of truth so long as the movement of mankind is hazardous. Let our heroes be joyous; but by conquering themselves, not by adopting children. The virtue of Mr. Anderson's book is that it is dynamic. His static ending is bad, because it breaks the rhythm. But it is worse since it slams the door on the vista of passionate inquiry which the book unfolds. Up to the end, we have a clear symbol of America's groping. At the end, we have nothing—in lieu of the suggested everything. But, of course, we may ignore the end. Or, in its fatuous simplicity, we may read still another symbol of America— token of what might happen to us, if we sought at this stage to read our lives as a conclusion, rather than a commencement.

I was not certain that Theodore Dreiser was a classic, until I had read this novel of Mr. Anderson. Its first half is a portal from which emerges an American soul. This portal is the immediate past, and in the works of Mr. Dreiser we find its definite expression. Beside their magnificent mass-rhythms, the opening chapters of Mr. Anderson are paltry. One feels, indeed, that the uneasy spirit of Sam McPherson has come forth, not from his own youth, not from his own pages, but from the choking structures of Mr. Dreiser.

Mr. Dreiser may of course yet surprise us by the sudden discovery of a new spiritual light. He has not stopped writing. But I feel in his work the profound massiveness of a completed growth. Mr. Dreiser has caught the crass life of the American, armoring himself with luxury and wealth that he misunderstands, with power whose heritage of uses he ignores. The tragedy of his hero is that of a child suddenly in possession of a continent; too unknowing to know that he is ignorant; too dazzled to be amazed. His books are a dull, hard mosaic of materials beneath which one senses vaguely a grandiose movement—like the blind shifting of quicksands or the imperceptible breathing of a glacier. This is

Mr. Dreiser, and this is enough. But with Mr. Anderson, the elemental movement begins to have form and direction; the force that causes it is being borne into the air.

Before Mr. Dreiser, there was "Huckleberry Finn"—there was, in other words, a formless delirium of color and of tangent. These are pre-cultural novels. And in the book of Mr. Anderson, I still find much of them. Indeed, the wandering of Sam McPherson has more than a superficial kinship with Huck Finn's passage down the Mississippi. The land that McPherson walks is still a land marred by men and women "who have not learned to be clean and noble like their forests and their plains." But Huck Finn is an animal boy, floating rudderless down a natural current, avid for food and play. And McPherson is a man, flung against his stream, avid for the Truth. . . .

In conclusion, let us not forget that this is Mr. Anderson's first book, and that a succession of them are already written and will appear in their turn. The fact that Mr. Anderson is no longer young is no hindrance to our hope of his growth. Genius in America, if it does not altogether escape America, rises slowly. For it has far to come. The European is born on a plateau. America is still at a sea-level. The blundering, blustering native was thirty-seven before he became **Walt Whitman**.

FRANCIS HACKETT

was typical of the few critics who liked Sherwood Anderson's second novel, Marching Men, *published in 1917. Hackett sympathized with the masses in their attempt to organize against oppression, but most people who read the book found Anderson's celebration of the raw physical power in massed men slightly disturbing. Americans were not certain in 1917 that they regarded the coming total organization of labor as reassuring; and it is ironic that Nazi Germany later apparently operated on Sherwood Anderson's theory of the Marching Men. This second "apprentice" novel, interesting only for its strange political philosophy, scarcely anticipates the writer's accomplishment in* Winesburg, Ohio, *published two years later.*

TO AMERICAN WORKINGMEN

Francis Hackett

It is Mr. Sherwood Anderson's distinction in Marching Men that he summons the rawest American people, brutal in their callous acceptance of their own ugly and shoddy material condition, flaccid in their personal tastes and futile in their spurts to escape from banality, barbarous in their solemnity about trivial things and their levity about serious ones, cruel in their enforcement of submissiveness and their drunken explosions against it, anarchic in their relation to any sustained purpose outside the immediacies of their food and shelter, their women and their progeny.

Having possessed himself of the vast part of the life of the vast proportion of the American people, Mr. Anderson wanted to do something besides represent its disorder and brutality and ineffectiveness. He wanted to show how it could be led. It is the failure of his book, as I see it, that he has made his hero a primordial figure about whom he is clearly infatuated. The sensational and spectacular scheme by which this Pennsylvania miner aspires to evoke the solidarity of labor hardly succeeds in escaping the ludicrous. But Marching Men is not a literal novel. It has, indeed, its large element of the caveman piffle that played such a part in the romanticizations of Jack London, but outside this puerility, this day-dream of the male egoist, there is a great deal of inspiring symbolism in Marching Men, and it is justifiably dedicated to American workingmen. Perhaps, as the success of Jack London intimates, it is necessary for the novel of the proletarian to reproduce for modern hero-worship the simple Herculean giant who invariably downs his enemy. It is not the prowess of McGregor that makes Marching Men a living presence, however, so much as the freshness of feeling about opinions, the flashes of energetic description, the perverse notions concerning women, the details of mining town and apple-warehouse and night restaurant and Chicago pulchritude, the reminiscence of 1893 and of First Ward infamies, the swiftness of incident. Mr. Anderson's subjects are handled with a verve so different from the tired matrimonialism of the professional novelist that an occasional naïveté is unimportant. Without naïveté he would probably not have had the courage to write so graphic a proletarian novel.

"Huge, graceless of body, indolent of mind, untrained, uneducated, hating the world," McGregor is the American whom time converts from a savage disgust with workingmen to a leadership that is ruthless love of order. "I hate you because you are disorganized and weak like cattle. I would like to come among you teaching the power of force. I would like to slay you one by one, not with weapons but with my naked fists. If they have made you work like rats buried in a hole they are right. It is man's right to do what he can. Get up and fight." This is the spirit that dominates McGregor when he is the joke of Coal Creek, "Beaut" McGregor, son of "Cracked" McGregor. But besides the quest of power that occupies his first years in Chicago, an ambition that regulates his sympathies and his passions, there is a self-identification with the working class by which his hatred is merely the obverse of his love. His success as a lawyer gives him a chance to leave his class, but his sense of solidarity prevails, and the rest of his struggle is a struggle to make an army out of labor by progress from the mere rhythm of marching to a rhythm of like-mindedness in society.

There are hints of the Peter of War and Peace in the figure of Mr. Anderson's McGregor, but it is only necessary to mention a Tolstoyan hero to mark the rudimentary portraiture of the American. He is not, primarily, an independent will. He is a purposeful creation of the author. We are introduced inside him, but only to discover that he is all of a piece, as simple as a sun-dial, and the mechanism by which he works requires a light from outside. His treatment in Coal Creek does supply some real motivation, and there are symptoms of spontaneous human nature in his relations with the undertaker's daughter, the milliner, the fashionable Chicagoan. But there is something about his devotion to a love of order, his recurrence to his simple sententiousness, that suggests a cuckoo-clock. The only way to overcome the difficulty of establishing an idea in a novel is to humanize every expression of its sponsor. This is not Mr. Anderson's way. His McGregor uniformly knocks men down, uniformly hates, uniformly suppresses women, uniformly spouts. He is fervid but rigid, a romancer's man.

The chief fact about Marching Men is not, however, its rhetoric, its grandiloquence. It is its apprehension of the great fictional theme of our generation, industrial America. Because the subject is barbarous, anarchic and brutal it is not easy for its story to be told. But the restless vitality of the thing itself is beginning to be felt, through layers of professorial censorship. Harsh voices, wild tongues of fire, ominous multitudinous mutterings, are at last striving up our horizon.

One is induced in reading Marching Men to theorize on the enormous gap between literate and unliterate America. The novel's weakness in throwing a rainbow across the gulf is a sign of the sundered realities. The explanation lies, perhaps, in man's faculty for ignoring the obvious, his great gift for evading glaring fact. It is not obtuseness that makes the chauffeur ignore hitching-posts or makes the admirer of Elihu Root fail to see the importance of Bill Haywood. It is a difference of purpose. It seems to be the necessity and the penalty of jealous purpose to compel the evasion of glaring fact, to delete unacceptable fact from consideration. The youth who lives in a boardinghouse can walk his city forever without seing carpenters' shops or plumbers', groceries or meats, and his blindness is not that he cannot see these agencies of life but that he has no sufficient motive for seeing. We cannot observe, apparently, unless we expand our purposes to make a place for attendant fact. If fact is stubborn and we are not ready for it, there is every category of morals and taste to be enlisted to sidetrack it. The imagination is much more connected with will, much more the servant of habit and circumstance, than we are accustomed to admit. The first step in educating the imagination, indeed, is to remind ourselves that the shutter remains on the camera so long as we do not will to perceive.

By reason of these restrictions, it seems to me, the proletarian has had small place in American fiction. Under the ban of negligible ugliness, as the eminent novelists see it, comes the great majority of the people. They, the eminent ones, have principally been the children of circumspect parents, Presbyterians or Baptists, middle class in social and moral habits and unlikely to be hospitable to the primordial. Outside their view lies the life of the proletarian except as it impinges on the middle class, and these rawnesses of American existence, so conceived, have as little part in a polite literacy as have peanuts in the poetry of

Oscar Wilde. It is not that the facts are seen and rejected. The facts are simply not open to the eminent novelists any more than to social-sentiment workers or bright reporters or class-hyphenates of the sweetest disposition. The proletarians are in a different universe of discourse, and one so unthinkable to eminent novelists that it is promptly ruled out, the way we humane people rule out the super-heated hell.

Where Marching Men succeeds is in thrusting the greater American realities before us, seen as by a workingman himself. It is a fragmentary novel, rhetorical in the atmosphere that surrounds McGregor and uncritical of its own notion of solidarity, but a narrative that suggests the presence in our fiction of a man who knows our largest theme.

REX BURBANK

has written in "The Populist Temper" the best examination of the early novels of Sherwood Anderson, wisely discussing together the first two, Windy McPherson's Son and Marching Men. While these works admittedly are "apprentice" novels, they merit more critical attention than has been given to them.

Burbank supplies that attention by analyzing Windy McPherson's Son and Marching Men as expressions of Anderson's own political background. "The Populist Temper" relies rather heavily on R. W. B. Lewis' The American Adam in order to show "the symbolic rise to consciousness and quest for innocence of the Midwesterner that Anderson drew after his own life and used as the structural and thematic basis for his later work."

[31]

THE POPULIST TEMPER

Rex Burbank

When he was writing the autobiographical *A Story Teller's Story* in August, 1923, Anderson wrote to Van Wyck Brooks that he was "frankly daring to proclaim" himself "the American Man." "I mean by that," he told Brooks, "to take all into myself if I can—the salesman, businessman, foxy fellows, laborers, all among whom I have lived. I do get the feeling that I, in a peculiar way and because of the accident of my position in letters, am a kind of composite essence of it all." [1] Well before 1923, he had transformed the main configurations of his own life into the psychological and moral metaphor that formed the thematic and structural framework of all his novels. His remark to Brooks was merely an open acknowledgment that he now consciously regarded the principal features of his life as a kind of summation of the essential American experience. Though *Windy McPherson's Son* and *Marching Men* are frequently stilted in diction and represent the work of a talented businessman rather than an accomplished artist, they reveal the nature of that metaphor and the moral and social ambiguities that helped shape the chief, significant contours of Anderson's work.

In both books we follow the heroes, Sam McPherson and Beaut McGregor, as they move (much as Anderson himself did) through three successive stages toward maturity and moral consciousness: the youth spent in a small town, the escape to the city and pursuit of

1. *Letters*, p. 104.

success, and the sudden abandonment of the success ethic. Unlike Anderson himself, whose break with convention was clearly a case of psychic necessity, McPherson and McGregor repudiate the individualistic values of a materialistic society for moral reasons; but, whereas Anderson's struggle was primarily one for psychological wholeness, theirs represent moral journeys first to consciousness and then to conscience.

Showing a moral strength Anderson himself could not muster, Sam and Beaut become reformers. Though the nature of their reform efforts differs, they have in common the rise from the spiritual and material poverty of their small-town youth to almost Napoleonic power as men of the people. McPherson, who becomes a business tycoon, plays the role of the "inspired millionaire," a kind of Frank Cowperwood who suddenly becomes conscience stricken. McPherson abandons the Darwinian world of business and throws his great personal strength into helping oppressed farm and factory workers in their conflicts against emotionally insulated capitalists, corrupt union officials, and brutal hireling managers. McGregor, who like McPherson ruthlessly tramples on those weaker than himself in his climb to success, also grows aware suddenly of his responsibilities to the exploited "little" people and organizes a mammoth Marching Men Movement in order to bring "old labour in one mass . . . before the eyes of men" and to "make the world see—see and feel its bigness at last." Neither has a discernible economic or political plan of action or goal, other than the determination to help the weak become strong enough to compete on equal terms with their industrial, financial, and political oppressors; and both fail in their reform efforts, though Anderson lets us believe they have achieved moral victories in making the effort.

Like Dreiser, Anderson presents a Naturalistic picture of people caught up in social "forces"—specifically, by a repressive, individualistic economic system and by an outworn Puritan morality which have defeated the weak and made egoistic monsters of the strong. But, unlike Dreiser, Anderson judges society against an ambivalent nature in which man may choose between harmony and discord, between a moral order based upon concord and a chaotic social system grounded in egoistic competitiveness. Though they "fall" into egoism and accept the community's ethics of competition, both of his strong men have an innate moral conscience which is not—as it is in Dreiser's Cowperwood— merely a social contrivance. Whereas Cowperwood struggles for survival in a Darwinian world that reflects a warring, amoral nature, Anderson's heroes fight their way to power and success in a society that has lost touch with a benevolent and harmonious nature and become egocentric.

Anderson departs further from the traditional Zolaesque and Dreiserian reductive Naturalism in providing his heroes with a choice between a nature of strife on the one hand and a nature of harmony on the other —between an egoistic, competitive life and one of sympathetic communion with others. During the course of his search for "truth" after abandoning the world of big business, McPherson one day observes the random fighting of two guinea hens:

> Again and again they sprang into the fray, striking out with bills and spurs. Becoming exhausted, they fell to picking and scratching among the rubbish in the yard, and when they had a little recovered renewed the struggle. For an hour Sam had looked at the scene, letting his eyes wander from the river to the grey sky and to the factory belching forth its black smoke. He had thought that the two feebly struggling fowls, immersed in their pointless struggle in the midst of such mighty force, epitomized much of man's struggle in the world. . . .

The background of factories clearly identifies modern, urban, industrial society and a decayed agrarian culture with a nature of brute conflict. But, in contrast to Dreiser's Cowperwood, who accepts a predatory human existence as a reflection of nature (recall, for instance, the famous scene in *The Financier* in which he observes a lobster devour a squid and concludes that that is the "way things are"), Anderson's McPherson charges the American people with moral responsibility for their failure to live in harmony with a benevolent nature. "American men and women," he declares, "have not learned to be clean and noble and natural like their wide clean plains." McGregor also makes a moral indictment as he rejects the idea of progress and contrasts a harmonious nature with American society: "Orators might have preached to him all day about the progress of mankind in America, flags might have been flapped and newspapers might have dinned the wonders of his country into his brain. He did not know the whole story of how men, coming out of Europe and given millions of square miles of black fertile land [,] mines and forests, have produced out of the stately order of nature only the sordid disorder of man." The economic struggle thus for Anderson becomes a psychological struggle, and the social conflict, moral; and, where Dreiser's naturalism is of the "scientific" variety that owes its origins to Zola, Anderson's is romantic and derives from indigenous sources, as we shall see.

Achievement of maturity for McPherson and McGregor comes when their innate need for order and communion becomes a conscious moral imperative; when aware of their share of their country's guilt, they rise to what Anderson later called—in reference to Twain—a "proud conscious innocence." [2] Both books are thus primarily psychological and moral in theme rather than political or economic, and we see in them the basic moral assumptions that are implicit in such later works as *Winesburg, Ohio*. McGregor and McPherson reject socialism as an alternative to an oppressive capitalistic system. In contrast to such contemporary heroes as Jack London's Ernest Everhard in *Iron Heel*, Anderson's two strong men are moral rather than utopian socialist leaders; the pattern of development they follow is one that takes them to social consciousness and conscience rather than to economic or political theory. Their sudden abandonment of the pursuit of their own self-interest represents a return to the community of oppressed, defeated people they have rejected and also a moral acknowledgment of social responsibility.

As Anderson's heroes move from the small towns to the larger world of Chicago and come into conflict with society on all levels, they follow the traditional pattern of one of the most common American literary heroes, the "American Adam." That pattern in its broadest outlines consists of what R. W. B. Lewis has termed "the ritualistic trials of the young innocent, liberated from family and social history or bereft of them; advancing hopefully into a complex world he knows not of, radically affecting that world and radically affected by it; defeated, perhaps even destroyed. . . . but leaving his mark upon the world, and a sign in which conquest may later become possible for the survivors." [3] Both McPherson and McGregor are initially innocent in the sense that they instinctively want to "draw close" to others in harmonious human relationships; but, repelled by the disorder and ugliness of their respective communities, they repudiate their hometowns, and in doing so, they undergo a "fortunate fall" into the very isolating egoism that causes the ugliness and disorder they have tried to escape. Thus, though isolated, they share the guilt of society, and their awareness of that guilt and their determination to atone for it comprise a symbolic moral rebirth—that is, the achievement of a "wise" innocence, now armed by experience and grounded upon understanding of its own ineradicable sense of guilt. [4]

2. *Letters*, p. 33.
3. R. W. B. Lewis, *The American Adam: Innocence, Tragedy, and Tradition in the Nineteenth Century* (Chicago, 1955), pp. 127–28.
4. See Frederic I. Carpenter, " 'The American Myth': Paradise (To Be) Regained," *PMLA*, LXXIV, 5 (Dec., 1959), 599–606.

As Lewis has well demonstrated, the myth of the American Adam is one of the more substantial in American literature; it finds expression notably in Thoreau's *Walden* and Whitman's *Leaves of Grass* and in works of Cooper, Hawthorne, Melville, James, Twain, Hemingway, Faulkner, and others. Variations on the theme are as numerous as the writers who have—consciously or unconsciously—used it; but it is most commonly expressed in terms of a moral journey, a loss of innocence and an effort to regain it. Lewis characterizes the Adamic narrative metaphor as "the birth of the innocent, the foray into the unknown world, the collision with that world, the 'fortunate fall,' the wisdom and the maturity which suffering produced." [5] Cooper's Natty Bumppo is the prototype of the innocent who shuns society for the innocence and purity of life in the wilderness; Hawthorne's Donatello and Miriam in the *Marble Faun* are innocents who fall prey to evil because they are unequipped by experience to cope with it, as do Melville's Billy Budd and such Jamesian protagonists as Christopher Newman, Adam Verver, Milly Theale, and Isabel Archer. And Mark Twain's Huck Finn defines his essentially innocent nature in acting against his socially developed conscience to help his friend Jim escape from slavery.

In the twentieth century the metaphor has become transfigured. The Adamic hero carries, from early in life, the burden of society's guilt; and, often in response to moral or psychic necessity, he embarks upon a quest for primal Edenic innocence and purity, a quest which culminates in psychic purification or moral rebirth through an elaborate ritual that renews his sentient and psychological contact with nature. Hemingway's Nick Adams and Faulkner's Ike McCaslin (in "The Bear") are among the most notable contemporary Adams who attempt to find a kind of primitive psychic innocence by means of a ritual contest (fishing and hunting, respectively) between themselves and nature.

Anderson's heroes follow a course in which they first fall prey to the corrupting effects of a materialistic and traditionally moralistic society; but then, as they become conscious of their "fall," they reject the values of convention and deliberately seek a revitalized innocence based upon experience. Consciousness or awareness of their "fall" comes to them suddenly as a result of a growing psychological reaction against the life they are living; and, as this natural psychological revulsion turns to a sense of guilt, the conventional becomes unnatural and therefore immoral, while the innermost, natural inclinations and needs become moral. Thus McPherson strives to quell the "man of achievement" in

5. Lewis, p. 154.

himself which has separated him from others and to respond to his second, "buried" personality, which draws him instinctively to others and compels him to "try to understand . . . other lives, to love."

The Adamic journey became the characteristic narrative metaphor in all of Anderson's subsequent novels, assuming social and psychological as well as moral and mythical dimensions. Like McPherson and McGregor, Hugh McVey of *Poor White* (1920), John Webster of *Many Marriages* (1923), Bruce Dudley of *Dark Laughter* (1925), Red Oliver of *Beyond Desire* (1932), and Kit Brandon of *Kit Brandon* (1936) embrace variously the ethics of success; the doctrine of progress; standardized, hypocritically sexual notions of love and courtship and marriage; or the bloodless piety of Puritan morality. And like McGregor and McPherson, they all rebel against the spiritual confinements of society and try to find and live by a principle of order in the face of the social disorder they have observed everywhere and the inner disorder they have felt in themselves and seen in others. All have a strong instinctive need for order—for example, McPherson's efforts to make an "art" of business and McGregor's obsession to "bring an end to disorder" in society—which reflects the chief cause of Anderson's own psychic crisis in 1912. And all escape from the disorder of their lives and begin a new life that develops into a moral quest, a groping effort to construct a new moral world.

Such a narrative metaphor lends itself to penetrating literary examinations of a cross-section of American life. The assumptions implicit in the moral journey Anderson's heroes take are not hard to identify, for they comprise the strange amalgamation of Jeffersonian agrarian primitivism and secular Calvinism that made up the "folklore of Populism" which was—and to some extent still is—a powerful ideological force in Anderson's Midwest. A brief examination of Populism and its "folklore" explains the thematic attitudes of *Windy* and *Marching Men* and enables us to assess them on their own terms.

Historian Richard Hofstadter distinguishes five chief themes in the Populist ideology, all of which may be identified in varying degrees in *Windy McPherson's Son* and in *Marching Men*: "the idea of the golden age; the concept of natural harmonies; the dualistic version of social struggles; the conspiracy theory of history; and the doctrine of the primacy of money." [6] The first two of these themes are primitivistic, and are historical remnants of Jeffersonian agrarianism. The idea of the golden age looks backward in time and is one of the oldest forms of chronological primitivism. For the Populists, the golden age lay in the

6. Richard Hofstadter, *The Age of Reform* (New York, 1955), p. 62.

pre-industrial era of the young Republic, when the hardy yeoman farmer, uncorrupted by city-bred notions of profit, worked harmoniously—and thus virtuously—with a benevolent nature.

One of the chief historical facts about the Populist Revolt is that it signified a shift in agrarian attitudes from hope for an agricultural Eden in the future to memory of an imagined golden age of the past. The agrarian myth, which had drawn settlers westward throughout the nineteenth century in search of a new Eden, changed after the Civil War as repeated natural disasters and growing problems with land speculators, mortgagors, and railroad monopolists turned the "garden of the world" into a "desert." [7] The growing agrarian sense of cultural failure which accompanied the Industrial Revolution and which was expressed in the Populist Party platform of 1892 [8] generated the conviction—seen in such other Populist writers as Masters and Lindsay —that, given an opportunity to begin life again in a new Eden, Americans had failed to build a society commensurate with the great abundance and beauty of the continent.

The "concept of natural harmonies," against which McPherson and McGregor judge the "sordid disorder" of the farms, the towns, and the industrial cities, commonly manifests itself as cultural primitivism, the conviction that life lived close to nature is wholesome and virtuous. In *Windy* and in *Marching Men* this theme is closely related to the nostalgic, agrarian Edenic myth. As youths, McPherson and McGregor respond simultaneously to the beauties of the idyllic countryside and mountain valleys. One morning when he is a boy, Beaut McGregor

7. See Henry Nash Smith's *Virgin Land: The American West as Symbol and Myth* (Cambridge, 1950), Ch. XVI, "The Garden and the Desert."

8. The Populist platform, as written by Ignatius Donnelly and presented to the convention in Omaha on July 4, 1892, was an indictment of both the Democratic and the Republican parties:

We meet in the midst of a nation brought to the verge of moral, political, and material ruin. Corruption dominates the ballotbox, the legislatures, the Congress, and touches even the ermine of the bench. The people are demoralized; . . . The newspapers are largely subsidized or muzzled; public opinion silenced; business prostrated; our homes covered with mortgages; labor impoverished; and the land concentrating in the hands of the capitalists. The urban workmen are denied the right of organization for self-protection; imported pauperized labor beats down their wages; a hireling standing army, unrecognized by our laws, is established to shoot them down, and they are rapidly degenerating into European conditions. The fruits of the toil of millions are bodily stolen to build up colossal fortunes for a few, unprecedented in the history of mankind; and the possessors of those in turn, despise the republic and endanger liberty. From the same prolific womb of governmental injustice we breed the two great classes—tramps and millionaires.

goes with his father to a valley over the mountain from the squalid town of Coal Creek and sees an agricultural Eden:

> On the first morning, when the boy sat on the hillside with his father, it was spring and the land was vividly green. Lambs played in the fields; birds sang their mating songs; in the air, on the earth and in the water of the flowing river it was a time of new life. Below, the flat valley of green fields was patched and spotted with brown new turned earth. The cattle walking with bowed heads, eating the sweet grass, the farmhouses with red barns, the pungent smell of the new ground, fired his mind and awoke the sleeping sense of beauty in the boy. He sat upon the log drunk with happiness that the world he lived in could be so beautiful. In his bed at night he dreamed of the valley, confounding it with the old Bible tales of the Garden of Eden, told him by his mother.

As McGregor grows to mature consciousness, the concept of natural harmonies becomes transformed into human terms, and the harmony of nature becomes the desired norm for harmonious psychological relationships—expressed by means of psychic collectivism or communion in *Marching Men*.

In the Populist ideology, the traditional primitivistic belief that society has deteriorated since the "golden age" of natural and human harmonies was charged with a latent Calvinistic moral Manicheanism which conceived a "dualistic" version of social struggles consisting of a clear-cut division between the demons of "money power, monopolies, and satanic mills" on the one hand and the simple rustic folk and workingmen on the other. Behind the evils of these Populist demons lay the lure of money, which in *Windy* brings about the "fall" of Sam McPherson. Like the manufacturer Ormsby in *Marching Men*—who was at one time an honest tradesman—Sam degenerates morally as he becomes rich; and we see him conspiring with other businessmen to manipulate the stock market and to capture control of his father-in-law's arms manufacturing company. The dualistic version of social conflicts is even clearer in Beaut McGregor's Marching Men crusade against the capitalists; and the "conspiracy theory" shows itself in the fact that the first glimmerings of social conscience come to him when he exposes a scheme by the corrupt business-controlled Chicago political machine to throw the blame for a murder upon one of its petty hirelings who is innocent.

The intellectual weaknesses inherent to the Populist folklore are obvious, and Anderson's attempts to confront complex political, social, and economic issues with psychological and moral solutions reflect the unfortunate (and dangerous) failure of the Populists to implement their moral fervor with intelligence. Unable to unite for any length of time on a political or economic program, generally unreceptive to theories of reform, and frustrated by their feeling of weakness before the great commercial powers, the Populists were responsive to the appeals of the strong-man hero of the people, the inspired political "white knight" who could articulate their grievances, marshall their diffused strength, and lead them in a crusade against a formidable—and sometimes nebulous—enemy. At times, as when they followed John Peter Altgeld, the hero who set free the men involved in the Haymarket Riots, they were fortunate enough to be led by a man of intelligence who combined vision with dedication to the cause of the "people" and personal disinterest. But they were by no means uniformly judicious or consistent in their choice of a leader; and they were often more susceptible to the blandishments of impassioned demagogues than to the articulation of a clearly defined political or economic course of action. The notion that a Napoleonic folk hero was needed was commonly held. In a biography of Napoleon published in 1902, Populist leader Thomas E. Watson saw the conquering Corsican as a "great democratic despot"; and the militant Mary E. Lease contended that "we need a Napoleon in the industrial world who, by agitation and education, will lead the people to a realizing sense of their condition and remedies." [9]

This Populist hero-worship—abetted by Anderson's reading of Carlyle and, probably, of Jack London's Nietzschean proletarian novels—surely lay behind the creation of Sam McPherson and Beaut McGregor. It is pervaded by a thinly veiled contempt for the masses with whose interests it purports to concern itself; McGregor and McPherson show a kind of Carlylean and Nietzschean scorn for the "rabble" even as they try to unite them, and both books reveal a Calvinistic concern for the secular elect, "extraordinary men" who "now . . . suffer terribly" in a democracy.

Grounded in the Populist ideology, with its political and social mindlessness, such power- and hero-worship is potentially fascistic. As Anderson later ruefully admitted, the peculiar type of collectivism drawn in *Marching Men* was effected by the fascist dictators in Italy, Germany, and Spain during the 1920's and 1930's.[10] The brand of anti-

9. Hofstadter, *op. cit.*, p. 92 and note.
10. *Memoirs*, p. 284.

commercial sentiment seen in McPherson's "rebellion" is scarcely as far removed from the business ideology as it might appear to be, for McPherson remains a businessman-hero to the end; and we are given to believe—in a style that sometimes sounds like an advertising blurb—that he has achieved a neat, comfortable moral awakening: "He is a rich man, but his money, that he spent so many years and so much of his energy acquiring, does not mean much to him. What is true of him is true of more wealthy Americans than is commonly believed. . . . Men of courage, with strong bodies and quick brains, men who have come of a strong race, have taken up what they had thought to be the banner of life and carried it forward."

The intellectual problems implicit in confronting a corrupt and complicated modern society with an Adamic hero equipped with little more than a strong but recently gained moral conscience were to plague Anderson to the end of his career. But traces of the kind of work he was to do in *Winesburg, Ohio* are evident in these books, particularly in *Windy;* and suggestions of a more useful character type than the Adamic hero—distinguished by a perverse obsession with an innocence that violates conventional modes of behavior—appear in the early sections of both books. A number of admirable scenes involve minor characters who are beaten by life, grotesques of the villages and cities who adumbrate the twisted figures of *Winesburg* and the ones that appear in the better tales of *The Triumph of the Egg* and *Horses and Men.* In his portrayal of the abrupt initiation into their world of young McPherson and McGregor and of the painful loss of youthful detachment from the adult world, we see the combination of characters, narrative techniques, and style that brought Anderson's art to its peak of perfection.

These scenes are for the most part found in the first two sections of both books before McPherson's life "ceases to be the story of a man and becomes the story of a type, a crowd, a gang," and before McGregor becomes a proletarian organizer. These scenes are characterized by the fact that McPherson and McGregor act as centers of consciousness who absorb the life about them in the form of impressions. Though rendered objectively in a realistic, reportorial style, the best scenes are filtered through the sensitive inner lives of the heroes and dramatize both the externally observed action and the observers' feelings and thoughts. Thus, like Stephen Crane, Anderson portrays the initiation of his heroes into a complicated world by disclosing their complex responses to the world they are involved in. They grow in consciousness as they absorb the impressions everywhere of defeat and failure.

The successful fusion of Anderson's early impressionistic style with his indirectly stated themes of cultural failure and psychic defeat may best be seen when as youths McPherson and McGregor observe, with shocked and outraged innocence, the cruelty, callousness and meanness of life in the villages and in Chicago, where their fathers—the "war touched" Windy and "Cracked" McGregor—and their careworn and overburdened mothers have become human fragments; where the most intelligent and sensitive people, like the intellectual John Telfer and the school teacher Mary Underwood in *Windy,* and McGregor's father in *Marching Men,* are either tolerated as amusing eccentrics or persecuted by village gossip; and where the timid and meek are social cripples, like the generous Chicago hatmaker, Janet Eberly in *Windy,* and the shy milliner Edith Carson in *Marching Men.*

The most striking episode in either book is that in which the drunken, boastful Windy, who has persuaded himself that he was a heroic figure in the Civil War, dresses in full military regalia for the veterans' parade, mounts a splendid horse, and rides majestically to the center of town intending to open the parade with a magnificent bugle call, only to reveal—and discover—in his abortive performance that he doesn't even know how to play the bugle. In another brilliant episode, a young man named McCarthy, jailed for murder, confronts a heckling mob from his jailhouse window and jeeringly exposes the supposedly respectable women in the crowd whom he has seduced.

Such episodes as these are more common in *Windy* than in *Marching Men,* and they make it the superior work; for in those scenes Anderson's heroes are unhampered by the conscious moral purpose that turns them into the simple-minded reformers of the later sections. His best work in *Winesburg,* in *The Triumph of the Egg,* in *Horses and Men,* and in *Death in the Woods* was to be that which—as in these episodes—the frightening complexity, the puzzling contradictions, the perplexing ambiguities of the adult world first impinge upon the simple and morally ordered world of a youth and shatter his or her comfortable childhood innocence.

The form Anderson found most agreeable to that particular experience was that of the tale. With their moral legends that approach allegory and with their stylized heroes who became psychological archetypes (and thus too often lose their flesh-and-blood identity), *Windy, Marching Men* and all of Anderson's subsequent long narratives are, strictly speaking, romances rather than novels. They emphasize the subjective portrayal of heroic individuals and the growth of their inner lives and are thus to be distinguished from novels which, as

Northrop Frye has usefully shown,[11] more objectively render "real" personalities in vital involvement with others in an "actual" society having the sort of balanced order and commonly accepted modes of behavior we see in the works of Jane Austen and Henry James. The tale and the short story, as Frye points out, are shorter species of the romance and the novel, respectively. It was in the tale, concerned primarily with the inner life of the individual rather than with the social relations of the group, that Anderson was to excel in writing. If he was unable to solve the problems of the individual in American society through the moral journey of his Adamic heroes in the romances, he did successfully portray in the tales that make up *Winesburg, Ohio* both the broken inner lives that characterized that society and the growth to maturity and consciousness of a Midwestern youth.

11. *The Anatomy of Criticism* (Princeton University Press, 1957), pp. 303–14.

BERNARD DUFFEY

has told the story of the Chicago Renaissance, that flowering of a new spirit in the midst of the sterility of American literature in the early twentieth century. This renaissance, ultimate source of much of the later achievement in our literature, was to Sherwood Anderson a "robin's-egg renaissance" that never fulfilled its promise. But to this movement Anderson owes his first acquaintance with the literary figures whose talk and books were to shape the development of his work.

In this selection from The Chicago Renaissance in American Letters, Bernard Duffey discusses Anderson's famous rejection of the business ethic, his associations with the leaders of the Chicago Renaissance, and the effects of that movement in Anderson's novels, stories, and poetry.

From *THE CHICAGO RENAISSANCE IN AMERICAN LETTERS*

Bernard Duffey

The cause and ground of the later Chicago renaissance, the solvent which made of it a homogenous entity, was a struggle against withering restraint. Many in the movement were dedicated to the struggle itself and satisfied by its negative aims. But of the major writers, three at least owed their distinction to the efforts they made, while accepting the Liberation as a beneficent first step, to proceed thence to affirmation, to make their writing speak the Yea which a fulfillment of the Liberation required. Sherwood Anderson, Carl Sandburg, and Vachel Lindsay were wholly of the Liberation. Each of them lived in it and, in part, from it. But each felt the need of a world-view in which one need not always be a rebel. What, after freedom had been achieved, should be the realization? This was the question which they sought to answer.

I.

Sherwood Anderson's history was one of affirmation made through a process of denial and torturous re-learning, a case of conversion in which the lines ran one way until suddenly they broke into confusion and indecision, and then, after a sorting period, gradually reasserted themselves in a new direction. He was born in Camden, Ohio, in 1876, but grew up largely in the near-by town of Clyde where his father had established himself as a house painter and odd-job man. He worked briefly in Chicago as a laborer, served in the Spanish-American War, spent a year at Wittenberg Academy in Ohio, and, in 1900, came again to Chicago to work as an advertising copy writer and begin what seemed an ordinary promising business career. He not only wrote copy for the Frank B. White Co., but for a time conducted columns in *Agricultural Advertising* in which he expressed optimistic and go-getting sentiments appropriate to his calling. In 1904 he married Cornelia Lane, and in 1906 moved to Cleveland into the nominal presidency of a merchandising organization. This venture, however, proved disappointing, and in 1907 he settled in Elyria to the management of a paint-sales business. Then, in 1912, he experienced what was his great crisis, the turning of his back upon the business world and a deliberate estrangement from the only life and values he had known.

His business, increasingly, had seemed sheer involvement without interest or satisfaction; his acquaintance in the city meant less and less; and his home life gave him little satisfaction. With a motive which was in the beginning perhaps purely one of flight he turned to writing, but the positive direction of his work was made clear even in his first effort. This work, he recorded, was called "Why I Am a Socialist," and, although the manuscript itself he later destroyed, the title remained significant. In this instance the primary aim was that of self-definition. As the conflicts of the Elyria years sharpened, Anderson's experience was stretched more and more threateningly between the poles of his business career and his growing sense of literary dedication. In the first he felt increasingly little reality while the second exerted a stronger and stronger pull. These years of strain saw the writing of his first two published novels, *Windy McPherson's Son* and *Marching Men*. He had read Whitman and indulged in literary conversations with professors from a nearby college, perhaps Oberlin, against whose taste he attacked Howells. He neglected his business increasingly for writing and for conversation upon art and life with congenial cronies. The inevitable break came in the fall of 1912 when Anderson walked out of his office under considerable nervous strain, made his way to Cleveland where he spent a mysterious few days from which he recovered in a hospital of that city, and then returned to Elyria convinced that he must scuttle his business commitments and adopt a new life. This aim he realized when in December he left Elyria for Chicago.

Though its ultimate importance has been brought into question by later writers, Anderson's action had always a major significance for himself. It is correct to suggest that he exaggerated, that his accounts of

his departure from his paint warehouse grew more dramatic and more
distorted with the telling, that actually he was as much running away
from a shaky business enterprise as he was projecting himself into a life
of mind and imagination. But such qualifications are more easily made
after the fact by too detached observers than the whole truth may
require. As Anderson was a man always profoundly stirred by his own
image of himself, so one must understand and accept that image if one
is to understand the causes of his behavior and the forces conditioning
his writing. There was, moreover, an objective reality in his choice.
Born and reared in a lower class family, from his earliest years he had
worked within the structure and values of a mobile world. As a
youngster he acquired for himself the nickname "Jobby" because of his
eagerness and skill in making money through scraped-up opportunities.
He had always clung to such main chances as came his way and used
them bit by bit to make of himself a case of that classic and accepted
American type, the man who has risen. He was far from achieving
success in his business ventures by the time of the Elyria period, but in
turning his back upon them, in shaking off as much as he could of his
old character, he did not so much slide down the rungs of American life
as cast off his hold upon the very ladder itself. His earlier efforts had
been mixed, but they had been in character; his successes and failures
had been definable to himself and his world. Upon his arrival in
Chicago, however, in December of 1912, he was for the time a man
without place or identity.

The Elyria episode was no doubt a flight. Because Anderson wrote
again and again of flights, because his style and structure were
deliberately fugitive and elusive in character, because of his many
marriages, because in a genuine sense his life for the nearly thirty years
after 1912 hinged around repeated flights, it is easy to see in his work
nothing but flight—that, of course, being one from reality. Such a
judgment is not wholly false, but it is partial. And what it leaves out is
best suggested by a contrast between the whole career of Anderson and
of another member of the Liberation, like Margaret Anderson, to whom
rejection and rebellion were in fact the only cogent modes of belief and
action. Anderson, for his part, was more seeker than fugitive. What he
found was without doubt nebulous, but his search was none the less
genuine. In his writing there was little to suggest that he ever came
upon a body of finally satisfying ideas or experiences, but, if one look at
his work rather than through it, the achievement of Anderson's search
can be defined. It was nothing less than a sense of self, to be achieved
in the craft of writing, which the world of business and middle class

propriety had destroyed. He, in a radical sense, had rejected that world, but having done so he turned to the creation of another world which could be put in its place. His effort, no doubt, was quixotic, but in one way it accomplished its end. Anderson did in a genuine sense, define himself in his best work. Stories of the quality of "Death in the Woods," "The Man Who Became a Woman," or "The Egg," gave to him what he sought, and they conveyed an act of fulfillment to the reader. They were realizations of what, potentially, Anderson could be —the imaginatively honest and acute narrator of his own bewildering quest. His achievement was lyrical, but, within that limit, one of occasional high success.

Windy McPherson's Son and *Marching Men*, however, had been largely written before Anderson's fulfillment, in Elyria, though one cannot be sure how much they may have been altered between 1912 and their publication in 1916 and 1917. In 1915, for example, Anderson wrote [Floyd] Dell, who had carried *Marching Men* to New York with him, "Send Marching Men to me, I am ready to do some patient sustained work on it."[1] As early work, his novels partook of his earlier sense of tension rather than his later fulfillment. They spelled out a shaky but revealing pattern. Sam McPherson, the hero of the first, was precisely Anderson, the business man in self-discovery and revolt, with a good deal of autobiography thrown in for good measure. Beaut McGregor, hero of the second, was all this plus Anderson's early vision of himself as he might be, the idealist, visionary leader of men, who was perhaps the self-envisaged author of "Why I Am a Socialist." Neither book succeeded as literature or as self-fulfillment. Anderson the rebel was to find ends and means wholly different from Sam McPherson's while Anderson the visionary was to realize his hopes as a writer rather than a leader. But both stories were marking-wands along the path of a liberated midwesterner in search of affirmation.

They shared equally a sense of strain caused by their uneasy balance between objective and inner narrative. Sam McPherson's story was that of a small town boy who, like Anderson, had grown up under a double heritage and double loyalty. He absorbed the standard of success which his world put faith in and, indeed, excelled in its pursuit. Like his author he bore the nickname, Jobby, but he retained also a deep hunger for self-realization unrelated to worldly success. After exhausting the business possibilities of the home town of his story, he proceeds to Chicago and there rises rapidly by a ruthless dedication to business and a total denial of his instinctive self. In becoming a millionaire, however,

1. Anderson to Dell, July 27, 1915. Floyd Dell Collection, Newberry Library.

Sam retains his sense of himself as seeker, and when his business success is shown to involve his father-in-law's suicide, and his own estrangement from his wife, he decides with reason that his personal being must now be given its play. His achievement has turned to ashes, business holds no further lure for him, and on the spur of the moment he makes an about face. Disposing of his business affairs and packing a bag, he strikes alone into the country determined to find out what in life he has missed.

The story, of course, was to be Anderson's own. He plotted out for himself in this novel the course which he himself was to follow except for the bumbling way in which the last third of the book attempted to find a solution for Sam. That hero suffers from the persecutions of a corrupt and driving boss. He joins with laborers and leads a strike for them. He communes with nature. He sinks into dissipation. These experiences all have a redemptive value, but none of them is satisfying. Finally he chances on a drunken and dissolute mother who wants to abandon her children. Sam adopts them, brings them home to his wife, who has lost several children through miscarriages, and reconcilement takes place.

The tale is a wandering and indecisive one entirely congruent with Anderson's frame of mind before the 1912 break. His state of indecision in regard to the story was indicated by his dissatisfaction with the original ending and his plan of writing a new one for the book's republication by Ben Huebsch in 1922. He wished then to take the children back to their own mother, apparently in an effort to show finally that Sam realizes the evils he has turned away from cannot be overcome by a sentimental gesture, even as Anderson's own plight was not to be solved simply by leaving his paint business. One might guess, however, that the real failure in the ending of *Windy* was not that of lighting upon the wrong kind of event, but just that of trying to solve Sam's problem by events at all. This, of course, was also Anderson's problem, and Anderson himself had not in these early years found the consummate experience which he needed to bring Sam's troubles to a convincing end.

The book, as a result, was only the beginning of a search, or the postulation of its necessity, rather than any substantial advance toward ending it. It had value as it gave definition to the dilemma upon which Anderson's consciousness was hung—that lying between the meaninglessness of life for the aspiring individual in the middle-class world and the elusiveness of fulfillment in the pure act of rebellion. *Marching Men* explored the third choice which was necessary if the matter was to be resolved. Though its hope, that of a natural and mystical brotherhood of the men who had been made strangers to each other by an urban and industrial civilization, was rejected in the end, it came from deep in Anderson's feelings and remained in changed form and emphasis a chief element in much of his later work. Sanity, and perhaps survival, depended upon the re-establishment of instinctive human contact. The world in Anderson's view could be made habitable only by love. Individuals could be redeemed only by the same force.

Such for Anderson was the great goal of human life. In 1931, on grounds that Communism was institutional and puritanical, he rejected Dreiser's proposal that he enter the Communist Party. At best it was irrelevant to the deepest human needs and at worst it was a tyranny. Four years later, a letter to Dreiser summed up much of what nearly twenty years of Anderson's writing had been saying. "Now what I have been thinking is that we need here among us some kind of new building up of relationship between man and man." [2] Such too was the theme of *Marching Men,* the deep need for human solidarity and the hopes that lay in such a fulfillment. The book ended, however, with the collapse of Beaut McGregor's vision—that of organizing bodies of workmen and training them to march in disciplined silence so to produce a sense of unity among them deeper and more instinctive than any political scheme. His failure came when, on the brink of success, he found it necessary to relapse into talk, to explain and justify. Anderson, not yet prepared with a concept of natural talk, could not yet prevail against divisive artificialities of civilization.

Unlike *Windy, Marching Men* was content to record a failure. It did not make an effort to patch up. And here lay great hope for Anderson's later work. With the many faults which weakened these two earliest novels, they possessed one solid quality. In them Anderson, as he had one of his characters say of all worthy writers, did seek to reach that point of complete devotion to the demands of his craft summed up by the phrase, imaginative honesty. Janet Eberly, in *Windy McPherson's Son,* chides Sam, "Books are not full of pretense and lies; you business men are . . . What do you know of books? They are the most wonderful things in the world. Men sit writing them and forget to lie, but you business men never forget." For Anderson, the telling of truth could never become a matter of writing in such a way that his work would correspond to whole and objective situations. The dramatic imagination was not his. But he could, in his best work, rise to the point

2. Anderson to Dreiser, January 1, 1935. Sherwood Anderson Collection, Newberry Library.

where he did not delude himself. *Windy* had had an element of self-delusion in it, for Sam McPherson was a heroic, a melodramatized, and finally a fulfilled Sherwood Anderson—but only by power of fancy. *Marching Men* moved on a step. Anderson's hope for himself and for mankind was there considered and rejected because it was stretched over too broad a field. His chief Chicago writing, *Mid-American Chants, Winesburg,* and a number of the stories collected in *The Triumph of the Egg,* was first to reduce that field and then re-define it. In this way a victory became possible.

Chicago presented Anderson with two major gifts. First, through an encounter with Gertrude Stein's *Tender Buttons* he found the possibilities of expressive style. His first novels, he felt later, suffered from imitativeness. They were not sufficiently himself, and the fulfilled Anderson was to be in his own writing his own man. But this new turn came largely through a second gift of Chicago to him, the chance he found, particularly in the 57th street colony, to live as an explorer of the Liberation. Both his introduction to Gertrude Stein and to the 57th street group were brought about by his brother, the painter Karl Anderson, and it was in correspondence with Karl that he defined his theory of art as successful intuition, the basic apologia of his developed work. "What we have got to do," he wrote, "is to feel into things. To do that we only need learn from people that what they say and think isn't of very much importance." [3] And after *Marching Men* had been published in 1917, Anderson emphasized to Karl his lack of sympathy with any merely intellectual view of his writing. "It is very amusing to see our American intellectuals taking me so seriously." [4] They could not know that Anderson was discovering not ideas but a whole person, himself.

The effect of the Liberation was to focus new lights in a brightening sense of self-discovery, and it was thus that Anderson recorded a shock of recognition caused by Dell's praise in the *Friday Literary Review.* "Why how exciting," he exclaimed. "There I was, as Dell was saying in print, in a newspaper read as I presumed by thousands, an unknown man (I do not now remember whether or not he mentioned my name) doing, in obscurity, this wonderful thing. And with what eagerness I read. If he had not printed my name at least he had given an outline of my novel. There could be no mistake. 'It's me. It's me.' " [5] By March of

3. Howard Mumford Jones, in association with Walter B. Rideout, *Letters of Sherwood Anderson* (Boston, 1953), 42.
4. Jones and Rideout, 20.
5. *Sherwood Anderson's Memoirs* (New York, 1942), 235.

1914 Anderson could contribute to the first number of the *Little Review* an essay on the contemporary movement, expressed now in terms precisely of what were to be the two chief attainments in his own work. There was, first, the discovery of a sense of craft, of the writer's identity as writer rather than as advertiser, reformer or self-instructor. And, second, the necessary condition to this discovery, the freeing of the writer from any responsibilities except those he took upon himself. "In the trade of writing," as Anderson put it, "the so-called new note is as old as the world. Simply stated, it is a cry for the reinjection of truth and honesty into the craft; it is an appeal from standards set up by money-making magazines and book publishers in Europe and America to the older, sweeter standards of the craft itself; it is the voice of the new man come into a new world, proclaiming his right to speak out of the body and soul of youth rather than through the bodies and souls of the craftsmen who are gone." [6] Anderson was no youth when he wrote these words, but he was indeed a new man. No longer was he writing out a substitute for an unsatisfactory world as he had in *Windy* or *Marching Men*. His work now became an end in itself by which the writer participated in real life—that of his fulfilled individuality.

In 1933 he wrote to a friend, "My first conception of literature was through Margaret Anderson who started the *Little Review* in Chicago," [7] and, though Anderson wrote many things to many people, there is reason to seize upon this remark as a significant one. Taken in conjunction with his declaration in "More About the New Note" appearing in the second number of the *Little Review* it points revealingly to the discovery Anderson's Chicago experience was to give him. He remained devoted to his concept of love as a saving force, but he found that love was not to be obtained by constructing a fanciful simulacrum of it in his novels. Rather, the writer must lavish love upon his creations themselves. He must become a lover to satisfy his need for love. His craft, and a devotion to it, was the indispensable link between mankind and himself, and love lay in a preservation and exploitation of such links. Thus, for Anderson, came a crucial change, that from writing vitalistic propaganda to himself, or of plotting his course in his writing, to imaginative creation for its own sake. This was the essential difference between the two early novels and the great stories of *Winesburg, The Triumph of the Egg*, and *Horses and Men*, and it remained throughout his career the difference between all his work of the first rate and that below first rate. Literature was a creating of

6. "The New Note," *Little Review*, I (1914), 1, 23.
7. Jones and Rideout, 274–275.

persons, a respecting of them, and a realizing by the writer's imagination of their truth. Anderson as craftsman, his key word in this regard, was to be two things simultaneously. He was the artist of language and the artist of life. In discerning and arranging one, he arranged and so discerned the other. In realizing one he realized the other. The two could not in his view be separated without destroying the very nature of literature. Thus Anderson had no hesitance in founding his critical thought upon a concept of craft despite the latter's seeming incongruity with his passion for life. "The writer is but the workman whose materials are human lives," he wrote in 1925. "It is as true as there is a sun in the sky that men cannot live in the end without love of craft. It is to the man what love of children is to the woman." [8] Later, "The real reward, I fancy, lies just in the work itself, nowhere else. If you cannot get it there, you will not get it at all." [9] Craft, in Anderson's view was not formalistic and not vitalistic, it was both. It was the element common to life and to art. "The imagination must constantly feed upon reality or starve. Separate yourself too much from life and you may at moments be a lyrical poet, but you are not an artist. Something within dries up, starves for the want of food." But it was equally true that, "the life of the imagination will always remain separated from the life of reality. It feeds upon the life of reality, but it is not that life—cannot be." [10] The heart of the matter lay in the inescapable duality of the writer's task.

One more direction was to be tried however before Anderson achieved his first clear success in the new, double vein. That was the composition of his free-verse poems which were collected and published under the title *Mid-American Chants* in 1918. In these, as it were, he abruptly cut the gordian knot of mixed purpose which had been so debilitating a weight on the early novels to launch himself upon outright and unrestrained lyricism—pure expression and undivided feeling. The literary results for the most part were atrocious, perhaps as bad a case of maundering and abortive work as the whole Chicago Liberation, so ready in formless effusion, was to produce. The poems were written during the early years in Chicago. In Anderson's own chronology they followed *Marching Men* and "led into *Winesburg, Poor White,* and *The Triumph,*" which, though there is no other positive evidence for so early a date, would put their composition

8. *The Modern Writer* (San Francisco, 1925), 29.
9. *Modern Writer,* 44.
10. "A Writer's Concept of Realism," quoted from Paul Rosenfeld (ed.), *Sherwood Anderson Reader* (Boston, 1947), 344.

previous to late 1915. Whatever their lack of quality, they were unquestionably of first-rate importance for their author. They marked, first of all, an end to personal rebellion as the great prop of his work. They were testaments of affirmation. *Windy* and *Marching Men,* he wrote to Paul Rosenfeld, had been "the effects of a reaction from business men back to my former associates, the workers. I believe now it was a false reaction. . . . That went. A break came. You will see it in *Mid-American Chants.*" [11] The poems declared, in effect, their author's acceptance of Anderson's own region and its characteristic life. The change, of course, was not a simple flip of the mind to uncritical acceptance. But it was a deep conversion from fear and bewilderment at the Midwest and its ways to a sympathetic concern for it. There was, in the *Chants,* a deliberate effort to say yea, not to all Anderson had formerly denied, but to the inevitable essence of his own development and his work. His new acceptance depended on hope and imagination: new perceptions, that is, of qualities in Midwestern people and their lives which not only gave a different tone to the region than he had formerly recorded but also and more important made it available for imaginative and sympathetic scrutiny. The early Anderson had been, as much as he could, a pessimistic rebel crying to himself the news of doom. After *Mid-American Chants* with their broad acceptance, he could pick up the pieces of what he still regarded as a spoiled and broken life for detailed and genuinely loving treatment. *Winesburg* and the *Triumph* stories were not acts of judgment but of commiseration and understanding.

> *Back of Chicago the open fields—were you ever there?*
> *Trains coming toward you out of the West—*
> *Streaks of light on the long gray plains?—many a song—*
> *Aching to sing.*
>
> *I've got a grey [sic] and ragged brother in my breast—*
> *That's a fact.*
>
> *Back of Chicago the open fields—were you ever there?*
> *Trains going from you into the West—*
> *Clouds of dust on the long grey plain.*
> *Long trains go West, too—in the silence*
> *Always the song—*
> *Waiting to sing.*[12]

11. Jones and Rideout, 78.
12. *Mid-American Chants* (New York, 1918), 81.

Anderson's new approach to the Midwest drew its strength from humility and love. There was also the unabashed lyricism which, though it was to be transmuted in the later work by sympathy, here cut loose from the clogs of realistic convention. But particularly, the *Chants* revealed a concentrated effort to make poetry out of Anderson's own language. This was simple and limited, frequently not sufficient to the demands he put upon it. In the *Chants,* for the first time, he came down upon his language, not to prune and order, but to let come from it whatever was, in nature, there. This was a part of his acceptance. He had felt in Gertrude Stein the achievement of poetry in the aggressively simple. And that, in a literary way, was where his own work must begin and end. He wrote to Paul Rosenfeld, "Being as I have said slow in my nature, I do have to come to words slowly. I do not want to make them rattle. And well enough I know that you, Waldo [Frank], [Van Wyck] Brooks might do in a flash what I will never be able to do. You may get to heights I can never reach. That isn't quite the point. I'm not competitive. I want if I can to save myself." [13]

Such imaginative fulfillment was not conducted in a social vacuum. The change from Elyria to the metropolis had served not only as a change of place, but more deeply as a change in the texture and direction of Anderson's whole life. He left an existence which had been divided among office, home, and country club for a re-alliance with his Chicago advertising firm as a free-lance copywriter, rooms in a boarding house on 57th street, and an intimacy with his artist-brother, Karl, with Floyd Dell and other members of the 57th street group. He could, once again, gratify his taste for flamboyant clothes. He replaced his necktie by a scarf drawn close around his throat with a ring. In the winter of 1913 Anderson and his wife spent some weeks in a cabin in the Ozarks, he with the double purpose of concentration upon his writing and an effort to cement a failing marriage. In the Spring of 1914 he returned to the agency where he wrote furiously at his stories while supposedly turning out advertising copy. During 1914 he also met Tennessee Mitchell, sculptress and suffragette who, Edgar Lee Masters later claimed, had been the great love of Masters' life and was portrayed as Deirdre in his autobiography. He spent the summer of 1915 with her at Lake Chateaugay in the Adirondacks. Here he met Trigant Burrow, one of the early American psychoanalysts, with whom he formed a close friendship. Burrow the medical man and Anderson the writer found an absorbing common ground in their psychological interests.

After this summer Mrs. Cornelia Anderson was to obtain a divorce from the author so that he returned to Chicago in the fall a single man.

13. Jones and Rideout, 79.

He took an attic room at 735 Cass Street where he had as neighbors a group of artistically minded and bohemian friends. Chief among them was George Daugherty, a fellow copy writer with Anderson at the Critchfield agency and one of the early admirers of his work. There were also Jerry Lane, a pianist and a writer, Bill Hollingsworth, a painter, and Max Wald, a musician. This group surrounded him during the composition of the bulk of the Winesburg stories in late 1915 and early 1916.

In August of 1916 he married Tennessee Mitchell. By that time also he had met Waldo Frank and through Frank was made known to the staff of *The Seven Arts,* particularly Van Wyck Brooks. These acquaintances led on to a friendship with Paul Rosenfeld which was to last for a number of years and which sealed his acceptance by the New York intellectual circle of the Liberation. This, though like the Chicago group in important particulars, was possessed of greater literary and intellectual sophistication—attainments which attracted and repelled Anderson alternately until his eventual drift away from the New Yorkers during the twenties. In 1918 Anderson spent much of the year in New York and so continued a movement away from Chicago which had begun with his summers at Lake Chateaugay in 1915 and 1916. In 1920 he was in Alabama where he wrote *Poor White.* His first visit to Europe came in 1921 with Rosenfeld, and in 1922 he made his final break with Chicago, moving to New York, to Reno for a divorce from Tennessee, to New Orleans, and finally to Virginia.

The new attitude expressed by Anderson in *Mid-American Chants* was contemporary with the early links in this chain of events. The first two novels, having been finished substantially before Anderson's move to Chicago, were dominated by a tone of solitary plotting against a hostile and unlovely world. The writing which grew subsequently from an achieved freedom and a steadily widening acceptance by the midwestern and eastern literary groups reflected equally a new self-confidence and a new hope. Anderson's ability, by the time of writing *Mid-American Chants* in 1914 or early 1915, to conceive of himself as a loving artist rather than an alienated and confused prophet must have been greatly heightened by the marked enthusiasm of his new friends for his work. Dell, soon after meeting Anderson in 1913, warmed to his writing and undertook to find publishers for *Windy* and *Marching Men.* Margaret Anderson invited him to write for the *Little Review.* George Daugherty was excited by his stories, and his new love, Tennessee Mitchell, thought highly of his achievement. Anderson the unsuccessful and rebellious salesman had been adopted into the liberated community of the arts in Chicago. It was natural that he should in his first years there have gained a new view of himself as artist, that which he summed up in his ruling idea of craft and expressed first in the achievement of the *Winesburg* and *Triumph* stories. Having been baptized into the community of the Liberation, Anderson received the fruits of its spirit.

The first harmonizing of Anderson's new-found sympathy and newly implemented lyricism in an appropriate form was to come in the narrative sketches of the *Winesburg* volume where he based his characters upon originals of his own acquaintance, an exercise of imaginative sympathy quite foreign to the early work in which he alone had been the focus. As in the case of Masters' *Spoon River*, the achievement of literary identity here followed upon the discovery of a proper subject and the granting to that subject an ultimate control over the whole work. The great bulk of the characters in *Winesburg*, like the town itself, grew from Anderson's own experience. By his own account, his fellow lodgers at 735 Cass Street served as models, but much also came from his years in Clyde. The layout of Winesburg was markedly similar to that of Clyde. In both towns, the imaginary and the real, were a Heffner block of store buildings and a Sinning's Hardware Store. In Winesburg stood Ransom Surbeck's Pool Room while Clyde included a Ransom Surbeck's Cigar Store. A nurseryman, French, in Clyde became a nurseryman, Spaniard, in Winesburg. Jesse Benton, the original settler in Clyde, emerged as the Jesse Bentley of Anderson's story. A Skinner Letson of Clyde had his name changed to Leason only by an afterthought when the original name in the *Winesburg* manuscript was crossed out and the new inserted. Correspondences with Elyria also appeared. Dr. Reefy of "Paper Pills" had the same name as a newspaper-editor friend of Anderson's in Elyria. And Anderson himself made a partial identification of Joe Welling, hero of "A Man of Ideas" with an Elyria printer whom he had found a congenial conversation partner.

The figures of his stories were fully realized, unlike each other, and different from Anderson himself. This set them apart from Sam McPherson and Beaut McGregor who, in character, were nearly interchangeable with their author or with one another. However, in Wing Biddlebaum, the inhibited lover; Doctor Parcival, discoverer of the great truth that "everyone in the world is Christ and they are all crucified;" Jesse Bentley, convinced of a divine vocation to patriarchy; or the Reverend Curtis Hartman, who perceived the strength of God working upon him through the naked body of Kate Swift, enabling him to put her aside—in these was a collection of persons with whom Anderson could sympathize, but who were far from being just puppets or mouthpieces for their author. Each had identity and individual existence. Neither here nor elsewhere did Anderson achieve dramatic validity. Each of his figures sustained a narrative sketch entirely from his own nature without an independent or complicating structure of its own. But each was moving and real.

The resulting literary achievement was curiously ambiguous but also wholly authentic in its impact. It made Anderson a master of the revealing glimpse. Though interested in Freud, Anderson had rejected the idea of clinical Freudianism. Such practice, he felt, tampered too dangerously because too ineptly with the private and inviolable sources of individuality. These yielded up their secrets only to intuition; the artist's sympathy and craft could perhaps suggest something of their nature and importance. In this way literature came to grips with actuality by its own means. It yielded news of the human situation in its own way. And, by its attainments, it gave distinction and identity to its creator.

Anderson's later years brought no drastic change from the discovery and the achievement which Chicago had given him. His writing was an extension with variations of the *Winesburg* pattern. The relative lack of success of his novels bespoke no failure of his powers but rather the basic and obvious inconsistency of his particular method with the demands of the novel. He found happiness in his last marriage, achieved a degree of settlement at Ripshin Farm in Virginia, and continued to produce work of distinction. His later life, at the same time, had its share of troubles. But it did not, in any case, precipitate a further crisis of the kind which had sent him to Chicago in 1912 or offer any discoveries as significant as that which had led him to *Winesburg*. As a writer he had been perfected so far as it lay within him, and the pattern which had brought him fulfillment continued without basic change. "Artists," he said in a summary of his own discovery, "do not want to cut down trees, root stumps out of the ground, build towns and railroads. The artist wants to sit with a strip of canvas before him, face an open space on a wall, carve a bit of wood, make combinations of words and sentences as I am doing now—and try to express to others some thought or feeling of his own. He wants to dream of color, to lay hold of form, free the sensual in himself, live more fully and freely in this contact with the materials before him than he can possibly live in life." [14] These sentiments, for Anderson, were the creed which Chicago had given him. They marked his way of accepting the universe through his own literary vocation.

14. *A Story Teller's Story* (New York, 1924), 300–301.

WILLIAM L. PHILLIPS

has made the most extensive study of the writing of Winesburg, Ohio, *the book that is certain to assure fame to Sherwood Anderson as long as American literature is read. And yet, although* Winesburg, Ohio *has been enjoyed since 1919 by four generations in all major languages, relatively little was known about the circumstances and method of its composition until William Phillips completed his thorough examination of the manuscript. The conclusions reached by Phillips, presented in the March, 1951, issue of* American Literature, *must now be considered in any serious discussion of* Winesburg, Ohio.

HOW SHERWOOD ANDERSON WROTE
WINESBURG, OHIO

William L. Phillips

I.

Probably the most illuminating of the Sherwood Anderson papers recently made available for study is the manuscript of *Winesburg, Ohio*.[1] There on several pounds of yellowed paper lie the answers to questions which have been only hazily answered by critics content to draw their discussions of Anderson's literary habits from his own highly emotionalized accounts. The manuscript reveals Anderson's methods of work and, as a consequence, the limited extent to which his writing may be called "artless." With particular reference to *Winesburg* itself, moreover, it indicates that the book was conceived as a unit, knit together, however loosely, by the idea of the first tale, "The Book of the Grotesque," and consisting of individual sketches which derived additional power from each other, not, as anthologists of Anderson repeatedly suggest,[2] a collection of short stories which can be separated from each other without loss of effect.

1. The Sherwood Anderson Papers, Newberry Library, Chicago. Excerpts from unpublished letters and manuscripts in the Newberry collection are here printed with the generous permission of Mrs. Sherwood Anderson and Dr. Stanley Pargellis, Librarian of the Newberry Library.
2. The most recent, Horace Gregory, in his introduction to the *Portable Sherwood Anderson* (New York, 1949), p. 42, states the prevalent view in

The manuscript, first of all, makes possible a rather accurate dating of the writing itself, a matter not unimportant in the discussion of influences upon Anderson's fiction. In this connection, Anderson's own accounts in his *Memoirs* of the writing of the tales need to be examined as to accuracy. There he said:

> I had been published. Books, with my name on their backs standing on a shelf over my desk. And yet, something eating at me.
>
> "No. I have not yet written."
>
> . . . upon the particular occasion I am speaking of . . . it was a late fall night and raining and I had not bothered to put on my pajamas.
>
> I was there naked in the bed and I sprang up. I went to my typewriter and began to write. It was there, under those circumstances, myself sitting near an open window, the rain occasionally blowing in and wetting my bare back, that I did my first writing.
>
> I wrote the first of the stories, afterwards to be known as the Winesburg stories. I wrote it, as I wrote them all, complete in the one sitting. I do not think I afterwards changed a word of it. I wrote it off, so, sitting at my desk, in that room, the rain blowing in on me and wetting my back and when I had written it I got up from my desk.
>
> The rest of the stories in the book came out of me on succeeding evenings, and sometimes during the day while I worked in the advertising office. At intervals there would be a blank space of a week, and then there would be two or three written during a week. I was like a woman having my babies, one after another but without pain.[3]
>
> I had been working so long, so long. Oh, how many thousands hundreds of thousands of words put down. . . .
>
> And then, on a day, late in the afternoon of a day, I had come home to that room. I sat at a table in a corner of the room. I wrote.
>
> There was the story of another human, quite outside myself, truly told.
>
> The story was one called "Hands." It was about a poor little man, beaten, pounded, frightened by the world in which he lived into something oddly beautiful.

justifying his omission of "The Book of the Grotesque": "The loose construction of *Winesburg, Ohio* makes it possible to present the best of its stories without loss to the reader, and it should be remembered that the tales of *Winesburg, Ohio* were conceived and written as short stories before they appeared under the title of a book."

3. *Sherwood Anderson's Memoirs* (New York, 1942), pp. 286–288. Reprinted with the permission of Harcourt, Brace and Company, publishers.

The story was written that night in one sitting. No word of it
ever changed. I wrote the story and got up. I walked up and down
in that little narrow room. Tears flowed from my eyes.

"It is solid," I said to myself. "It is like a rock. It is there. It is
put down. . . ."

In those words, scrawled on the sheets of paper, it is
accomplished.[4]

The romantic subjectivity of these two accounts indicates the
importance of the *Winesburg* stories as a turning point in Anderson's
writing career, at least as he saw it; but the same subjectivity suggests
that the facts surrounding the composition of the stories should be
studied in the light of other evidence. Indeed the mention of the
typewritten story in the first account and of the "words, scrawled on the
sheets of paper" in the second should warn Anderson's biographers of
his lack of interest in fact when invention would make a better story.[5]

If we assume that in the first account when Anderson speaks of "the
first of the stories, afterwards to be known as the Winesburg stories" he
is referring to "The Book of the Grotesque," the time indicated by the
first paragraph is incorrect. This story, actually the first of the
Winesburg tales to be written and the first to be published, appeared in
the *Masses* in February, 1916,[6] and thus must have been written at least
as early as November, 1915. In November, 1915, Anderson could not
have had "books with [his] name on their backs" on his shelf, since his
first book, *Windy McPherson's Son*, was not published until September, 1916, and since his second book, *Marching Men*, was not
published until the autumn of 1917.[7] If, on the other hand, Anderson
in the first account is speaking of the story "Hands," specifically

4. *Ibid.*, pp. 279–280. For two similar accounts, both of which specifically
mention "Hands" as the story the writing of which marked the turning point in
his career, see "A Part of Earth" in the *Sherwood Anderson Reader*, ed. Paul
Rosenfeld (Boston, 1947), pp. 321–328, probably a rejected variant of one of the
Memoirs passages quoted above, and a letter from Anderson to Roy Jansen, April,
1935, Newberry Library Collection.

5. Cf. *Memoirs*, p. 7: "Facts elude me. I cannot remember dates. When I deal
in facts, at once I begin to lie. I can't help it. I am by nature a story teller."

6. *Masses*, VIII, 17. The magazine publication of this story was not noticed by
Raymond B. Gozzi in his "Bibliography of Anderson's Contributions to
Periodicals, 1914–1946," *Newberry Library Bulletin*, pp. 71–82 (Dec., 1948);
Paul Rosenfeld erroneously gave its date of composition as 1918 in the *Sherwood
Anderson Reader*, p. v.

7. Cf. Harry Hansen, *Midwest Portraits* (New York, 1923), p. 121, which
includes statements from the publisher of the books.

mentioned in the second account, the paragraph still is inaccurate, since "Hands" was published in the *Masses* in March, 1916,[8] six months before the publication of his first novel and a year and a half before that of his second.

Furthermore, although Anderson insisted that after writing the story "Hands," "no word of it ever changed," the manuscript shows that the tale underwent extensive revisions of words and phrases after it had been written. And in addition to the manuscript revisions, the first five paragraphs of the *Masses* version of "Hands" are a re-arrangement of the corresponding first two paragraphs of the manuscript version, indicating that Anderson reworked the first part of the story before submitting it to the *Masses*.[9]

Two more accounts of the writing appear in Anderson's unpublished papers. On April 21, 1938, he wrote to his friend Roger Sergel that he had recently found a complete manuscript of *Winesburg, Ohio* in an old box of papers; and, explaining the fact that the manuscript was on cheap newsprint paper, he said: "When I wrote the book I was employed in the copy department of an advertising agency and used to cop print paper. The mms is [*sic*] partly on the back of earlier attempts at novels and is mostly in long hand . . . pen, partly pencil." [10]

Anderson's statements in the letter to Sergel agree with the note which Anderson attached to the manuscript which he had found. There he said:

> At the time these stories were written, the author was employed as a copy writer in a Chicago advertising agency and the paper is no doubt that used for roughing up advertisements. It is likely the stories were written two or three times, in the writer's room, in a rooming house in Cass Street in Chicago, or in hotels as he traveled about, visiting clients of his employers. It is the author's notion that the manuscripts which only showed up after many years in a box of old manuscript, is the one prepared for the making of a fair copy by a stenographer. At the time these stories were written the author had already published two novels and had made beginnings and sketches for others and some of this

8. *Masses*, VIII, 5, 7.

9. According to Floyd Dell, then coeditor of the *Masses* with Max Eastman, any changes not made by the author would have been made by Dell or Eastman; each in a letter to the writer has denied changing any of the tales. The only result of the *Masses* revision is a slightly more abrupt opening to the story.

10. Newberry Library Collection.

manuscript is on the back of sheets covered with these abandoned efforts.

This last account again raises the problem as to when the stories were written. But, as we have shown earlier, Anderson had not "already published two novels" at the time of the writing of the first two stories, and there is good evidence that, as Anderson has indicated in the *Memoirs* passage quoted earlier, many of the stories were written in a short space of time.

The surviving manuscript consists of drafts of each of the *Winesburg* stories, seven of which are written on the cheap, now yellowed print paper used in blocking out advertisements. The other eighteen tales (counting the four parts of "Godliness" as individual tales) are written on the backs of twenty-one separate fragments of early writing, which are, in the main, parts of a novel concerning a character named Talbot Whittingham and variously called "The Golden Circle," "Talbot the Actor," and "Talbot Whittingham." [11]

Since most of the stories are written on the backs of these earlier attempts, and since several *Winesburg* narratives may appear on the back of one fragment, it is possible to set up a chain of the composition of this draft of the tales. The supposition is that if a pile of scrap manuscript were to be used for writing, the entire pile would be turned over, and what was the last page of the abandoned fragment would appear as the first page of the new story. Thus, for example, when pages 2 to 12 of the manuscript "The Book of the Grotesque" appear on the backs of pages 15 to 5 of an earlier penciled story about a boy named Paul Warden, and the first four pages of the manuscript "Hands" continue down through the pile of the Paul Warden story to complete pages 4 to 1 of the fragment, it seems clear that Anderson wrote the two stories without a delay which would disturb the order of the pile of abandoned attempts.

By the use of such a chain of manuscripts, the order of composition for three groups of tales may be established.[12] In the first group the

11. This was a novel parts of which Anderson brought with him to Chicago from Elyria, Ohio, in early 1913, and which he worked on intermittently until his death. Several large bundles of "Talbot Whittingham" are now in the Newberry Library Collection. For comment concerning the merits of the novel, see Hansen, *op. cit.*, pp. 117, 122.

12. For a detailed description of the process, see William L. Phillips, "Sherwood Anderson's *Winesburg, Ohio*: Its Origins, Composition, Technique, and Reception" (unpublished doctoral dissertation, University of Chicago, 1949), Appendix.

following stories appear on the backs of manuscripts the pages of which interlock:

1 "The Book of the Grotesque"   7 "Surrender (Part Three)"
2 "Hands"   8 "Nobody Knows"
3 "Paper Pills"   9 "Respectability"
4 "Tandy"   10 "The Thinker"
5 "Drink"   11 "Terror (Part Four)"
6 "Mother"

The second group begins a second chain of manuscripts, beginning with pages removed from the fragment on which "Mother" (Number 6 above) was written, and continuing on the back of another manuscript:

1 "Godliness (Part One)"
2 "Godliness (Part Two)"

The third group consists of five tales written on the backs of nine fragments, the pages of which do not follow an exact chain but which indicate that the tales were all written on the same small pile of abandoned manuscript. The probable order of these tales is:

1 "Adventure"   4 "Loneliness"
2 "The Strength of God"   5 "An Awakening"
3 "The Teacher"

This third group has connections to the pages of manuscripts on the backs of "The Thinker," "Surrender," and "Terror" in the first group.

Since the first three of the *Winesburg* tales ("The Book of the Grotesque," "Hands," and "Paper Pills" in Group 1) were published in magazines in February, March, and June of 1916 in that order,[13] it seems reasonable to assume that the drafts of all the stories written on the backs of abandoned manuscripts were written in the fall of 1915 and the winter of 1916. It seems proper to assume that over anything but a short period of time, the pile of manuscripts would have been disturbed to such an extent that a grouping like that above would not

13. "The Book of the Grotesque" in *Masses*, VIII, 17; "Hands" in *Masses*, VIII, 5, 7; and "Paper Pills" under the title of "The Philosopher" in *Little Review*, III, 7–9. An entirely different story appeared as "The Philosopher" in *Winesburg, Ohio*, a point which has been overlooked in Gozzi, *op. cit.* Rosenfeld in the *Sherwood Anderson Reader* erroneously dates "Paper Pills" as written in 1918.

have been possible, and thus it seems clear that Anderson has correctly indicated that "the rest of the stories came out of me on successive evenings, and sometimes during the day while I worked in the advertising office. At intervals there would be a blank space of a week and then there would be two or three written during a week."

The remaining seven stories, written on the print paper, may well be the stories composed "in the advertising office" or "in hotels as he traveled about visiting clients of his employers." These are "The Philosopher," "A Man of Ideas," "Queer," "The Untold Lie," "Death," "Sophistication," and "Departure." Since two of the seven were published in magazines in December, 1916, and January, 1917,[14] at least those two may be placed with the stories jotted on the backs of manuscripts; some of the other five, as we shall see, were written later.

Anderson's statement that the manuscript represents "one prepared for the making of a fair copy by a stenographer" suggests that he felt that the manuscript was a late one, prepared just before the collection of the tales into a volume. This, however, is not the case. The preparation of a fair copy for a stenographer would probably have followed the order of the tales in the volume, whereas the order of the manuscripts suggests rather the order of *composition* of the tales. Furthermore, each manuscript contains evidence of extensive revision on the manuscript itself, the results of which revision appear in the magazine version of the tale. A manuscript prepared for the gathering of the tales into a volume might contain revisions from the magazine version to a final version, but could hardly contain revisions from an earlier writing to a magazine version.

Finally, Anderson's statement that "it is likely that the stories were written two or three times" needs to be examined. The revisions on the manuscripts indicate that Anderson was thinking his way through the stories as he wrote them, and that if there were earlier versions, they were mere outlines. Unless this kind of writing were considered a first draft and the revisions made on the manuscripts themselves considered a third draft, Anderson's *Memoirs* statement that "I wrote it, as I wrote them all, complete in one sitting," is closer to the actual manner of composition, although not wholly accurate, as we shall see when we come to consider the revisions themselves. Thus, from Anderson's varying accounts and from the evidence of the manuscripts we may conclude that the *Winesburg* stories were written during a relatively

14. "Queer," *Seven Arts*, I, 97–108 (Dec., 1916); "The Untold Lie," *Seven Arts*, I, 215–221 (Jan., 1917).

short period of time, one leading to another, and that this period of time was late 1915 and early 1916.

2.

The first *Winesburg* story, as we can see from Anderson's own accounts of its composition, was a starting-point for a career in short story writing which was to lead Anderson to international fame in the genre. One is naturally curious about the conception of the first tale, how its basic idea and the details of its rendering came about. Such a scene as this can be reconstructed: on a late fall day in 1915 Anderson had come home from his desk at the advertising office of the Critchfield Company to the third floor of a rooming house at 735 Cass Street in Chicago, just a few blocks away from the offices of Harriet Monroe's *Poetry* and Margaret Anderson's *Little Review*. He had perhaps stopped on a bridge over the Chicago River to try to fathom the expression on a face he had passed in the street, and then he had gone up to his room to write at a long table with a bare electric light over it. For nights before, figures had been passing before his eyes as he lay on the bed which he had had built up for him so that he could look out over the Loop.[15] Concerned for his own future as a writer, feeling himself one who "had known people, many people, known them in a peculiarly intimate way," he searched himself by throwing himself into the imagined life of another. That other, an old man with a white mustache, lay on *his* raised bed and watched in a half-dream the procession of figures before his eyes. They were all grotesques, and the old man wrote a book which he called "The Book of the Grotesque." [16]

Whether the conception of Anderson's own book of grotesques came before or immediately after he wrote this first *Winesburg* story, "The Book of the Grotesque," his own gallery of imaginary figures offered him more than enough characters for his book. For the past several years he had been writing novels about a Talbot Whittingham who had lived in a town called Winesburg, Ohio, so far as Anderson knew not a real Ohio town, but one which had the characteristics of Clyde, Ohio,

15. For information concerning Anderson's circumstances in Chicago in 1915–1916 I am indebted to Mr. George Daugherty, Mr. Max Wald, and Mr. Mitchell Dawson, all of Chicago, and to Mr. Marco Morrow, of Topeka, Kansas. For Anderson's accounts, see *Memoirs*, pp. 227–233, 277–280.

16. *Winesburg, Ohio* (New York, 1919), pp. 1–5. This edition will be referred to throughout this paper; since the Modern Library reprint was printed from the original plates, the page numbers noted also apply to it.

where he had spent his boyhood.[17] The name of the town had perhaps been suggested by Wittenberg, the academy which he had attended, or perhaps there had remained in the back of his mind, lost to consciousness, the real town of Winesburg, to which he may have sent "Roof-fix" from his Elyria paint factory. The name of George Willard was similar in sound to the names of George Bollinger, Joe Welliver, and Trigant Williams which appeared on the pages of the rejected manuscript on which he wrote the *Winesburg* stories. Now he could tell how Tandy Hard got her name; he had told his friends in the rooming house that he was writing a trilogy about a woman named Tandy Hard; and Max Wald, the musician, had said that the name reminded him of nothing but hard candy.

The first figure to be clothed was that of the frightened little man who seemed to be afraid of his hands. Anderson once suggested that the impulse to write about Wing Biddlebaum came from his jokingly calling a friend "Mabel" in a bar and watching the knowing looks of the other men at the bar,[18] but the idea of writing about a man "in whom the force that creates life is diffused, not centralized" must have occurred to him earlier when he questioned a group at the Floyd Dells' parties about Freud's views on homosexuality, two years before.[19] After he had lifted Wing Biddlebaum of Winesburg from the life of imagination into the life of reality, the other "figures on the doorstep of his mind" stood "waiting to be clothed." There was the figure of Dr. Reefy, who, like the father of Talbot Whittingham in the pile of rejected attempts at novels, was a small-town doctor with radical ideas; there was Tandy Hard, the girl whose strange name needed explanation; there were the friends of George Willard, his mother, his father. All of these people were grotesques, suffering from the universal illness

17. For Anderson's life in Clyde, drawn on in the *Winesburg* stories and others, cf. Evelyn Kintner, "Sherwood Anderson: Small Town Man" (unpublished M.A. thesis, Bowling Green State University, 1942), and William Alfred Sutton, "Sherwood Anderson's Formative Years (1876–1913)" (unpublished doctoral dissertation, Ohio State University, 1943).

18. *Sherwood Anderson Reader*, pp. 325–327.

19. *Memoirs*, pp. 243–244. The matter of Anderson's knowledge of Freudian psychology is a complicated one, and it has been made no less so by Frederick J. Hoffman's discussion of it in his *Freudianism and the Literary Mind* (Baton Rouge, 1945), pp. 230–255. Although the proof cannot be reproduced here, it may however be said that Anderson first encountered Freudian terminology at the apartment of Floyd Dell in the late summer of 1913, and that by the time the *Winesburg* stories were written he was intimately acquainted with at least one practising psychiatrist, Dr. Trigant Burrow, to whom he had been introduced by his second wife, Tennessee Mitchell Anderson.

of isolation and frustration, and they all belonged in "The Book of the Grotesque."

Here was an opportunity for the novel writer who had not been published; the manuscripts of *Windy McPherson's Son* and *Marching Men,* almost wholly written before he had left his Elyria paint factory in late 1912, were still being peddled from publisher to publisher by Floyd Dell.[20] Perhaps already Anderson was aware of the faults of these books, difficulties which he had not been able to overcome. In a gallery of portraits, a book of grotesques, there would be an opportunity to search back into his boyhood to exploit the material which had provided the most appealing parts of his two early novels. Here was an opportunity to allow the center of the stage to the characters in episodes who had kept intruding into the plots of his earlier novels; here he could build a series of incidents like the tale of Windy McPherson's attempt to blow a bugle in the Fourth of July parade,[21] an episode much more appealing as a portrait of Windy than as a contribution to the growth of Windy's son, the chief character of the novel. Windy really belonged in a "book of the grotesque."

One other factor helped to crystallize Anderson's conception of a "book of the grotesque"—Edgar Lee Masters's *Spoon River Anthology.* When the reviewers of *Winesburg, Ohio* in 1919 made the obvious comparison between the two books, Anderson's publishers replied with an announcement that "Mr. Anderson's 'Winesburg' stories appeared in magazines before Mr. Masters's work appeared," clearly a misstatement of the facts.[22] But Anderson himself, despite the critics' suggestions of influence, kept silent on the matter, while he strongly denied the influence of "the Russians" and Theodore Dreiser. Fortunately, some new evidence has appeared which helps to determine the facts of the matter. Mr. Max Wald, one of the "Little Children of the Arts" who lived with Anderson in the Cass Street rooming house, recently recalled in an interview that shortly after *Spoon River Anthology* appeared in book form (April, 1915), he bought a copy, read it, and spoke admiringly of it to Anderson. Anderson, after remarking that Tennessee

20. See Floyd Dell, *Homecoming* (New York, 1933), pp. 253–254, for the most accurate account.

21. *Windy McPherson's Son* (New York, 1916), pp. 22–23.

22. The statement was reported in the *Bookman,* L, x (Sept., 1919). Masters's *Spoon River* portraits had begun to appear in *Reedy's Mirror* in the issue of May 29, 1914, and had been collected into a book published in April, 1915; the first *Winesburg* story was not published until Feb., 1916. Thus it is at least *possible* for Anderson to have had a copy of *Spoon River Anthology* before him as he wrote the *Winesburg* tales in the winter of 1915–1916.

Mitchell (soon to become his wife) knew Masters, took the book to his room and returned it in the morning, saying that he had stayed up all night reading the poems and that he was much impressed by them.[23] Very probably this reading of Masters's book just six months before the writing of the first *Winesburg* story helped shape the "book of the grotesque" into a collection of sketches in which the characters would be related in their environment and treated as a cross section of village life. It may be suggested furthermore that Anderson's reticence to discuss Masters's work in print may have resulted from his awareness of the past relationship of Tennessee Mitchell (his wife by the time of the book publication of *Winesburg*) and Edgar Lee Masters. Tennessee Mitchell was the "Deirdre" of Masters's *Across Spoon River,* scathingly denounced by him in that work; she had, apparently, been his mistress for eighteen months in 1909 and 1910, and, according to Masters, had been responsible for widening the breach between Masters and his first wife.[24] If Anderson had been aware of the extent of Tennessee Mitchell's alleged involvement with Masters,[25] he could hardly have failed to identify the original of "Georgine Sand Miner" and "Tennessee Claflin Shope" in *Spoon River Anthology* and "Deirdre" in the later *Across Spoon River,* and he may very well have preferred not to open the subject of his relations with Masters. In any event, it seems extremely likely that Anderson's admiration for Masters's portraits and his knowledge of their enthusiastic reception by the Chicago critics may have hastened his development from *Windy McPherson's Son* to "The Book of the Grotesque," later to be called *Winesburg, Ohio.*

The manuscript shows that from the first the *Winesburg* stories were conceived as complementary parts of a whole, centered in the background of a single community. In the first individual story, "Hands,"

23. Statements in interview with the writer, Chicago, June 24, 1949.

24. *Across Spoon River* (New York, 1936), pp. 295–313. Masters verified the identification of Tennessee Mitchell as "Deirdre" in a letter to the writer, May 25, 1949. It must be said that the authenticity of the "Deirdre" episode rests solely on Masters's testimony; those close to Anderson at the time—Dr. Trigant Burrow, Mr. Karl Anderson, Mr. Max Wald, Mr. George Daugherty, Mr. Marco Morrow, and others—recall only that Anderson first met Masters through Tennessee Mitchell, who had known him before Anderson came to Chicago. Masters wrote of his acquaintance with Anderson: "After meeting I do not remember how often we saw each other; not often. I do remember he came to my house one night. I never discussed *Spoon River* with him, but I do think it had influence upon his *Winesburg, Ohio.*"

25. In his *Memoirs,* p. 453, one of the few instances in which Anderson wrote of Tennessee Mitchell, he said: ". . . Tennessee—someone away back in your childhood had done you a great wrong. You could never quite tell of it, although you wanted to. Or perhaps it was some man later—some poet—you had a passion for poets."

Anderson had called his town "Winesburg, Ohio"; in "Paper Pills," the next tale to be written, only "Winesburg" appears on the manuscript as the name of the town. In the second story he introduced "the Heffner Block," an actual group of buildings in the Clyde, Ohio, of his boyhood, and "John Spaniard," the disguised nurseryman French of Clyde.[26] In the first story he had mentioned that George Willard was the son of the proprietor of the New Willard House; the third story to be written, "Tandy," might well take place on the steps of the New Willard House. Tandy lives on a road leading off Trunion Pike, a new geographical detail added to the growing conception of the town of Winesburg; in the fourth story to be written, "Drink," the opening paragraph contains a reference to Trunion Pike, and added in this story to the physical picture of the town are Duane Street, the name of a Clyde street, and "Hern's Grocery," the disguised name of Hurd's grocery where Anderson worked as a boy in Clyde. Much of the action of this story takes place in the office of the *Winesburg Eagle,* which had been mentioned earlier in "Hands." One can see how each scrap of description tended to fill in the environment of Winesburg—its stores and its streets—and how after Winesburg was furnished with a Main Street, it would be easy to have a Duane Street, a Buckeye Street, and a Maumee Street branching from it.

As the streets led to each other, and all branched from Main Street, so one scrap of action led to another, and each had some reference to George Willard. In "Drink" it was mentioned in passing that George Willard, like Tom Foster, had a "sentiment concerning Helen White" in his heart. From this brief casual reference must have grown the conception of George Willard's love affair with Helen White which furnishes part of the interest in "The Thinker" and the entire interest in "Sophistication," both later stories, and which in turn suggested George Willard's adventures with the two other girls of the town, Louise Trunnion and Belle Carpenter, in "Nobody Knows" and "An Awakening." George's walk with Belle Carpenter in "An Awakening" provided a beginning for Wash Williams's lecture on women to George in "Respectability." The outbreak of George's schoolteacher in "The Teacher" led Anderson to wonder what effect she had on others of the town, and in "The Strength of God" he described her impact upon the Presbyterian minister. Kate Swift's naked form at prayer beside her bed

26. The most convincing evidence that Anderson was thinking of Clyde characters as he filled out the *Winesburg* stories is his use of "Skinner Leason" for the name of the Winesburg grocer (*Winesburg, Ohio,* p. 28). There was a Skinner Letson in Clyde, and the name on the manuscript appears as "Letson" crossed out, with "Leason" substituted.

suggested to him another sexually frustrated spinster, Alice Hindman, who runs naked into the street in "Adventure." Reading the stories in the order of their composition, one can watch Anderson follow the excursions of his own imagination, while the town of Winesburg becomes completed in its physical setting and the people of Winesburg become tangled in their relations to each other, in either their awareness of each other or their significant unawareness of each other.

3.

A study of the manuscript furthermore reveals something of the way in which the individual *Winesburg* tales were written. No outlines or early half-formed versions of the stories exist, although there may have been some for a few of the tales. On the backs of the Newberry manuscripts of "Mother" and "Drink," however, is an earlier story which has been preserved in an early draft. The manuscript begins with eighteen words and phrases scrawled in a column down a page, forming a brief outline, one which might have been jotted down in a few seconds in an attempt to catch the characteristics of a figure in Anderson's fancy. Following this outline are thirty pages of a story, never completed, about a George Bollinger and his love affair with an Alice Hassinger.

Such brief outlines may or may not have been used for the *Winesburg* tales; with such a story as "Hands" it is likely that the story was written in one frenzied rush of the pencil. Anderson once said: "I am not one who can peck away at a story. It writes itself, as though it used me merely as a medium, or it is n.g. . . . The short story is the result of a sudden passion. It is an idea grasped whole as one would pick an apple in an orchard. All of my own short stories have been written at one sitting." [27] Let us examine for evidence of his working habits the manuscript of "Hands," which Anderson most admired and which he singled out for mention as one that had never been changed in a word.

The manuscript of this story consists of twenty-seven pages written in a penciled scrawl on the backs of three fragments of earlier stories. The handwriting is legible only with difficulty, and it becomes less legible toward the end of the story and in several sections in which the ideas apparently flowed more rapidly than the hand could put them down. Nowhere in the manuscript is there a rearrangement of the parts of the story, the deletion or addition of a paragraph, or even the deletion or addition of a complete sentence, indicating that Anderson followed the order of narration which came most natural to him, in some instances

27. *Memoirs*, pp. 286, 341.

an order which violated the usual chronology of a short story. There are no revisions so far as major changes in the story are concerned, and in this respect Anderson's comment that "no word of it ever changed" is correct; the story was "grasped whole."

There are, however, almost two hundred instances in which earlier words and phrases are deleted, changed, or added to, to provide the readings of the final published version of the story. The larger part of these revisions were apparently made after the story had been written through once, since they are made over the lines and in the margins. But about one-tenth of the revisions were made during the first writing, since they appear on the line of writing before it continues.

Such revisions as were made during the first writing provide an interesting picture of Anderson's habits, his manner of working through a story. He can be seen taking great care in the selection of the exact word for the idea to be expressed, sometimes rejecting one word for another only to reinsert the first one before the rest of the sentence was finished.[28] Occasionally the creative process was stopped while Anderson, always a bad speller, corrected his misspelling of a simple word.[29] One can observe the consolidation of ideas, and in some instances the dawning of new ideas which were then incorporated into the story and developed. Indeed, the entire idea regarding the need for a poet to tell the story of Wing Biddlebaum's hands may have come from Anderson's dissatisfaction with a word used in the first writing and immediately changed. In the first passage mentioning the need for a poet, the story of Biddlebaum's hands originally was called merely "strange"; then for "strange" (a word much used by Anderson and often deleted) was substituted "worth a book in itself." The sentence about the need for a poet then followed: "The story of Wing Biddlebaum's hands is ~~strange~~. worth a book in itself. Sympathetically set forth it would tap many strange, beautiful qualities in obscure men. It is a job for a poet." [30] It is not too fanciful to suggest that in searching for a better word than "strange" Anderson hit upon the idea of the need for a poet to write the story, a motif repeated later [31] which adds to the frequent intrusion of the author into this tale.

The revisions which Anderson made *during* the first writing,

28. For example, "With a shiver of ~~dread fear~~ dread the boy arose. . . ." The final reading may be found in *Winesburg, Ohio*, p. 12. In notes following, the location of only the final reading will be indicated; each revision considered is representative of others which cannot be reproduced for lack of space.
29. ". . . a part of the ~~towhn~~ town where . . ." (*ibid.*, p. 8).
30. *Ibid.*, p. 10.
31. *Ibid.*, pp. 12–13.

however, are greatly in the minority; about nine-tenths of the changes were made after a first draft had been completed. And it seems clear that the story, although first drafted in a "sudden passion," was reworked several times, since occasionally words which were added above the line of writing of the first draft were later themselves deleted. Most of the revisions of words and phrases were made only once, however. Of these it is significant that while there were 99 *substitutions* of words and phrases for earlier expressions and 58 *additions* of expressions, there were only 21 instances in which expressions were deleted and not replaced by others. Anderson's first writing of the story must have seemed to him sufficiently economical in its treatment, so that instead of paring the story further he was concerned with filling it out.

In the main his deletions simply removed overworked or awkwardly used words, although in one instance he added to the universality of the story by deleting the single word "his": "The story of Wing Biddle-baum is a story of ~~his~~ hands." [32] But the substitutions and additions which he made to the story show more clearly his attempts to give an accurate rendering of the fanciful figure of Wing Biddlebaum and his hands. Anderson was first of all aware that he would have to avoid any details about Wing's case that would disgust the "normal" reader if he were to treat the homosexually inclined character with sympathy. He must avoid the suggestion that Biddlebaum's attraction to George Willard is wholly erotic in nature. Thus he added the qualifying "something like" in "With George Willard . . . he had formed something like a friendship"; [33] instead of "he still hungered for the boy" he wrote "he still hungered for the presence of the boy"; [34] and he replaced "[Biddlebaum's hands] stole to George Willard's shoulders" with "[Biddlebaum's hands] stole forth and lay upon George Willard's shoulders." [35]

Often his revisions increased the suggestiveness of the tale with symbolic details. Instead of an ordinary veranda, Wing's porch was made a "half-decayed veranda," suggesting the state not only of the veranda but of the man who walked upon it; and the field which stood near Biddlebaum's house, originally a corn field grown with "weeds," was changed to "a field that [had] been seeded for clover but that had

32. *Ibid.*, p. 9. One cannot, of course, be certain *why* Anderson made any of the revisions. It must be assumed that when a change achieves a new effect Anderson by his revision intended that effect.

33. *Ibid.*, p. 8.

34. *Ibid.*, p. 16.

35. *Ibid.*, p. 12.

produced only a dense crop of yellow mustard weeds." [36] Wing Biddlebaum's hands were described as beating like "the wings of an *imprisoned* bird," and were made to appear as something outside himself, uncontrollable, unattached to himself by the change of *"his* hands" to *"the* hands."

     the
Again he raised ~~his~~ hands to caress the boy. . . . Again and again the fathers of the boys had talked of ~~his~~ the hands.[37]

Some of the stylistic traits that have been noticed in Anderson's prose —colloquialisms, repetitive patterns, and frequent auctorial intrusions— can be seen to have arisen in the revisions. He can be seen changing a more formal, Latinate expression to a colloquial, Anglo-Saxon one: "At times an almost overwhelming curiosity had taken ~~possession~~ hold of him." [38] He added the last name of Wing Biddlebaum three times and of George Willard twice in the story, so that neither of the men is ever called by a single name. This repetitive trick, probably learned from Gertrude Stein's "Melanctha," [39] achieves the simple, causal effect of language comparatively free of pronominal antecedents. Although in "Hands" there are no passages with marked patterns of repetition of the kind to be found elsewhere in the tales,[40] the revisions of the story indicate that Anderson tended to select a descriptive detail for a character or place which he repeated whenever the character or place was again mentioned. For example, in the opening sentence of the story Wing Biddlebaum is pictured walking upon the "veranda of a small frame house that stood near the edge of a ravine"; near the end of the story when Wing continues to walk "upon the veranda of his house," Anderson added "by the ravine," and a few lines later he changed the original "he went again to walk upon the porch" to "he went again to walk upon the veranda." [41] Finally, the intrusions of the author into this

 36. *Ibid.*, p. 7. The book version and its later reprints read *"has* been seeded for clover," a typographical error; the manuscript has the more grammatically proper "had."
 37. *Ibid.*, pp. 9, 12, 15. Italics mine.
 38. *Ibid.*, p. 10.
 39. In a letter to Gertrude Stein preserved in the Yale University Library, Anderson expressed his admiration for "the first thing of yours I read—in the Three Lives—about the nigger woman." Such repetitive patterns are also characteristic of the King James Version of the Bible and *Huckleberry Finn*, both of which Anderson much admired.
 40. Cf. *Winesburg, Ohio*, pp. 4–5, 38–39, 168–169, 206–207, 219.
 41. *Ibid.*, p. 16.

story, characteristic of oral storytellers and of Anderson's borrowing of their technique, did not go unnoticed by him; they were not merely the slips of an untrained fiction writer. Although the intrusions appear in the first writing of the story and were not added later, Anderson in several instances smoothed off his entrance into the tale and made his intrusion seem less blunt. For example, "We will look briefly into the story of the hands. It may be our talking of them will arouse the poet . . ." was softened to "Let us look briefly into the story of the hands. Perhaps our talking of them will arouse the poet . . ." [42] as though the storyteller realized that he might offend his audience by directing their attentions too obviously.

The process of writing "Hands," then, was much as Anderson suggested; the story was "an idea grasped whole as one would pick an apple in the orchard." But, to continue his figure, the manuscript indicates that after Anderson had picked the apple he examined it carefully for bad spots and polished its minor imperfections.

4.

When a number of the *Winesburg* stories had been written and revised, Anderson set about getting the individual tales into print. Because of their unconventional subject matter and treatment, they were not likely to be acceptable to the popular magazines; but Anderson was known to the editors of several "little magazines." Since Floyd Dell still had the manuscript of *Windy McPherson's Son* and was still convinced that Anderson was a writer who should be published, he was likely to accept some of the tales for the *Masses,* of which he and Max Eastman were co-editors. Anderson apparently sent the early tales to Dell in the order that he wrote them, since "The Book of the Grotesque" and "Hands," the first two of the tales to be written and published, appeared in that order in the February and March, 1916, issues of the *Masses.* Later in the year Dell published "The Strength of God," but soon a dissatisfaction with the stories arose in the editorial offices of the *Masses,* and the later tales were voted down by the editors.[43]

In the meantime one of the stories, "Paper Pills," had appeared in Margaret Anderson's *Little Review.* Anderson had contributed articles to the first two issues of this magazine in 1914, and he continued to publish sketches there during 1915 and 1916. Since the magazine was at this time still being published in Chicago, and since Anderson was a

42. *Ibid.,* p. 12.
43. Letter to the writer from Floyd Dell, Dec. 12, 1948. Cf. Hansen, *op. cit.,* p. 123, and Dell, *op. cit.,* p. 256.

frequent visitor to Margaret Anderson's North Shore gatherings, it was not surprising that one of the early *Winesburg* tales should have been published in the *Little Review*.[44]

The beginning of plans in the winter of 1915–1916 for a new "little magazine," the *Seven Arts,* offered another outlet for the stories. Edna Kenton had met Anderson in Chicago in the early winter of 1916 and had read several of his stories. She sent Anderson's name to Waldo Frank, one of the men who was slated to become an editor of *Seven Arts* when it began publication. Anderson and Frank corresponded during the winter and spring of 1916, and Frank was enthusiastic about a number of the *Winesburg* stories which Anderson sent him. In the summer of 1916 Anderson invited Frank to come to Lake Chateaugay in upper New York for a vacation, and the two spent much time during June and July discussing Anderson's work. By that time, Frank has recently remarked, Anderson had "already written at least a majority of the Winesburg tales." [45] Frank's admiration for Anderson's work grew during this summer, so that for the first issue of *Seven Arts,* in November, 1916, he wrote the commendatory article, "Emerging Greatness," concerning Anderson's first novel (which by this time had been published). The second issue of *Seven Arts* had as its leading story "Queer," by Sherwood Anderson; the third issue printed "The Untold Lie" and announced that other *Winesburg* tales would follow. Two other tales did follow—"Mother" and "The Thinker"—before *Seven Arts* lost its subsidy and ceased publication.[46]

Except for "An Awakening" and "A Man of Ideas," which were printed in the *Little Review* some months later,[47] these were all of the *Winesburg* tales which appeared in magazines before their publication in book form in 1919. For the ten stories, Anderson later remembered, he received only $85, since of the three magazines in which they had appeared, only *Seven Arts* paid for its material.[48] But for a writer who had published only three short stories before,[49] the reception of the

44. Cf. n. 13. For an account of Anderson's relations with the *Little Review,* see Margaret Anderson, *My Thirty Years' War* (New York, 1930), pp. 90–91.

45. Letter to the writer, March 23, 1949.

46. "Mother," *Seven Arts,* I, 452–461 (March, 1917), and "The Thinker," II, 584–597 (Sept., 1917). With its next issue, the journal ended.

47. "A Man of Ideas," *Little Review,* V, 22–28 (June, 1918); "An Awakening," *Little Review,* V, 13–21 (Dec., 1918). The latter story has been omitted from Gozzi, *op. cit.*

48. *Memoirs,* p. 288.

49. "The Rabbit-pen," *Harper's,* CXXIX, 207–210 (July, 1914); "Sister," *Little Review,* II, 3–4 (Dec., 1915); and "The Story Writers," *Smart Set,* XLVIII, 243–248 (Jan., 1916). These do not include Anderson's contributions during 1902–1905 to *Agricultural Advertising,* the house organ of the Chicago advertising firm for which he worked, some of which were fictional sketches.

Winesburg tales by Floyd Dell, Margaret Anderson, and Waldo Frank must have led Anderson to believe that in such tales as these he had found his medium of expression.

Certain changes in the stories were made before Anderson submitted them to the magazines. Most of these were minor changes—revisions of punctuation and occasional changes of wording—but two were extensive. One was the rearrangement of the story "Hands" in the version published in the *Masses* mentioned earlier,[50] noteworthy only since this is the story of which Anderson said, "No word of it ever changed." But the second, involving the *Seven Arts* version of "The Untold Lie," is more striking. In *Seven Arts,* the story opens:

> When I was a boy and lived in my home town of Winesburg, Ohio, Ray Pearson and Hal Winters were farm hands employed on a farm three miles north of us. I cannot for my life say how I know this story concerning them, but I vouch for its truth. I have known the story always just as I know many things concerning my own town that have never been told to me. As for Ray and Hal I can recall well enough how I used to see them on our Main Street with other country fellows of a Saturday afternoon.[51]

The first person narrator continues, telling the story exactly as it is told in the book version, except for frequent intrusions like "as I remember him" and "I myself remember." Since in the book version the only entrance into the tale of characters in earlier tales is a brief mention of "boys like young George Willard and Seth Richmond," [52] which might easily have been added to tie this tale loosely to the others, one might think that the *Seven Arts* version was an earlier one which had been reworked to fit into the collection of tales. This possibility has been seized upon by a student of Anderson who has recently suggested that not only did Anderson revise the magazine version of "The Untold Lie" to make it conform to the focus of narration of the other tales, but that the frequent intrusions of the author into the other tales are the results of faulty revisions of *their* earlier "I" (first person) versions. This writer concludes:

> It is quite likely, I should say, that some of these stories were originally written from a first-person observer focus and then revised to tone down the "I"; others were written from the

50. See n. 9, above.
51. I, 215 (Jan., 1917).
52. *Winesburg, Ohio,* p. 245.

omniscient author focus. . . . The impression that one gains of most of the *Winesburg* stories is that they were written with the author doing the telling as an "I," and that this "I" appeared wherever it was necessary for him to do so. Later the number of "I's" was cut down either by direct elimination (and making the necessary changes) or by substitution of "George Willard." [53]

This ingenious theory is, however, disproved by the manuscripts of the stories which are now available for study. None of the manuscript versions is of the "I" variety; and the manuscript of "The Untold Lie," like the others an omniscient author version, contains frequent revisions the *results* of which appear in the magazine version. Thus, as he revised "Hands" before submitting it to the *Masses,* Anderson must have revised "The Untold Lie" immediately before sending it to Waldo Frank for publication in *Seven Arts;* the "I" version was not the first but a revised one, and the original omniscient author version stayed in the pile of manuscripts to be used in *Winesburg, Ohio.*[54]

5.

Most of the *Winesburg* stories must have been written, as Anderson said, in a short period of time with one providing the germ for another. But a few of the stories seem surely to have been written later. We have seen that eighteen of the twenty-five tales were written on the backs of the interlocking earlier manuscripts and thus must have been composed together. Of the seven stories on the yellow advertising copy paper (and therefore suspect of being later) two, "Queer" and "The Untold Lie," were published in the first two issues of *Seven Arts* and thus must have been written before, or at the latest, during Anderson's correspondence with Waldo Frank in the spring of 1916. A third, "A Man of Ideas,"

53. Jarvis A. Thurston, "Sherwood Anderson: A Critical Study" (unpublished doctoral dissertation, State University of Iowa, 1946), pp. 98–99, 110. The unpublished material in the Newberry Library Collection was not available at the time of Mr. Thurston's study.

54. It is difficult to see, nevertheless, why Anderson should have made such a change. The awkwardness with which "I" has to account for his knowledge of the story detracts from the plausibility of the tale itself. The "I" character is not affected by the events which he tells about; "I" is not anxiously thinking "I Want to Know Why," or explaining why "I'm a Fool." He is rather telling a story which could more plausibly have been told by an omniscient author. The only reasons for the change which may be suggested are admittedly questionable ones. Perhaps Anderson wished to achieve some variety of telling in the four stories which appeared in *Seven Arts,* or perhaps he was hesitant about including George Willard in all the stories which he published in magazines, thinking that George's appearance as a connecting force in the final collection would dissipate its novelty in magazine appearances.

was published in the *Little Review* soon after the *Seven Arts* ceased publication, and before the publication in the *Little Review* of "An Awakening," one of the early tales. The remaining four—"The Philosopher," "Death," "Sophistication," and "Departure"—are the only ones which seem to have been written later.

There are two indications that "The Philosopher" was a later addition to the group of tales. The story written as "Paper Pills" and published under that title in the 1919 volume was first published in the *Little Review* as "The Philosopher" in June, 1916, when, according to Waldo Frank, a majority of the tales had been written.[55] It is not likely that Anderson would take the title of a story which was waiting to be published and put it on another story. Furthermore, it will be noticed that as the tales were written more and more details of setting were added, so that in contrast to "Hands" and "Paper Pills," which have only modest references to Main Street or the New Willard House, the later stories are filled with names of streets, business houses, and minor characters. "The Philosopher" is such a story; here, although half of the comparatively short story is taken up by Dr. Parcival's tale of his earlier life away from Winesburg, the rest of the narrative is filled with allusions to the *Winesburg Eagle,* its editor Will Henderson, Tom Willy's saloon, the baggage-man Albert Longworth, Main Street, Biff Carter's lunch room, and the railroad station, all of which had been mentioned in earlier stories.

"Death," "Sophistication," and "Departure," the remaining tales of those written on the advertising copy paper, are the last three tales in the *Winesburg* volume. None was published in a magazine, and all are filled with allusions to names and places which had been mentioned earlier. "Death" is actually two stories, the account of the love affair of Dr. Reefy and Elizabeth Willard and the story of George Willard's reaction to the death of his mother. It is preceded in the *Winesburg* volume by "The Untold Lie" and "Drink," tales which have their chief interest in characters outside the Willard family. But in "Death" the interest shifts back abruptly to Elizabeth Willard and her struggle with her husband over George's future. Dr. Reefy had not been mentioned since the early story "Paper Pills," but here he becomes Elizabeth Willard's lover just before her death, as the two most sympathetically treated of the mature characters in the book are brought together in a brief moment of escape from isolation. It seems as if Anderson realized that his "Book of the Grotesque" had become filled, and that to keep the novelistic quality of the work he would have to bring his chief

55. Letter to the writer, March 23, 1949. Cf. n. 13 above.

characters to some end. Just as in *Windy McPherson's Son* and *Marching Men* it is the deaths of the mothers of Sam McPherson and Beaut McGregor which stir them to leave their villages permanently, so Elizabeth Willard's long-awaited death is the event which sends George Willard out of Winesburg and which prepares for the short résumé of his career in "Departure."

"Sophistication" is the culmination of the George Willard–Helen White affair which had been touched upon in several earlier stories, but which had not been given a full treatment. In it Anderson was able to show not only the final stage of George Willard's feeling for Helen White but also the growing sophistication which had resulted from his listening to the stories of the grotesques of Winesburg. Thus in the last two tales George Willard's affairs in Winesburg are brought to a close with the death of his mother and the establishment of a more mature relation with Helen White; he is ready for "Departure."

Whether a publisher suggested that the last stories be written to round out the career of George Willard or whether Anderson felt that they were needed to make his "Book of the Grotesque" something more than a mere collection of short stories cannot be determined. It is probable that the latter was the case. Anderson later said that although he had secured publication in magazines for some of the tales he wanted them put together in a single volume. "The stories belonged together," he said. "I felt that, taken together, they made something like a novel, a complete story [which gave] . . . the feeling of the life of a boy growing into young manhood in a town." [56]

But getting the items in "The Book of the Grotesque," as Anderson then spoke of it to Floyd Dell, published in a volume was a difficult matter. Anderson submitted the stories to John Lane, the English publisher of his first two novels, but the Lane firm had lost confidence in Anderson after the weak sales of his early books, and they refused the *Winesburg* stories on the ground that they were "too gloomy." [57]

Anderson's early work, however, had found admirers in people like Waldo Frank, Floyd Dell, Theodore Dreiser, Ben Hecht, Margaret Anderson, and Francis Hackett. And it was Francis Hackett, then literary editor of the *New Republic,* who showed the manuscript of "The Book of the Grotesque" to Ben Huebsch, owner and editor of a small publishing house in New York which had already published Joyce's *Dubliners* and *A Portrait of the Artist as a Young Man* and

56. *Memoirs*, p. 289.
57. Letter to the writer from B. W. Huebsch, June 22, 1949. For an account of the poor sales of the early books, see Hansen, *op. cit.,* pp. 121–122.

Lawrence's *The Prussian Officer* and *The Rainbow*. Huebsch became interested, obtained Anderson's release from John Lane, and suggested the title *Winesburg, Ohio* for the stories.[58] Finally, in April, 1919, fully three years after most of them had been written, the episodes which had begun with the conception of a "Book of the Grotesque," written (in the main) as a connected series, were published as *Winesburg, Ohio*.

58. *Ibid.*

"M. A."

can be identified only as the au-
thor of this article, which appeared in the June 25, 1919, issue of
The New Republic, shortly after the publication of Winesburg,
Ohio. "A Country Town" is reprinted here because it remains
historically interesting as a contemporary review of Sherwood
Anderson's best-known work and because it is typical of the critical
acclaim given to Winesburg, Ohio at its appearance. The reviewer
recognizes the "new note" that the volume struck in American
literature, and he readily praises Sherwood Anderson for the
salutary boldness of that note. But the tone of cautious praise points
toward the fact that only slowly and over a period of several years
was Winesburg, Ohio admitted to the ranks of the American
classics.

A COUNTRY TOWN

M. A.

Every middle westerner will recognize Winesburg, Ohio, as the town in which he grew up. Devon, Iowa, would have furnished forth just such a book as this had an incisive historian made the community his own; so would Minnewaukan, North Dakota, or Wolf Point, Montana, or any one of ten thousand others. The story of a small town anywhere is the story of the revolt of youth against custom-morality; with youth winning only occasionally and in secret, losing often and publicly. In the middle west the dominant morality of the cross-roads is a puritan inheritance. Puritanism went over to Ohio from New England with the settlers, and has taken a firmer hold on the minds and lives of the inhabitants of the Mississippi valley than it ever had in the east. Hell-fire begins to look a trifle comical in Massachusetts. There is a wide-spread recognition of other inconveniences more direct and immediate. But in Kansas and Nebraska the most potent terror is still the anger of a deity.

The Winesburg of twenty years ago was like the Kansas of today, at least in philosophy. The known and accepted standards were those laid down some thousands of years ago by the leader of one of the nomadic tribes of Asia Minor, crudely adjusted to fit a more complex situation. In many ways the ancient laws could not be adjusted at all; they seem to have confused and darkened more often than they shed light. The wonder is that so few shins were broken on the ten tables of stone. Five hundred sensitive individuals isolated in a haphazard spot on the prairie and seeking to express themselves through the forms of a religion ill-understood, the methods of a business system inherently unjust, and the social customs of a more brutal and bitter era were fated to come upon tragic and pathetic difficulties. For that matter there has never been any truth in the notion of pensive hamlets and quiet little villages. Cranford may have dozed. There were no men in Cranford. But the dwellers in -villes and -burgs and -towns from Jamestown in Maine to Jamestown in California can tell you truths about their neighbors that will shatter forever what remains of the assumption that life seethes most treacherously in cities and that there are sylvan retreats where the days pass from harvest to harvest like an idyl of Theocritus. There is outward repose over Winesburg, a garment of respectable repose covering alike the infinite pain, the grief, the agony of futile grouping, the momentary flare of beauty or passion of which the citizens are ashamed.

We are given our view of Winesburg through twenty-three sketches dealing with the crises in as many lives. The lives are inter-related, and a multitude of subsidiary figures drift through the incidents, appearing and disappearing, grouping and changing, in the manner of pedestrians along a by-street. The stories are homely and unemphatic. Crime and love and merry-making come casually into being; chance exalts and flatters, thwarts and subdues. The character that re-emerges oftenest is George Willard, reporter for the Winesburg Eagle. He is the ordinary, bumptious young man with dreams of getting "away from all this" and doing "something" huge and vague in distant cities. To him the town is dull and queer. Save when shocked or startled into a mood of insight he sees little but news values. It was old Parcival who first shocked him. He "began to plead with George Willard, 'You must pay attention to me,' he urged. 'If something happens to me perhaps you will be able to write the book that I may never get written. The idea is very simple, so simple that if you are not careful you will forget it. It is this—that everyone in the world is Christ, and they are all crucified. That's what I want to say. Don't you forget that. Whatever happens, don't you dare let yourself forget.'"

The most satisfactory of the sketches is the one called Paper Pills, a bit from the lives of Doctor Reefy and the tall dark girl who became his wife. There are only five pages of it, and it is told effortlessly, almost carelessly, yet it suggests better than any of the more conscious attempts the theme that engages Mr. Anderson throughout, the loneliness of human life, the baffled search of every personality for meanings and purposes deeper than anything that may be said or done, answers that will cut under the superficial axioms by which we are judged.

> The girl and Doctor Reefy began their courtship on a summer afternoon. He was forty-five then, and already he had begun the practice of filling his pockets with the scraps of paper that became hard balls and were thrown away. The habit had been formed as he sat in his buggy behind the jaded grey horse and went slowly along country roads. On the papers were written thoughts, ends of thoughts, beginnings of thoughts. One by one the mind of Doctor Reefy had made the thoughts. Out of many of them he formed a truth that arose gigantic in his mind. The truth clouded the world. It became terrible and then faded away and the little thoughts began again.

The girl had come to him because she was pregnant, and there was nobody else to confide in. We hear nothing of their talk together.

> The condition that had brought her to him passed in an illness, but she was like one who has discovered the sweetness of the twisted apples, she could not get her mind fixed again on the round perfect fruit that is eaten in the city apartments. In the fall after the beginning of her acquaintanceship with him she married Doctor Reefy and in the following spring she died. During the winter he read to her all of the odds and ends of thoughts he had scribbled on the bits of paper. After he had read them he laughed and stuffed them away in his pockets to become round hard balls.

As a challenge to the snappy short story form, with its planned proportions of flippant philosophy, epigrammatic conversation, and sex danger, nothing better has come out of America than Winesburg, Ohio. Because we have so little in the field it is probably easy to over-estimate its excellence. In Chekhov's sketches simplicity is an artistic achievement. With Sherwood Anderson simplicity is both an art and a limitation. But the present book is well within his powers, and he has put into it the observation, the brooding "odds and ends of thoughts" of many years. It was set down by a patient and loving craftsman; it is in a new mood, and one not easily forgotten.

IRVING HOWE

                             published his Sherwood Anderson *in 1951 as an attempt to understand why the writer remained an outstanding artist for his good work and why he had produced so many unsatisfactory books. Howe wrote with the assumption that Sherwood Anderson was, after all, but a minor figure in American literature, and this assumption lessens the reliability of his study. Yet Irving Howe's discussion of* Winesburg, Ohio *is an invaluable treatment of the literary backgrounds of the work and the reasoned effort which Anderson put into the book that was to be recognized as his masterpiece.*

THE BOOK OF THE GROTESQUE

Irving Howe

Between Sherwood Anderson's apprentice novels and *Winesburg, Ohio* there stands no intermediary work indicating a gradual growth of talent. *Mid-American Chants* testifies to both an increasing interest in the possibilities of language and a conscious submission to literary influence, but it is hardly a qualitative advance over its predecessors. From Anderson's Elyria work to the achievement that is *Winesburg* there is so abrupt a creative ascent that one wonders what elements in his Chicago experience, whether in reading or personal relations, might have served to release his talents.

The list of writers to whom Anderson acknowledged a serious debt was small: George Borrow, Mark Twain, Ivan Turgeniev. In the early 1920's D. H. Lawrence was added to the small group of masters who had decisively impinged on him, but in 1915 and 1916, the years when he wrote *Winesburg*, Anderson had, of course, not yet read Lawrence.

While his attachment to Borrow antedates his public career as a writer, it also testifies to a wish, once that career had begun, to fondle a certain image of himself as a literary personality. To Anderson, the artist always seemed a peculiarly fortunate being who could evade much of the drabness of daily life. By ordering his experience through the canny artifice available only to himself, the artist could establish a margin for the half-forgotten life of flair and largesse, could find a way of surmounting the barren passage of the routine. Unlike those

American writers who take great pains to insist that their occupation is as "normal" as any other, Anderson liked to proclaim the uniqueness of the artist's life.

To a writer enamored of such a notion, the figure of George Borrow would naturally seem attractive. Borrow's picturesque narratives of gypsy life, virtually unclassifiable among the traditional genres, seemed significant to Anderson because they flowed from a conscious rejection of conventionality and charming because they did not flinch from the romantic, the garrulous, and the merely odd. Borrow provided Anderson with an image of a potential self: the sympathetic auditor of his people's inner history; and for the Borrovian hero who wanders among "backward peoples" he had a considerable admiration, particularly during those burdened years in Elyria when he thought the literary career an avenue to a liberated and adventurous life. Yet there are no significant traces of Borrow in any of Anderson's books; neither in subject matter nor in structure is there an observable line of descent from, say, *Lavengro* to *Winesburg*. The relation is one of personal identification rather than literary influence; Borrow, it seemed to Anderson, was above all a guide to how a writer might live.

If Borrow suggested an attractive style of life, Turgeniev's *Memoirs of a Sportsman*, "like low fine music," set the very tone Anderson wished to strike in his prose. In Turgeniev's masterpiece he admired most that purity of feeling which comes from creative tact, from the author's strict refusal to violate or impose himself on his characters. Between *Memoirs of a Sportsman*, which Anderson called "the sweetest thing in all literature," and *Winesburg* there are obvious similarities: both are episodic novels containing loosely bound but closely related sketches, both depend for impact less on dramatic action than on a climactic lyrical insight, and in both the individual sketches frequently end with bland understatements that form an ironic coda to the body of the writing. These similarities could certainly be taken as tokens of influence—if only we were certain that Anderson had actually read Turgeniev before writing *Winesburg*.

When critics in the 1920's discovered that Anderson was indebted to Chekhov and Dostoievsky (which he was not), he gleefully denied having known the Russian novelists until after the publication of *Winesburg*. This denial, however, is controverted by two statements in his correspondence, a remark in his *Memoirs*, and a recollection in an autobiographical fragment. His credibility as a witness of his own past is further damaged by the fact that in the early 1920's his publisher, probably at his instigation and certainly with his consent, issued a public statement denying that Anderson had read *Spoon River* before writing *Winesburg* and insisting that Masters's book appeared after the *Winesburg* sketches came out in magazines. Though the publisher was wrong on both counts, Anderson did not trouble to correct him. Like many untrained writers, he may have feared than an acknowledgment of a literary debt would cast doubt on the value or at least the originality of his work.

But if Turgeniev's influence on *Winesburg* is not quite certain, there can be no doubt about Mark Twain's. Between the America of Anderson's boyhood, which is the setting of his best work, and the America of Huck Finn there are only a few intervening decades, and the nostalgia for a lost moment of American pastoral which saturates *Huckleberry Finn* is also present in *Winesburg*. Twain's influence on Anderson is most obvious in the early portions of *Poor White* and some of the stories in *The Triumph of the Egg*, but it can also be seen in *Winesburg*, particularly in Anderson's attempt to use American speech as the base of a tensed rhythmic style. His identification with Borrow was to some extent a romantic whimsy, but his identification with Twain had a strong basis in reality. As he wrote to Van Wyck Brooks, Twain had also been an untrained man of natural talent "caught up by the dreadful cheap smartness, the shrillness that was a part of the life of the country"; Twain had also been bedeviled by the problem of success and the need to conciliate the pressures of East and West.

These were pervasive influences; none of them could have provided the immediate shock, the specific impetus that turned Anderson to the style and matter of *Winesburg*. Such an impetus, if one can be singled out at all, came not from any individual writer but from Anderson's dramatic exposure in 1913–15 to the Chicago literary world. When Max Wald, one of "the little children of the arts," lent him a copy of *Spoon River*, Anderson raced through it in a night. This, he excitedly told his friends, is the real thing—by which he meant that Masters, in his imaginary Midwestern village, had bared the hidden lesions of the American psyche. Had Anderson stopped to notice the appalling frustration that motivated Masters's book he might have been somewhat less enthusiastic, but for the moment *Spoon River* suggested that in a prose equivalent Anderson might find a form allowing more freedom that the conventional novel and yet resulting in greater complexity of meaning than could be had in any individual sketch. Masters hardly influenced the vision behind *Winesburg*, but he did provide intimations of how it might be organized.

At about the same time Anderson was introduced by his brother Karl to the early writings of Gertrude Stein. Anderson has recalled that he "had come to Gertrude Stein's book about which everyone laughed but about which I did not laugh. It excited me as one might grow excited in going into a new and wonderful country where everything is strange. . . ." The truth, however, was somewhat more complex than Anderson's memory. His first reactions to Stein were antagonistic: at a Chicago party in 1915 he told Edna Kenton that he thought it merely funny that anyone should take *Tender Buttons* seriously, and shortly afterwards he even composed a parody of Stein for his advertising cronies.

But his inaccurate recollection had, as usual, a point of genuine relevance. For though he laughed at Stein when he first read her, she seems to have stimulated him in a way few other writers could. Nearly always one parodies, for good or bad, those writers who deeply matter. To Anderson Stein suggested that, at least in the actual process of composition, words could have an independent value: they could be fresh or stale, firm or gruelly, colored or drab. After reading the fanatically monosyllabic *Three Lives* Anderson would hardly try again, as he had in his first two novels, to write "literary" English. But despite such surface similarities as repetition of key words and an insistently simple syntax, their styles had little in common. Stein's language was opaque, leading back into itself and thereby tending to replace the matter of fiction, while the language of *Winesburg* was translucent, leading quickly to the center of the book's action. Stein was the best kind of influence: she did not bend Anderson to her style, she liberated him for his own.

And that, essentially, was what the Chicago literary milieu did. It persuaded Anderson that American writers needed an indigenous style which, if only they were bold enough, they could then and there construct; it taught him that before language could be used creatively it might have to be crumbled into particles; and it made him conscious of the need for literary consciousness. For the time being that was enough.

Anderson has recalled that during the years immediately preceding *Winesburg* he would often take with him on advertising trips pages torn from Gideon Bibles, which he read over and over again. This recollection tells us most of what needs to be known about the making of *Winesburg*. Its author had not the slightest interest in religion, but his first involvement in a literary environment had made him aware of writing as writing and had taught him where to find its greatest English source. He had begun to work as a conscious craftsman: the resulting ferment was *Mid-American Chants*, the substance *Winesburg*.

The history of *Winesburg* is a curious instance of the way criticism, with its passion for "placing," can reduce a writer to harmless irrelevance. At various times the book has been banished to such categories as the revolt against the village, the rejection of middle-class morality, the proclamation of sexual freedom, and the rise of cultural primitivism. Whatever the justification for such tags may once have been, it is now quite obvious that Anderson's revolt was directed against something far more fundamental than the restrictions of the American village and was, for that matter, equally relevant to the American city; that *Winesburg* is not primarily concerned with morality, middle-class or otherwise, if only because most of its characters are not in a position to engage in moral choice; that while its subject is frequently tangential to sex it expresses no opinions about and offers no proposals for sexual conduct, free or restricted; and that its style is only dimly related to anything that might be called primitive. If read as social fiction *Winesburg* is somewhat absurd, for no such town could possibly exist. If read as a venture into abnormal psychology the book seems almost lurid, for within its total structure the behavior of its hysterics and paranoids is quite purposeless and, in the absence of any norms to which their deviations might be compared, even incomprehensible. In fact, if read according to the usual expectations of 20th-century naturalistic or conventionally realistic fiction, *Winesburg* seems incoherent and the charge of emotion it can still raise inexplicable.

In its fundamental quality *Winesburg* is nonrealistic; it does not seek to gratify the eye with a verisimilitude to social forms in the way a Dreiser or a Lewis novel does. In rather shy lyrical outbursts the book conveys a vision of American life as a depressed landscape cluttered with dead stumps, twisted oddities, grotesque and pitiful wrecks; a landscape in which ghosts fumble erratically and romance is reduced to mere fugitive brushings at night; a landscape eerie with the cracked echoes of village queers rambling in their lonely eccentricity. Again and again *Winesburg* suggests that beneath the exteriors of our life the deformed exert dominion, that the seeming health of our state derives from a deep malignancy. And *Winesburg* echoes with American loneliness, that loneliness which could once evoke Nigger Jim's chant of praise to the Mississippi pastoral but which has here become fearful and sour.

Winesburg is a book largely set in twilight and darkness, its backgrounds heavily shaded with gloomy blacks and marshy grays—as is proper for a world of withered men who, sheltered by night, reach out for that sentient life they dimly recall as the racial inheritance that has been squandered away. Like most fiction, *Winesburg* is a variation on the theme of reality and appearance, in which the deformations caused by day (public life) are intensified at night and, in their very extremity, become an entry to reality. From Anderson's instinctively right placement of the book's central actions at twilight and night comes some of its frequently noticed aura of "lostness"—as if the most sustaining and fruitful human activities can no longer be performed in public communion but must be grasped in secret.

The two dozen central figures in *Winesburg* are hardly characters in the usual novelistic sense. They are not shown in depth or breadth, complexity or ambiguity; they are allowed no variations of action or opinion; they do not, with the exception of George Willard, the book's "hero," grow or decline. For Anderson is not trying to represent through sensuous images the immediate surface of human experience; he is rather drawing the abstract and deliberately distorted paradigm of an extreme situation, and for that purpose fully rounded characterizations could only be a complicating blemish.

The figures of *Winesburg* usually personify to fantastic excess a condition of psychic deformity which is the consequence of some crucial failure in their lives, some aborted effort to extend their personalities or proffer their love. Misogyny, inarticulateness, frigidity, God-infatuation, homosexuality, drunkenness—these are symptoms of their recoil from the regularities of human intercourse and sometimes of their substitute gratifications in inanimate objects, as with the unloved Alice Hindman who "because it was her own, could not bear to have anyone touch the furniture of her room." In their compulsive traits these figures find a kind of dulling peace, but as a consequence they are subject to rigid monomanias and are deprived of one of the great blessings of human health: the capacity for a variety of experience. That is why, in a sense, "nothing happens" in *Winesburg*. For most of its figures it is too late for anything to happen, they can only muse over the traumas which have so harshly limited their spontaneity. Stripped of their animate wholeness and twisted into frozen postures of defense, they are indeed what Anderson has called them: grotesques.

The world of *Winesburg*, populated largely by these back-street grotesques, soon begins to seem like a buried ruin of a once vigorous society, an atrophied remnant of the egalitarian moment of 19th-century America. Though many of the book's sketches are placed in the out-of-doors, its atmosphere is as stifling as a tomb. And the reiteration of the term "grotesque" is felicitous in a way Anderson could hardly have been aware of; for it was first used by Renaissance artists to describe arabesques painted in the underground ruins, *grotte,* of Nero's "Golden House."

The conception of the grotesque, as actually developed in the stories, is not merely that it is an unwilled affliction but also that it is a mark of a once sentient striving. In his introductory fantasy, "The Book of the Grotesque," Anderson writes: "It was the truths that made the people grotesques . . . the moment one of the people took one of the truths to himself, called it his truth, and tried to live his life by it, he became a grotesque and the truth he embraced a falsehood." There is a sense, as will be seen later, in which these sentences are at variance with the book's meaning, but they do suggest the significant notion that the grotesques are those who have sought "the truths" that disfigure them. By contrast the banal creatures who dominate the town's official life, such as Will Henderson, publisher of the paper for which George Willard works, are not even grotesques: they are simply clods. The grotesques are those whose humanity has been outraged and who to survive in Winesburg have had to suppress their wish to love. Wash Williams becomes a misogynist because his mother-in-law, hoping to reconcile him to his faithless wife, thrusts her into his presence naked; Wing Biddlebaum becomes a recluse because his wish to blend learning with affection is fatally misunderstood. Grotesqueness, then, is not merely the shield of deformity; it is also a remnant of misshapen feeling, what Dr. Reefy [*sic* for the third-person narrator] in "Paper Pills" calls "the sweetness of the twisted apples."

Winesburg may thus be read as a fable of American estrangement, its theme the loss of love. The book's major characters are alienated from the basic sources of emotional sustenance—from the nature in which they live but to which they can no longer have an active relationship; from the fertility of the farms that flank them but no longer fulfill their need for creativity; from the community which, at least by the claim of the American mythos, once bound men together in fraternity but is now merely an institution external to their lives; from the work which once evoked and fulfilled their sense of craft but is now a mere burden; and, most catastrophic of all, from each other, the very extremity of their need for love having itself become a barrier to its realization.

The grotesques rot because they are unused, their energies deprived of outlet, and their instincts curdled in isolation. As Waldo Frank has noticed in his fine study of *Winesburg,* the first three stories in the book suggest this view in a complete theme-statement. The [first] story, "Hands," through several symbolic referents, depicts the loss of creativity in the use of the human body. The second story, "Paper Pills," directly pictures the progressive ineffectuality of human thought, pocketed in paper pellets that no one reads. And the third story, "Mother," relates these two themes to a larger variant: the inability of Elizabeth Willard, *Winesburg's* mother-figure, to communicate her love to her son. "The form of the mother, frustrate, lonely, at last desperate," Frank writes, "pervades the variations that make the rest of the book: a continuity of variation swelling, swirling into the corners and crannies of the village life; and at last closing in the mother's death, in the loss forever of the $800 which Elizabeth Willard had kept for twenty years to give her son his start away from Winesburg, and in the son's wistful departure." In the rupture of family love and the consequent loss of George Willard's heritage, the theme-statement of the book is completed.

The book's central strand of action, discernible in about half the stories, is the effort of the grotesques to establish intimate relations with George Willard, the young reporter. At night, when they need not fear the mockery of public detection, they hesitantly approach him, almost in supplication, to tell him of their afflictions and perhaps find health in his voice. Instinctively, they sense his moral freshness, finding hope in the fact that he has not yet been calloused by knowledge and time. To some of the grotesques, such as Dr. Reefy and Dr. Parcival, George Willard is the lost son returned, the Daedalus whose apparent innocence and capacity for feeling will redeem Winesburg. To others among the grotesques, such as Tom Foster and Elmer Cowley, he is a reporter-messenger, a small-town Hermes, bringing news of a dispensation which will allow them to re-enter the world of men. But perhaps most fundamentally and subsuming these two visions, he seems to the grotesques a young priest who will renew the forgotten communal rites by which they may again be bound together. To Louise Trunnion he will bring a love that is more than a filching of flesh; to Dr. Parcival the promise to "write the book that I may never get written" in which he will tell all men that "everyone in the world is Christ and they are all crucified"; to the Reverend Curtis Hartman the willingness to understand a vision of God as revealed in the flesh of a naked woman; to Wash Williams the peace that will ease his sense of violation; and to Enoch Robinson the "youthful sadness, young man's sadness, the sadness of a growing boy in a village at the year's end [which can open] the lips of the old man."

As they approach George Willard, the grotesques seek not merely the individual release of a sudden expressive outburst, but also a relation with each other that may restore them to collective harmony. They are distraught communicants in search of a ceremony, a social value, a manner of living, a lost ritual that may, by some means, re-establish a flow and exchange of emotion. Their estrangement is so extreme that they cannot turn to each other though it is each other they really need and secretly want; they turn instead to George Willard who will soon be out of the orbit of their life. The miracle that the Reverend Curtis Hartman sees and the message over which Kate Swift broods could bind one to the other, yet they both turn to George Willard who, receptive though he may wish to be, cannot understand them.

In only one story, "Death," do the grotesques seem to meet. Elizabeth Willard and Dr. Reefy embrace in a moment of confession, but their approach to love is interrupted by a stray noise. Elizabeth leaves: "The thing that had come to life in her as she talked to her one friend died suddenly." A few months later, at her deathbed, Dr. Reefy meets George Willard and puts out "his hand as though to greet the young man and then awkwardly [draws] it back again." Bloom does not find his Daedalus; the hoped-for epiphany comes at the verge of death and, as in all the stories, is aborted; the ritual of communal love remains unrealized.

The burden which the grotesques would impose on George Willard is beyond his strength. He is not yet himself a grotesque mainly because he has not yet experienced very deeply, but for the role to which they would assign him he is too absorbed in his own ambition and restlessness. The grotesques see in his difference from them the possibility of saving themselves, but actually it is the barrier to an ultimate companionship. George Willard's adolescent receptivity to the grotesques can only give him the momentary emotional illumination described in that lovely story, "Sophistication." On the eve of his departure from Winesburg, George Willard reaches the point "when he for the first time takes the backward view of life. . . . With a little gasp he sees himself as merely a leaf blown by the wind through the streets of his village. He knows that in spite of all the stout talk of his fellows he must live and die in uncertainty, a thing blown by the winds, a thing destined like corn to wilt in the sun. . . . Already he hears death calling. With all his heart he wants to come close to some other human, touch someone with all his hands. . . ." For George this illumination is enough, but it is not for the grotesques. They are a moment in his education, he a confirmation of their doom. "I have missed something. I have missed something Kate Swift was trying to tell me," he says to himself one night as he falls asleep. He has missed the meaning of Kate Swift's life: it is not his fault: her salvation, like the salvation of the other grotesques, is beyond his capacities.

In the story "Queer" these meanings receive their most generalized expression, for its grotesque, Elmer Cowley, has no specific deformity: he is the grotesque as such. "He was, he felt, one condemned to go through life without friends and he hated the thought." Wishing to talk to George Willard, he loses courage and instead rants to a half-wit: "I had to tell some one and you were the only one I could tell. I hunted out another queer one, you see. I ran away, that's what I did." When Elmer Cowley does call George Willard out of the newspaper office, he again becomes tongue-tied in his presence. Despairing over "his failure to declare his determination not to be queer," Elmer Cowley decides to leave Winesburg, but in a last effort at communication he asks George Willard to meet him at the midnight local. Again he cannot speak. "Elmer Cowley danced with fury beside the groaning train in the darkness on the station platform. . . . Like one struggling for release from hands that held him he struck, hitting George Willard blow after blow on the breast, the neck, the mouth." Unable to give Elmer Cowley the love that might dissolve his queerness, George Willard suffers the fate of the rejected priest.

From the story "Queer," it is possible to abstract the choreography of *Winesburg.* Its typical action is a series of dance maneuvers by figures whose sole distinctive characteristic is an extreme deformity of movement or posture. Each of these grotesques dances, with angular indirection and muted pathos, toward a central figure who seems to them young, fresh, and radiant. For a moment they seem to draw close to him and thereby to abandon their stoops and limps, but this moment quickly dissolves in the play of the dance and perhaps it never even existed: the central figure cannot be reached. Slowly and painfully, the grotesques withdraw while the young man leaves the stage entirely. None of the grotesques is seen full-face for more than a moment, and none of them is individually important to the scheme of the dance. For this is a dance primarily of spatial relationships rather than solo virtuosity; the distances established between the dancers, rather than their personalities, form the essence of the dance. And in the end, its meaning is revealed in the fact that all but the one untouched youth return to precisely their original places and postures.

When Anderson first sent his *Winesburg* stories to the *Masses, Seven Arts,* and the *Little Review,* he intended each of them to be a self-contained unit, as in fact they may still be regarded. But there was clearly a unifying conception behind all the stories: they were set in the same locale, many of the characters appeared in several stories, and there was a remarkable consistency of mood that carried over from story to story. Consequently, when Anderson prepared them for book publication in 1919, he had only to make a few minor changes, mostly insertions of place and character names as connectives, in order to have a unified book.

Particularly if approached along the lines that have been suggested here, *Winesburg* seems remarkably of a piece. The only stories that do not fit into its pattern are the four-part narrative of Jesse Bentley, a failure in any case, and possibly "The Untold Lie," a beautiful story measuring the distance between middle-age and youth. Of the others only "Tandy" is so bad that its omission would help the book. On the other hand, few of the stories read as well in isolation as in the book's context. Except for "Hands," "The Strength of God," "Paper Pills," and "The Untold Lie," they individually lack the dramatic power which the book has as a whole.

Winesburg is an excellently formed piece of fiction, each of its stories following a parabola of movement which abstractly graphs the book's meaning. From a state of feeling rather than a dramatic conflict there develops in one of the grotesques a rising lyrical excitement, usually stimulated to intensity by the presence of George Willard. At the moment before reaching a climax, this excitement is frustrated by a fatal inability at communication and then it rapidly dissolves into its original diffuse base. This structural pattern is sometimes varied by an ironic turn, as in "Nobody Knows" and "A Man of Ideas," but in only one story, "Sophistication," is the emotional ascent allowed to move forward without interruption.

But the unity of the book depends on more than the congruous design of its parts. The first three stories of *Winesburg* develop its major theme, which, after several variations, reaches its most abstract version in "Queer." The stories following "Queer" seem somewhat of a thematic afterthought, though they are necessary for a full disposal of the characters. The one conspicuous disharmony in the book is that the introductory "Book of the Grotesque" suggests that the grotesques are victims of their wilful fanaticism, while in the stories themselves grotesqueness is the result of an essentially valid resistance to forces external to its victims.

Through a few simple but extremely effective symbols, the stories are both related to the book's larger meaning and defined in their uniqueness. For the former of these purposes, the most important symbol is that of the room, frequently used to suggest isolation and confinement. Kate Swift is alone in her bedroom, Dr. Reefy in his office, the Reverend Curtis Hartman in his church tower, Enoch Robinson in his fantasy-crowded room. Enoch Robinson's story "is in fact the story of a room almost more than it is the story of a man." The tactful use of this symbol lends *Winesburg* a claustrophobic aura appropriate to its theme.

Most of the stories are further defined by symbols related to their particular meanings. The story of the misogynist Wash Williams begins by rapidly thrusting before the reader an image of "a huge, grotesque kind of monkey, a creature with ugly sagging, hairless skin," which dominates its subsequent action. And more valid than any abstract statement of theme is the symbolic power of that moment in "The Strength of God" when the Reverend Curtis Hartman, in order to peek into Kate Swift's bedroom, breaks his church window at precisely the place where the figure of a boy stands "motionless and looking with rapt eyes into the face of Christ."

Though *Winesburg* is written in the bland accents of the American story teller, it has an economy impossible to oral narration because Anderson varies the beat of its accents by occasionally whipping them into quite formal rhetorical patterns. In the book's best stretches there is a tension between its underlying loose oral cadences and the stiffened superimposed beat of a prose almost Biblical in its regularity. Anderson's prose is neither "natural" nor primitive; it is rather a hushed bardic chant, low-toned and elegiacally awkward, deeply related to native speech rhythms yet very much the result of literary cultivation.

But the final effectiveness of this prose is in its prevalent tone of tender inclusiveness. Between writer and materials there is an admirable equity of relationship. None of the characters is violated, none of the stories, even the failures, leaves the reader with the bitter sense of having been tricked by cleverness or cheapness or toughness. The ultimate unity of the book is a unity of feeling, a sureness of warmth, and a readiness to accept Winesburg's lost grotesques with the embrace of humility. Many American writers have taken as their theme the loss of love in the modern world, but few, if any at all, have so thoroughly realized it in the accents of love.

EDWIN FUSSELL

here discusses the relationship of the artist to society as Sherwood Anderson revealed that relationship in Winesburg, Ohio. Fussell equates George Willard with the writer, seeing in his similarity to the "grotesques" of Winesburg the essential loneliness and incompletion of all people. Yet George Willard, as a "portrait of the artist as a young man," escapes being a complete grotesque through his intense awareness that all people are warped by their truths. The artist is thus separate from the mass of grotesques only by knowing the extent of the isolation of individuals and of his own separate isolation as an artist.

WINESBURG, OHIO:
ART AND ISOLATION

Edwin Fussell

In 1915–16, when the sketches collected in *Winesburg, Ohio* were written, American culture was in the process of making its way from muck-raking to depth psychology; they have in common the discovery of hidden truth behind false appearances, and no one is going to be much surprised at the fact that such a deeply representative work of the time is likewise organized around the prevailing idea of "revelation" ("The people of the town thought of her as a confirmed old maid. . . . In reality she was the most eagerly passionate soul among them").[1] Anderson called attention to this aspect of the book's method when he dedicated it to the memory of his mother, "whose keen observations on the life about her first awoke in me the hunger to see beneath the surface of lives." All observation of the book is more or less constrained to begin from this primary motivation—"to see beneath the surface of lives"—and to proceed to admit the improbability of there arising from this motivation fiction of the kind that we call realistic or naturalistic (those kinds being much less in a hurry to leave the surfaces behind). Recent readings are thus rightly concerned with revision of the 1920s' picture of a "realistic" Anderson—in the 1920s anyone who tried to tell the truth was a "realist"—and with the

1. *Winesburg, Ohio* (New York: Modern Library, 1919), p. 191.

elucidation of Anderson's more lyric achievement: they are properly concerned with defining the emotions that sustain *Winesburg, Ohio*, for example, and with observing the means by which Anderson was occasionally able to render these emotions with such sweetness and clarity.

It goes without saying that the emotions are loneliness and incompletion, particularly as these emotions take their source from some failure of affection or of creative expression. There is no disagreement on this score: the new criticism takes up where the old criticism left off. Whether viewed as a writer of "exposé" or as a minor poet in prose, Anderson is indisputably the man who writes about discontinuity among persons and about the behaviors and feelings that spring from that discontinuity. Stated so baldly, it does not perhaps at once strike us as a theme capable of supporting a very ambitious fictional *oeuvre* (though it is not quite fair to imply that Anderson has nothing else to say); and we may even feel that without some act of judgment entered by the participating intelligence, or alternatively some connections made with other and more general truths, this vision of isolation may not be capable of supporting more than a static description of a pathetic situation. Yet it is particularly the possibility of such an act of judgment on Anderson's part, or of such a general extension of meaning, with respect to the pathos of his materials, that is most persistently ignored (perhaps because the pathos is in its own way so good); so that readers who come to *Winesburg*, or who come back, fresh from the criticism of it—and who reads even the minor classics these days entirely apart from the offices of criticism?—are likely to see in it mainly a reflection of the passivity of its critics and their easy satisfaction with its pathos. Meanwhile its original impact becomes every year more difficult to recapture or explain.

But upon the possibility of there really being in *Winesburg* such a contribution of intelligent judgment consonant with truths of broad applicability and thus qualifying and refining the vision of grotesque isolation, would seem to depend the book's chances of survival as more than a landmark in literary history. It is this question that the present essay seeks to engage, if not definitively to answer. Obviously the answer can be neither unassailable nor triumphant: *Winesburg* has been repeatedly read, and if its acts of judgment were conspicuous they would have been found out. We must be prepared to accept a modest result and to content ourselves with remembering that the addition of a single note can change the character of a chord.

We may make a beginning by noticing how ambivalent, if not

confused, Anderson's feelings were toward the usual substance of his fiction. The ambivalence could doubtless be documented from a variety of fictional and biographical records; but a single passage from *Poor White* (the novel immediately following *Winesburg*) is entirely adequate to the outline and dimensions of Anderson's dilemmas.

> All men lead their lives behind a wall of misunderstanding they themselves have built, and most men die in silence and unnoticed behind the walls. Now and then a man, cut off from his fellows by the peculiarities of his nature, becomes absorbed in doing something that is impersonal, useful, and beautiful. Word of his activities is carried over the walls.[2]

Perhaps the most obviously glaring anomaly in this passage is the way it envisages the artist, like all other men, living in isolation and working out of it, yet sees in his case the isolation mysteriously leading to creation instead of destruction. The distinction is not explored, nor even, apparently, recognized. Moreover, there is curious uncertainty in the phrase "cut off from his fellows by the peculiarities of his nature," which seems to imply that the "fellows" (whom Anderson has been describing in *Winesburg* as almost universally "grotesque") are somehow less "peculiar," more "normal" perhaps, than this artist who devotes himself to the "impersonal, useful, and beautiful." Finally, there is a contradiction which if we notice it at all must strike us as even more bewildering than the creation-destruction confusion, and which is equally unresolved: in the second sentence the artist is described as one "cut off from his fellows," as if the "fellows" were in happy communion with each other and therefore to be regarded as a homogeneous group from which *his* peculiarities have alienated him; yet in the first sentence Anderson tells us, sounding a little like Thoreau and at the same time echoing both doctrine and metaphor from *Winesburg,* that "all men lead their lives behind a wall of misunderstanding they themselves have built."

It will be said that of course Anderson is not skillful in expository prose and that it is therefore quite beside the point to submit to rational analysis a piece of writing so murky as the passage from *Poor White.* That would be true if the criticism were undertaken for any other purpose than to locate a center of tension in Anderson's feelings about this theme. That center of tension may now be broadly defined as the

2. *Poor White* (New York, 1920), p. 227.

polarity of artist and society (and from Anderson's biography we should expect no less), particularly as both terms are illuminated (or muddied) by the shifting values that it is possible to attach to the words "normal" and "isolated." In order to see *Winesburg* clearly and as a whole, it is essential to bear in mind both ends of the polarity and not allow ourselves to be tempted, either by Anderson's ability to "see beneath the surface of lives" or by the fantastic pathos of the *Winesburg* victims, to focus all our attention on the grotesques. To do so is at a stroke to give up half the book; worse than that, to give up the half which furnishes perspective and therefore significance to the other.

If we approach the novel from the direction of George Willard, the young reporter presumably on the threshold of his career as a writer, instead of from that of the *subjects* of the sketches, *Winesburg* composes as a *Bildungsroman* of a rather familiar type[,] the "portrait of the artist as a young man" in the period immediately preceding his final discovery of *métier*. In order to arrive at the rare excellence of *Winesburg*, we must first see that it is a book of this kind; and then we must go on to see in what ways it is not typical of the *genre*, for it is in the differences that Anderson's merits are revealed. An initial formulation of this difference would mainly call attention to Anderson's almost faultless holding of the balances between his two terms, artist and society, a delicacy that was perhaps made easier for him by the genuine uncertainty of his feelings. To put it bluntly, there are few works of modern fiction in which the artist's relations with ordinary men are seen with such a happy blend of acuity and charity, few works of any age in which the artist and ordinary men are seen so well *as fitting together* in a complementary union that permits us to make distinctions of relative value while at the same time retaining a universally diffused sense of equal dignity. We need look no further for the cause of the remarkable serenity of tone of *Winesburg*.

This balancing of forces is the thing to hang onto; and it thus seems to me a mistake for Irving Howe, in his beautifully written description of *Winesburg*,[3] to call so much attention to the grotesques' pathetically eager need to draw sustenance from George Willard without equally emphasizing how many of them come to him convinced that it is *they* who have something to give. It is only a superficial irony that so few of the gifts (like the mother's $800) can possibly have for the young writer the same values that have been assigned to them by the givers.

3. *Sherwood Anderson* (New York, 1951), pp. 102–106.

Their understanding is inevitably not the same as his, which is one of the general truths *Winesburg* readily enforces; but another is that without their gifts there would be no writer at all.

Everyone is ready to give George Willard good advice. Doctor Parcival urges him to write a book saying that all men are Christ and that all are crucified. Wash Williams is anxious to save him needless pain and trouble by putting him on his guard against "bitches." Joe Welling is pleased to confide in him a few secrets about the art of writing. Kate Swift, his former English teacher, tries to tell him to "know life" and "stop fooling with words." Perhaps none of this advice, in the form in which it is offered, is wholly sound. But it is well-intentioned, and one of the most engaging things in *Winesburg* is the way George Willard, on his part, is always ready to credit the local talkers with more wisdom than they may strike us as having. " 'I have missed something,' " he says, " 'I have missed something Kate Swift was trying to tell me' " (196); and he might as well be saying it of them all.

His mother has a more intimate and more comprehensive under-standing of his needs and is thus appropriately the one who is able to articulate the representative prayer of all the grotesques: that " 'this my boy be allowed to express something for us both' " (26). For finally what the characters want of George Willard is to have their stories told (they are quite literally characters in search of an author); at the same time, they wish to have a stake in the way the stories are going to be told. Or say that they insist on having some share in the making of the artist whose task will be to expose them as they really are. Each in turn comes forward to offer his secret (the material of art) and to give up whatever fragmentary wisdom he may possess toward the development of the artist who will be the spokesman for everyone. Each one implicitly expects a reward for his contribution: the "release" into expressiveness which each needs but which only the artist may in real life encompass. Seen this way, the book begins to take on some of the formal quality of a procession, imbued like a ritual pageant with silent and stately dignity.

It has other kinds of motion, too; the relationship between writer and subject may, for instance, also be put in terms of an antithesis between development and fixity, an antithesis which we may not notice at first because George Willard's progress is so easygoing compared with the more explosive gestures of the grotesques. But throughout *Winesburg* runs the slow and often hidden current of George Willard's growth toward maturity; often the stream is subterranean and we are surprised to see where it comes out; sometimes it appears to lose itself in backwaters of irrelevance or naiveté. But all the time the book's current is steadily setting toward the ultimate "Departure." The torpidity of that stream is best taken as an expression of Anderson's humility, his refusal to sentimentalize the figure of the writer.

But we must not ignore the drift, for Anderson is equally clear (novelistically speaking) that the artist's essential quality must be defined as a capacity for the growth which he refuses to attribute to any of the grotesques. It is indeed the very description of their grotesqueness that each of them is forever frozen somewhere below the level of a full and proper development. Sometimes this incompletion is "their fault," sometimes not (unless it be more true to say that such a question of ultimate responsibility is meaningless); but there can be no doubt about Anderson's clear perception of the *fact*.

It is not enough, however, to see these figures as incomplete and to sense the pathos of their plight. It is not enough even to see that it is the glimmering awareness of their inadequacy that drives them to their futile efforts at revelation and communion. Ultimately it is only a sentimental reading of *Winesburg, Ohio* that fails to recognize that the grotesques' anxiety to escape their isolation is in itself excessive and truly symptomatic of their grotesquerie. It is of the utmost importance that their counterweight, George Willard, is almost alone among the inhabitants of *Winesburg* [4] in being able to accept the fact of human isolation and to live with it. His willingness to do so is at once the sign of his maturity and the pledge of his incipient artistic ability.

The view of the artist presented in *Winesburg* is that of a man who joins sympathy and understanding to detachment and imperturbability. Anderson obviously sees the relation of art and life as from one point of view illuminated by an opposition between the freedom and flexibility which are necessary to the creative role and, on the other hand, the extremes of static and rigid over-commitment instanced by the grotesques. This is undoubtedly the distinction—flexibility versus rigidity—which Anderson rather unsatisfactorily tries to explain with a modern "humors" theory in the introductory "Book of the Grotesque." This book is clearly not unrelated to *Winesburg, Ohio* and is like it built on the "notion that the moment one of the people took one of the truths to himself, called it his truth, and tried to live his life by it, he became a grotesque and the truth he embraced became a falsehood" (5).

4. A possible exception is Alice Hindman in "Adventure," who at the end of the story "began trying to force herself to face bravely the fact that many people must live and die alone, even in Winesburg" (134). But her unmarried state, although desolate, is not the quintessential loneliness.

Anderson rather implies that what saved the old writer from becoming a grotesque himself (he is endangered by his obsession with his notion) is that he didn't publish the book. The clarity of Anderson's argument here is scarcely helped by his views about non-publication nor by his eccentric use of the word *truth;* but his general intention, a contrast between obsession and freedom, is plain enough. For the distinctions made in this introductory sketch are entirely continuous with the distinction made throughout *Winesburg* between George Willard and his fellow citizens, and are referable finally to one of those broad general truths or paradoxes about art and life that pervade the book, and in which Anderson's charity most winningly shows itself: namely, that the artist, in order to express the common passion, must remain free from entanglements with it, while those who actually *live* the common passion are by the very fact of their involvement prevented from coming to the threshold of complete self-realization and are thereby deprived of the release inherent in expression.

To remember that the "grotesques" are thus distorted and misshapen by their insistent involvement with life itself is to share Anderson's realistic perception of "normal" or "ordinary" people (as distinguished from the artist, who is "normal" in a different way); it is to participate imaginatively in Anderson's remarkable vision of humanity, a vision tender without sentimentality, tough without rancor. The grotesques must not be thought of as necessarily unattractive, for the truths that distend them include "the truth of virginity and the truth of passion, the truth of wealth and of poverty" (4), properties or conditions either good or neutral, and not wholly unlovely even when carried to the excess that lays the grotesques open to the charge of "abnormality." Actually it is almost useless to attempt to retain any usual conception of "normality"—except in the sense of more or less "developed"—when dealing with Anderson (we have seen how he confused himself trying to use the word), for at the heart of his feeling is his uncommon ability to like people for what they are instead of for what they might be (a common failing among minor writers) while in the very act of seeing them as they are. And even if the grotesques are not, by virtue of their inability to develop into full and various normality, quite like other people, there still remains a question whether their lopsidedness does not especially endear them; and I think we must finally say that it does, that they are like Doctor Reefy's "twisted apples": "into a little round place at the side of the apple has been gathered all of its sweetness" (20). What Anderson could never articulate in expository prose he manages so easily with the most commonplace image.

And so easy is it to allow one's attention to be monopolized by the grotesques! Their problem is presented first and their bizarre revelations continually keep it at the forefront of our perception. Meanwhile, as I have said, the current of the book is setting away from them toward the final story, "Departure," and, before that, the climactic tale, "Sophistication," wherein George Willard's maturity is to be realized and the final opposition between artist and society drawn. The placing of this climactic story is important: it immediately precedes "Departure," which is pointedly *anti*-climactic, and immediately follows "Death" (Elizabeth Willard). And it is in significant contrast with an earlier story, "Loneliness," about the artist *manqué* Enoch Robinson who "never grew up."

In "Sophistication" we may find—or infer—an attitude about art and loneliness sufficiently complex and sufficiently clear to enable us to read *Winesburg* without those distortions of meaning that follow upon the loss of any important part of an organic entity. It is one of the few stories in the book which has a happy ending and it concludes with what is for *Winesburg* a startling statement: "For some reason they [George Willard and Helen White] could not have explained they had both got from their silent evening together the thing needed. Man or boy, woman or girl, they had for a moment taken hold of the thing that makes the mature life of men and women in the modern world possible" (298). It would be difficult to imagine a passage more explicitly pointing to the presence of the book's overarching meaning; but this is not to say that that meaning is very easy to grasp or to conceptualize without offering violence to a story of incomparable tact and delicacy (stylistic qualities happily matching the virtues it recommends).

George Willard's maturity has of course been coming on for a long time. In "An Awakening" (his), for instance, he has been shown (1) trying to get "'into touch with something orderly and big that swings through the night like a star'" (219), (2) "muttering words" into the darkness, and (3) feeling himself "oddly detached and apart from all life" (221). But these inchoate impulses, although more or less in the right direction, are quickly brought to an end by his foolish involvement with the milliner Belle Carpenter. By the time of "Sophistication" he is older and wiser. His mother's death has intervened. It is this death, no doubt, that enables him now "for the first time [to] take the backward view of life," to realize with the "sadness of sophistication" that "in spite of all the stout talk of his fellows he must live and die in

uncertainty." The point of passage from adolescence to maturity is thus
defined as the moment one "hears death calling"; and the universal
response to an awareness of this moment is to "want to come close to
some other human" (286–287). But not too close; wherein lies the
moral of the story.[5]

"Sophistication" is nocturnal, but not that nightmare climate common to so many of the *Winesburg* stories, and as pleasantly informal as
the evening stroll that provides its slight framework. First we see
George Willard alone, "taking the backward view of life," and
anxiously waiting for the hour when he can share his new sense of
maturity with Helen White and perhaps compel her admiration of it.
Helen White is undergoing a rather parallel transformation into
womanhood, a transformation only vaguely felt by George Willard, and
comparatively unfocused for us, since her imputed maturity—real or
not, significant or not—is presented less for its own interest than as a
complementary background for George Willard's achievement of tran-
quility. ("The feeling of loneliness and isolation that had come to the
young man . . . was both broken and intensified by the presence of
Helen. What he felt was reflected in her") (294). Finally the two
young people come together (each one from an atmosphere of "noise,"
meaningless superficial talk), and walk silently through the streets of
Winesburg to the deserted grandstand at the fair grounds. So far as the
story informs us, they never say anything to each other.

In the grandstand they are confronted by "ghosts, not of the dead,
but of living people." One paradox leads to another: "The place has
been filled to overflowing with life . . . and now it is night and the
life has all gone away. . . . One shudders at the thought of the
meaninglessness of life while at the same instant, and if the people of
the town are his people, one loves life so intensely that tears come into
the eyes" (295). This is perhaps the climax of the story—and thus of
Winesburg, Ohio—for at this point Anderson's own ambivalent attitude
toward experience, and toward the art that arises from it to proclaim its

5. The best possible gloss for "Sophistication," and for this aspect of
Winesburg generally, would be the following passage from D. H. Lawrence,
"Poe," *Studies in Classic American Literature* (1922):

> The central law of all organic life is that each organism is intrinsically
> isolate and single in itself. . . .
> But the secondary law of all organic life is that each organism only lives
> through contact with other matter, assimilation, and contact with other
> life. . . . Men live by love, but die, or cause death, if they love too much.

(Quoted from Edmund Wilson, ed., *The Shock of Recognition*, New York,
1947, pp. 967–968).

ineradicable dignity, is fully embodied, not in terms of ideas (which Anderson never learned to manipulate) but in terms of their corresponding emotions encompassed in images.

Now that the summit of George Willard's emotional and aesthetic development has been attained, we have a final look at the artist's social role. It is all comprehended in a single sentence, again paradoxical: "He wanted to love and to be loved by her, but he did not want at the moment to be confused by her womanhood" (296). (Presumably she feels the same.) The point is that they recognize and respect the essential privacy (or integrity) of human personality: "In that high place in the darkness the two oddly sensitive human atoms held each other tightly and waited. In the mind of each was the same thought. 'I have come to this lonely place and here is this other,' was the substance of the thing felt" (296). The loneliness is assuaged—there is no other way—by the realization that loneliness is a universal condition and not a uniquely personal catastrophe; love is essentially the shared acceptance by two people of the irremediable fact, in the nature of things, of their final separateness. But these are truths beyond the comprehension of the grotesques, and one reason why they, who will not accept their isolation, are so uniformly without love; like Enoch Robinson, they never grew up.

The artist, then, is not necessarily different from other people, after all. Primarily, he is defined in terms of maturity and in terms of the practical mastery of his craft (throughout *Winesburg*, George Willard has been busy as a reporter, learning to fit words to life felt and observed). The craft is his special secret, and it is not required that "normal" or "ordinary" people have it. They will have other skills, other secrets. But what they might all share, ideally, is that mixture of participation and detachment, love and respect, passion and criticism, which is, Anderson tells us, the best privilege offered by the modern world to those who wish to grow up, and toward the attainment of which the writer's case—at first glance special, but ultimately very general—may serve as an eminently practicable pattern of virtue.

WALDO FRANK

wrote the first prophetic hope for
Sherwood Anderson in his "Emerging Greatness," a 1916 review of
Windy McPherson's Son. *Frank and Anderson remained close*
friends during the writer's lifetime; when Anderson died in 1941,
Story *asked Frank to write a reappraisal of* Winesburg, Ohio *for its*
Sherwood Anderson Memorial Number.

"Winesburg, Ohio after Twenty Years" is the finest critique of
Anderson's masterpiece ever written. The essay is highly sympa-
thetic toward the author's re-creation of a Midwestern town in the
late nineteenth century. Seen in its cultural setting, Winesburg,
Ohio *becomes the lyrical outpouring of the soul of the American*
small town.

WINESBURG, OHIO
AFTER TWENTY YEARS

Waldo Frank

Sherwood Anderson wrote his most famous book about a generation ago; and it reveals a Mid-American world that already then was a generation dead. A full half century therefore divides the mind that reads the book today from the life it portrays. Since, from this adequate perspective, the work stands firm in its form, true in its livingness, strong in its light upon our present, it is clear that "Winesburg, Ohio" is a classic.

I had not re-read the book since it was published. Many of its chapters were mailed to me in his own writing by Anderson himself, who then lived in Chicago and worked for an advertising house near Jackson Boulevard. I still see the long sprawling potent hand on the cheap paper, feel the luminous life that swelled miraculously from it. I recall sending him back one story which I wished to publish in *The Seven Arts,* because it was written down totally without commas; a few days later, it came back to me with commas sedulously spaced after each fourth or fifth word, irrespective of meaning. I had no doubt of the significance of this prose; otherwise, in 1916 I should not with such assurance have entitled my first essay on Anderson "Emerging Greatness"; but I know now that accidentals like the handwriting and the punctuation somewhat obscured for me, as the man's homespun did for many, the actual lineaments of this clear art. It is a dangerous hazard to re-read, after twenty-five years, a book involved in the dreams and fervors of one's youth; it is a blessing when that book stands forth from the test a rediscovery . . . indeed a prophecy and an illumination.

The first impressive realization that came to me with my re-reading was that "Winesburg" has form. The book as a whole has form; and most of the stories have form: the work is an integral creation. The form is lyrical. It is not related, even remotely, to the aesthetic of Chekhov; nor to that of Balzac, Flaubert, Maupassant, Tolstoy, Melville. These masters of the short story used the narrative or dramatic art: a linear progression rising to a peak or an immediate complex of character-forces impinging upon each other in a certain action that fulfilled them and rounded the story. For an analogy to the aesthetic of the Winesburg tales, one must go to music, perhaps to the songs that Schubert featly wove from old refrains; or to the lyric art of the Old Testament psalmists and prophets in whom the literary medium was so allied to music that their texts have always been sung in the synagogues. The "Winesburg" design is quite uniform: a theme-statement of a character with his mood, followed by a recounting of actions that are merely variations on the theme. These variations make incarnate what has already been revealed to the reader; they weave the theme into life by the always subordinate confrontation of other characters (usually one) and by an evocation of landscape and village. In some of the tales, there is a secondary theme-statement followed by other variations. In a few, straight narrative is attempted; and these are the least successful.

This lyric, musical form has significance, and the tales' contents make it clear. But it is important, first, to note that the cant judgment of Sherwood Anderson as a naïve, almost illiterate storyteller (a judgment which he himself encouraged with a good deal of nonsense about his literary innocence) is false. The substance of "Winesburg" is impressive, is alive, because it has been superbly *formed*. There are occasional superficial carelessnesses of language; on the whole, the prose is perfect in its selective economy and in its melodious flow; the choice of details is strict, strong, sure; the movement is an unswerving musical fulfillment of the already stated theme. Like Schubert, and like the Old Testament storytellers, the author of "Winesburg" comes at the end of a psychological process; is a man with an inherited culture and a deeply assimilated skill. He is a type of the achieved artist.

The theme of the tales taken as a whole follows the same pattern as the individual "chapters"—although less precisely. "Hands," the first chapter, tells of Adolph Myers, alias Wing Biddlebaum, the unfortunate schoolteacher with sensitive, wandering, caressing hands, who gets into trouble because his loving touch upon his pupils is misinterpreted by a half-wit boy and the crude obscene men of the town. Because the tale is concretely, poetically realized, its symbolism is true; and because this symbolism is not intellectualized, not schematized, it would be false to tear it from its flesh and blood texture. Suffice it to say that the story suggests the tragic ambivalence of hands, which is the fate of all the characters of Winesburg. Hands, at the turn of the century, were making machines, making all sorts of things ("the thing is in the saddle"); making the world that was unmaking the tender, sensitive, intimate lives of the folk in their villages and farms. Hands are made for loving; but hands making mechanical things grow callous, preoccupied . . . fail at love. The second story is a straight variant of the theme: here, it is not the hand, the maker, that goes wrong; it is *thought,* which Doctor Reefy turns into written words—ineffectual scraps of wisdom jotted down, that become paper pills cluttering his pocket. The third chapter, "Mother," completes the theme-statement. Woman, the creator, the lover: the principle incarnate in Wing Biddlebaum's hands and in Doctor Reefy's thoughts, states the theme centrally. The form of the mother, frustrate, lonely, at last desperate, pervades the variations that make the rest of the book: a continuity of variation swelling, swirling into the corners and crannies of the village life; and at length closing in the mother's death, in the loss forever of the $800 which Elizabeth Willard had kept for twenty years to give her son his start away from Winesburg, and in the son's wistful departure. "He thought of little things—" as the train pulled out; they have become motes and beams carrying a distant sun to the reader.

I have spoken of suggested symbols. Suggestion, if you will *indirection,* is the quality of this lyric form; and no more *direct* expression could have been devised for a book which so precisely portrays a world avid for the expression of eternal truths and forced, by the decay of its old cultural foundation, to seek truth anarchically, hopelessly, indirectly.

It has become a critical commonplace that Winesburg faithfully portrays the midwest village of two thousand souls during the post-civil war pre-motor age. Let us look. . . . No even bearably married couple is to be found in Winesburg; there are few marriages in the book, and these without exception are described as the harnessing together of strangers by the bondage of sex or a morality hostile to the spirit. There is no communion with children. There is no fulfilled sex life, sex being an obsession, a frustration and a trap. There is no normal sociability between men and women: souls lonely as carnivorae for once in their lives burst into melodic plaint to one another, and lapse into solipsistic silence. There is indeed more muttering than talk. There is no congregated worship, and no strength to organized religion except in the sense of a strong barrier; as in the piteous tales of the Reverend Hartman who sins by knocking a piece from his stained-glass church window (part of the figure of Christ) in order to gaze at the body of Belle Robinson [*sic* for Kate Swift] in bed. There is almost no joy, beyond the momentary joy of contemplating nature. And the most mature of the characters, Doctor Reefy, Seth Richmond, Elizabeth Willard, the Rev. Hartman, et al., do not evolve beyond a sharp negation of the things that *are*, in favor of a nebulous dream of "life."

Now, these omissions are purposive; and as aesthetically true as they are factually false. The author's art, perhaps unconsciously to himself, traces the frontier of emotional and spiritual action which, in that deliquescence of an agrarian culture which was rotten long ere it was ripe, was a line of *decay*, a domain of deprivation. In those very institutions and traditions which had been the base of the world's health, Winesburg was found wanting.

The positive substance of the book is the solitariness and struggle of the soul which has lost its ancestral props: the energy of the book is the release from these old forms into a subliminal search for new ones. The farms of Robert Frost's "North of Boston" are also peopled by broken, lonely lives; but their despair is hard, heroic. The folk of Winesburg are soft in a tenderness, in a nebulous searchfulness, that have gone farther in decay than the still standing families and churches of Frost's New England. In all the book, only irony—the author's irony—is hard.

This trait of Sherwood Anderson has been too little recognized. Consider the acrid irony in "Nobody Knows," where sex fulfillment ends in the boy's cowardly sigh of relief that "she hasn't got anything on me. Nobody knows"; in "The Awakening," that turns a moment of mystical insight into a brutal, humiliating sexual frustration; in "The Untold Lie" (one of the great stories of the world); in the chapters of Jesse Bentley, "the man of God" who is transformed by the sling of his grandchild, David, into a clumsy, puny, ineffectual Goliath. This hardness of irony in the author points to his spiritual transcendence over his subjects. Anderson has inherited intact a strength long since vaporized in Winesburg—and yet the heritage of Winesburg. His sureness of vision and of grasp enable him to incarnate in a form very precise the inchoate emotions of his people. To portray the deliquescence of America's agrarian culture beneath the impact of the untamed machine age required a man spiritually advanced beyond that culture's death. This is a law of art (and of ethic) ignored by the hardboiled Hemingway school, who depict their gangsters *on the level of the gangsters.*

Sherwood Anderson liked to think of himself as a primitive or neo-primitive artist; as a naïve unlettered storyteller. The truth is, that he belonged at the end of a cultural process, and shares the technical perfection which, within the limits of the culture's forms, only the terminal man achieves. One book was the pabulum of these people: the Bible. And a Testamental accent and vision modulate every page of Sherwood Anderson's great story. Moreover, the nebulosity of these poor souls' search is an end, a chaos *after* a world. That world was already drooping when it crossed the ocean; it had been, in England, a world of revealed religion and sacramental marriage, of the May dance and the sense of each man's life as mystery and mission. It lives in the past of Winesburg; it has become a beat and a refrain in the blood. In the actual experience of these men and women, it is a recidivism, a lapse away into organic echoes. Thus, of revealed religion and sacramental marriage, of the structures of social and personal responsi-bilities, nothing remains on the record but the memory and the dynamic yearning. Life has become a Prompter with the text of the dialogue and even the stage missing.

In sum, Sherwood Anderson is a mature voice singing a culture at its close; singing it with the technical skill of, literally, the *past master*. What in Winesburg, Ohio, of the year 1900 was authentic? The old strong concept of marriage? No: only the inherited knowledge that the embrace of man and woman must create a sacrament again. The old dogmas of the churches? No: only the inherited knowledge that there is God—even in sin, there is God; and that for want of a living Body formed of this new world, God is revealed in animistic gods of the corn, and even in the phallus. Thus the artist, distilling the eternal from the old doomed ways, becomes the prophet.

Sherwood Anderson's place at the end of a cultural cycle finds eloquent corroboration in the quality of his immediate imitators and disciples. Ernest Hemingway turned the nebulous seeking softness of the master's characters into a hard-shell bravado. Winesburg's men and women are old souls, inheritors of a great Christian culture who have been abandoned and doomed to a progressive emptiness by the invasion of the unmastered Machine. (This is a process now at its nadir in the world.) In Anderson, however, these lives are transfigured by a mature and virile artist who is able to crystalize what is eternal in them as an aesthetic value. In Hemingway, an adolescent rationalizes the emptiness (which flatters his own) into a rhetorical terseness which flatters the emptiness of the reader; and the essential formlessness of the story is slicked up into plots borrowed from the thrillers. In Thomas Wolfe, the same formlessness becomes grandiose, the nebulosity becomes an elephantiasis, the yearning and lostness discreetly lyricized in Winesburg becomes a flatulent, auto-erotic *Ding an Sich*. What is vital since Anderson in American letters (a great deal, varying from such men as Faulkner and Caldwell through Hart Crane to such young poets as Kenneth Patchen and Muriel Rukeyser) is independent of the Winesburg tradition. But that is another story. . . .

The perfect readability of this book within our agonizing world proves the potential that lived—needing only to be transfigured—within a world already gone when Winesburg was written. Here are intrinsically great stories: as great as any in our language. The author, intellectually bound to the decadence of the agrarian age that he revealed, proves in himself a vital spirit, a creative promise that are ours. The village of these queer men beating the innocent bystander to prove they are not queer, of these sex-starved women running naked through the summer rain, was after all pregnant of the Great Tradition. The tender and humbly precise artist who painted these portraits bespoke the Tradition's still unimagined future.

JOSEPH WOOD KRUTCH

wrote this review of Dark Laughter *in 1925, when he was becoming known as an exponent and popularizer of the Freudian approach to literary criticism. His psychologically oriented study,* Edgar Allan Poe: A Study in Genius, *appeared in 1926; and his Freudian condemnation of traditional American behavior,* The Modern Temper, *assured him fame in 1929.*

*Dark Laughter, which was the only book by Sherwood Anderson to achieve immediate financial success (*Winesburg, Ohio *has, of course, surpassed it in popularity over the years), is here compared with the work of Sinclair Lewis. To Krutch, Lewis is a man of action; Anderson is a man of reverie. With his inclinations toward Freudian theory, it may be thought strange that Krutch prefers Lewis' fiction to Anderson's, but he comments pointedly here on the necessity of reading Anderson's work as a poetic synthesis of the American experience.*

VAGABONDS

Joseph Wood Krutch

When one thinks of the contemporary commentators upon the American scene the names of Messrs. Sinclair Lewis and Sherwood Anderson come naturally to mind, and yet it is a curious fact that though these names are so frequently linked the men themselves belong to the two different classes into which all societies are divided. The mass of any population is composed of those whose nature it is to play, as it were, the game. They clear the forests when forests are to be cleared, they build the industries when industries are to be built, they catch the rhythm of the step when their comrades march away to war; and in whatever world they happen to be they definitely, in the words of the Hairy Ape, "belong." Mr. Lewis, by virtue of his peculiarly American vigor, of his zeal, and of his positive, confident determination, is a member, in so far as any artist can be, of this group; for satirist though he be his participation in the life of his time is active and enthusiastic. But there is another class, composed, like every class of big men and little men alike, of those who are the vagabonds of body or of mind. The spirit of their own or of any age seems never to grip them; they do not understand the value set by their fellows upon the prizes for which the races are run; and in the midst of the bustle they stand wondering by. When one of them charms us we call him a dreamer and when one, vaguely ineffectual in the performance of some task we have set him, moves our anger we call him shiftless; but we know the class to which

they all belong—they are the moonstruck ones who seem never able to
share the unquestioning faith in the worth of this or that which keeps
the others so intent on their pursuit of wealth, of fame, of respectability, and of comfort. The most articulate and the most self-conscious
of the class write the dreamy poems, essays, and novels which fascinate
without ever deeply entering into readers in whom the will is more
dominant; but even in the midst of the busy American civilization one
may see the lower ranks of the order who have calmly detached
themselves from the hurly-burly and are sitting, perhaps, by the banks
of some stream into whose waters they are contentedly dangling lines
never yet bitten by fish.

That Mr. Anderson's father was such a one Mr. Anderson revealed
by the delightful picture which he drew in "A Story Teller's Story,"
and that he is himself his father's son grown sophisticated and self-
conscious his own novels confess. The old man who could always find
some excuse to leave his family behind and wander about the country
fascinating the inhabitants of lonely farms by the resplendent and lying
tales which he could so readily imagine is the true begetter of the
novelist Anderson, for he too, when he lets his fancy wander, can form
the most delightful of day dreams. But partly because he happens to
have been born in an age but little inclined to yield to the charm of
fancy and partly because he has become too sophisticated naively to
indulge the day-dreaming faculty, he holds himself in check and
describes rather the deeds and the souls of those who, like himself,
belong to that moonstruck class whose members find themselves
temperamentally alien to the orderly and busy world in which they
happen to have been born. The hero of "Dark Laughter" is such a one,
and though he has a story—the story of how he escaped from the
routine life into which he did not fit, how he wandered dreaming here
and there in search of he knew not what, and how finally, with fitting
irony, he stole the wife of a respectable though unexciting manufacturer while the latter was taking part in an Armistice Day parade—this
story has actually neither beginning nor end, and the charm of the book
lies in the author's evocation of the vagabond mood.

Anderson is not a deep thinker, and it is one of the absurd results of
the conventional thought-pattern of our age that he is taken seriously as
a critic of society; but he is, nevertheless, a poet who feels things deeply
in his own particular way. His characters live chiefly by virtue of that
part of them which is himself; certainly his two most vivid personages
in the present book—the hero himself and that middle-aged fellow-
workman of his who is accustomed from time to time to slip away for a

night with his wife and a bottle of whiskey, ostensibly to fish, but really to lie in the moonlight by the river and feel himself as free as an animal from the thoughts and responsibilities of man—are vivid because of the extent to which their mood is his own; and he is best of all when he is communicating to the reader by delicate exposition, by vivid picture, or in Whitmanesque prose-poems that soft, vague reverie, too little definite to be called thought, which all have known in some moment of summer idleness but which is the natural mood of those who are born like himself to drift gently through life. In many a passage of "Dark Laughter," especially in those which describe the life along the river, he has caught it with a nearly flawless art, and realizing that it is an attitude to be felt rather than a philosophy to be intellectually defended or understood he has wisely refrained from argument and left it to be symbolized by that mellow, careless laughter with which the Negroes, the perfect vagabonds, greet the situations over which those of another race puzzle their heads and search their hearts. There are some who choose to breast a current, but there are others who find it sweeter to drift dreaming downstream.

WALTER B. RIDEOUT

was the first literary historian to examine carefully Sherwood Anderson's unique career as a country newspaper editor in rural Southwest Virginia. Many Americans have begun writing for newspapers and later achieved literary fame; among them are Benjamin Franklin, Washington Irving, William Cullen Bryant, Walt Whitman, Samuel Clemens, William Dean Howells, Stephen Crane, Theodore Dreiser, Robert Frost, Carl Sandburg, Sinclair Lewis, H. L. Mencken, and Ernest Hemingway. But Sherwood Anderson remains the only American author of admittedly high stature to forsake literary fame and society in order to operate obscure country newspapers.

The Marion Democrat and the Smyth County News were made famous by Sherwood Anderson, who owned, wrote, edited, printed, and reported for his two weekly newspapers. The happenings in Marion, Virginia, constituted Hello Towns!, the little-known but fascinating collection of Anderson's newspaper writing, published in 1929. Walter Rideout here discusses the most interesting facet of Anderson's newspaper days—the fictional character whom Anderson invented to act as his chief reporter.

WHY SHERWOOD ANDERSON EMPLOYED BUCK FEVER

Walter B. Rideout

When Sherwood Anderson was in his deeper moods of depression, he had a sharp physical image to describe his feelings. "With me," he writes, "the blues take a physical form sometimes. The black dog is on [m]y back." By the summer of 1927 he had been carrying the black dog about for months even though by outward fact he should have been entirely happy. His critical fame as one of America's leading short story writers still held, his novel *Dark Laughter* (1925) had been a best-seller, and he was at last settled in his handsome fieldstone house on Ripshin Farm near the little town of Troutdale in Southwest Virginia, the area he had fallen immediately in love with two years earlier because of its sensually rounded mountains, its woods and streams, its upland valleys where the reserved and independent mountain people lived in cabins on tiny farms.

But it was the inward facts that had put the black dog on Anderson's back and kept it there. While the house had been building in the previous summer, he had been too excited watching the work to concentrate properly on writing and then had felt too guilty about the watching to continue any of the starts he did make on a never-finished novel. Now in 1927 he was still going through the experience, trying for him, of attempting to direct the lives of his two sons by his first wife;

and discord had already begun between himself and his present, third wife, a discord rooted deeply in temperamental differences. He was especially disturbed by his contract with Horace Liveright, the publisher, which paid him $100 weekly on advance royalties in return for a book a year. Having nothing to do but write, he found himself unable to do it, unable even to get close to people in their everyday lives and thus attain that imaginative entrance into other personalities which lies at the bottom of all his best work. His second trip to Europe, in the winter of 1926–27, made in a frantic attempt to pull away from dead center, was because of physical, probably psychosomatic, illness an[d] emotional disaster.

So in the spring and summer of 1927, back at Ripshin Farm, he struggled through the days, writing, but hardly able to do more than string together single-sentence paragraphs that are almost individual cries of pain. Even his desperate breaking off of the Liveright contract did not help by this time. Then out of his sluggish torment he caught at an event which had been one of the joys of his life from early boyhood, the county fair. The Smyth County Fair, held in Marion, the shire town of the neighboring county, ran that year from August 30th through September 3rd; and on some one of those five days Anderson began a quick, if impermanent, recovery from despair. For as he sat in the grandstand watching his beloved horse races, perhaps recalling nostalgically the tangled but hopeful feelings of George Willard of Winesburg in the story "Sophistication," he got into conversation with a townsman, one Denny Culbert, who told him that the two small weekly newspapers of Marion were for sale. Here was suddenly an opportunity to throw the black dog off his back, and Anderson took it. The $5,000 needed for the purchase price he borrowed from a recently acquired friend in New York, a wealthy advertising man and bibliophile named Burton Emmett. On November 1, 1927, Anderson took possession of the papers.

The *Smyth County News* and the *Marion Democrat* had been quite typical country weeklies, the former containing eight pages, the latter only four, both thin on news and editorials and padded out with syndicated material, or "boilerplate." A standard amused comment on Anderson's venture has been that, though the papers were issued from the same office, the *News* was Republican and the *Democrat*, obviously, Democratic in political policy; but recent scholars have insisted that Anderson, who was not interested in politics anyway, solved the "problem" by assigning the political editorials to a Republican and a Democrat respectively. Actually Anderson merely continued the practice and the same political personnel long since employed by the previous editor, one Arthur L. Cox. That man's circumspection may also be gauged by the fact that two years earlier the papers had tacitly supported the cause of William Jennings Bryan and Old Time Religion in the Scopes Trial at Dayton in neighboring Tennessee, and they had always staunchly upheld the local sheriff's unending attempts to apply the 18th Amendment against the brisk moonshine activity in the surrounding mountains.

Contrary to common assumption, Anderson had only a few general notions as to future policy for his newspapers. In the eighth number he issued, after boasting that the papers had taken in 150 unsolicited new subscriptions, he admitted that he hadn't had much to say about policy and that "We have been feeling our way along." (More than two years later he was to announce that the papers were still feeling their way.) But he did have a few notions of policy, those one might expect from the author of *Winesburg, Ohio* turned country editor. According to published statements in early issues of both newspapers, what Anderson most clearly wanted was that the *News* and the *Democrat* "give expression to . . . all of the everyday life of a very typical American community." The papers were to be "intensely local"; and he asked for the help of his readers both in collecting local news items and in writing letters to the editor so that the papers could become "a sort of forum for the expression of public opinion." Because of his own lack of interest in politics, he would leave political comment to the designated contributing editors; instead he would speak editorially "on the life about me and"—here he admitted to interests beyond the city of Marion —"on the life of the outside world." He would print things that interested him: poems, famous short stories, some of his own tales, and "things seen and felt, strange happenings in this and other communities. . . . " The function of a country weekly was not to give state and national news, like the city dailies, but to help bind a community together, to help its people to understand each other. A weekly, he concluded, "should have some life in it, fun, a serious streak, plenty of home news, some good solid reading." Whatever the papers became, they must escape the curse of most modern publishing of newspapers and magazines; they must not be mass-produced, standardized, imper- sonal, anti-individualistic, or dull.

The specific changes which Anderson introduced were directed toward making the papers more personal and readable. His second son, John, who now publishes the weekly at nearby Abingdon, Virginia, recalls his father's dislike for the drab syndicated material, particularly that on the Hawaiian pineapple, which had usurped so much space under the previous editor. Anderson quickly threw out all such matter except for agricultural information that might be useful to the farmers of the area. Writing most of the papers himself except for the personal items sent in from outlying communities—as a former advertising man, he even composed some of the advertisements—he began to inject a personal note, sometimes humorous, sometimes serious, into the news stories, and to print brief characteristic observations of his own to fill out a column on any page: "If a great wind should suddenly tear off the front of your house, what would your life look like to people passing in the street?" Throughout the papers were scattered short or long editorials on things seen and felt by the editor—the beauty of an autumn maple tree or the fine lack of self-consciousness in dogs—while from the first issues a feature was his regular column, "What Say!"—a kind of running supplement to *Sherwood Anderson's Notebook*. Only occasionally, as when Hoover split the Solid South in the 1928 elections, did he run a story on a national event, but he derived great enjoyment out of Sheriff Dillard's raids on the stills of the mountain men, raids which he had a tendency to report as though they were pursuit sequences from the old Keystone Cops comedies. When news ran low some week, Anderson might print a story by Chekhov, or one of his own. At the time of the Smyth County Fair of 1928, he republished "Sophistication," here subtitled "A Fair Story of Youth."

During the year that had elapsed between fairs Anderson had found that having a job which supported him without requiring him to sell his powers as a creative writer kept the black dog off his back most of the time. Despite occasional brief attacks of depression and a continuing realization that ugly things could happen in Marion as well as in Winesburg or New York, his usual outward mood, as revealed in the papers, was one of warm interest in his new community and in the "educational experiment," as he later called it, which he was taking his editorship to be. Although he wrote little except newspaper copy, the contents of the two papers show that he had temporarily regained both his sense of humor and his sense of creativity. In a letter to his friend Ralph Church he explained that he was trying "to give the fancy a little play, create in the town imaginary figures of people and situations." Of these imaginary figures, who early began to take shape in the columns of the newspapers, the best known is that of a young mountain man, whose genesis had been explained, as much as Anderson ever explained it, in an earlier letter to Church: "As I couldn't afford a reporter, I invented one. I call him Buck Fever, a purely mythical being. Buck and

I do all the writing." Other figures were evolved, such as Mrs. Colonel Homing-Pigeon, a downy-bosomed Southern lady whose son Sullivan was in the Diplomatic Corps, and the mysterious Black Cat of Chilhowie, who had thirteen kittens and loped along the highway at a speed of thirteen miles an hour; but Buck Fever and the figures immediately surrounding him developed into an elaborate conception. In fact, somewhat as James Russell Lowell built up a whole milieu around Hosea Biglow or George Washington Harris around Sut Lovingood, Anderson, though in a way much less carefully controlled and certainly less impressive in its final literary result, built up a humorous character and a way of life.

As his letters show, Anderson knew Mark Twain's writings fairly extensively, and he must have been at least aware of such created figures in American journalism as the celebrated Mr. Dooley; yet there is no evidence to show any specific influence on him in the creation of his Southwest Virginia mountain man, Buck Fever. Buck's name first appears on the front page of the third issue of the *News,* that for November 17, 1927, signed to two brief news stories; but beyond a reference in one to his boyhood in a mountain town, Buck has not yet emerged as a created character, and the voice is still Anderson's. In the fifth issue (December 1st), however, an anonymous front-page letter, dated from "Coon Hollow" and filled with the misspellings dear to the funnybones of the 19th Century professional humorists, warns Buck against disgracing his family by becoming a newspaper man, while on the second page a similar warning is printed in a letter from Buck's mother, Malaria Fever. Paw Fever, Malaria goes on to say, is a mountain man, descendant of the ancient Virginia family of Fevers, and one-half of the firm of Fever and Ague, which runs a general store at the head of Coon Hollow. In this issue, Buck is clearly on his way to what his mother considers a vulgar career, for he signs three stories and is referred to by the editor as the paper's Coon Hollow correspondent. (The fictitious Coon Hollow, it turns out later, is up near the village of Troutdale in the vicinity of Anderson's Ripshin Farm.) With the sixth issue (December 8th), Buck has come down out of the hills to Marion and has inaugurated a front-page column, "Buck Fever Says," which appears with fair regularity in the following months.

From this point on Buck gradually acquires a history and a character. He is a young man, too young to have been in the First World War; he went to school with one Hannah Stoots, who writes letters about him to the Marion papers; now that he has come to town, he is dressing better, is studying spelling and grammar, and is clearly bound to rise despite

Malaria's objections. Strong and rather handsome, he likes pretty girls and in turn receives mash notes—printed in the papers, of course—from Bessy Wish of Roanoke or Girlie Gravey of Groseclose; nevertheless he is still unmarried and "has of course no children." Almost from his first appearance he has begun to ask "the boss" for a raise from his six-dollar-a-week salary, and Anderson's presumed reputation as an unrelenting tightwad becomes a recurrent target for Buck's sly abuse.

Bit by bit we learn more of the Fever family and life in Coon Hollow. Like the usual mountain woman, Malaria Fever does the work, while Paw loafs at the store and occasionally gets drunk on corn likker. There is a sixteen-year-old sister, Spring, who, like the other Fevers, can take care of herself; any man who gets gay with her will have to accept the consequences. The Fevers are poor but honest. A cousin once shot a revenue officer, "but that, as you well know or should know, is no disgrace among decent mountain people." From Coon Hollow "Personals" we hear that Miss Holly Tawney "grows one of the finest beards in Coon Hollow," that Buck's aunt, Old Miss Bone Fever, left him four acres of mountain land in her will but he has never climbed up to them yet, that Miss Hyacinth Wormwood has just had a baby, and that Old Uncle Henry Wormwood, a good church-going man who made more whiskey than anyone else in the Hollow and was jailed only three times, has died at the age of ninety-four.

Anderson's main use of Buck is not, however, as the center of a half-fanciful, half-realistic world, but rather as a shrewdly humorous reporter of and commentator on current events in Marion and Smyth County. In a style which fortunately does not rely on dialect forms or misspellings, but rather on the vocabulary and rhythms of average Southwest Virginia speech, Buck slyly or raucously pokes fun at the eccentricities and foibles of the townspeople as he recounts the events of the previous week. Most of his remarks are highly topical and local, but occasionally he comments in column or news story on national affairs and universal morality; thus he reports that Old Miss Sue Thomson of Coon Hollow was recently sent a book "all about President Harding and his private life," was so scandalized that she wouldn't keep it in the house, and so is lending it about over the Hollow "at fifty cents a reading and has already made over eight dollars for the foreign missionary society." Curiously, the conception of Buck and of his comic function shows resemblances, probably fortuitous ones, to each of the original four main traditions of American humor that Walter Blair has described in *Native American Humor*. As frequently with the comic Yankee type, Buck combines shrewdness and rusticity, while he can be related to the humorous frontiersman by virtue of his mountain origins and a tendency to boast of the fighting and drinking abilities displayed up in Coon Hollow. Buck's descriptions of everyday events occasionally remind one of the realism beneath the fun in the humor of the Old Southwest; in one issue he even tells his readers soberly and sensitively "the cold grey early morning truth" about two unpleasant incidents which show that "Life is pretty raw in some of these farms." Finally, the fact that Buck is a character created by a practising newspaper man, who used him as a kind of assumed personality, forms a link with the tradition of the professional humorists.

Doubtless Buck was often identified with his creator. In the issue for May 8, 1930, some months after Anderson's elder son, Robert Lane, had in effect taken over management of the papers, Anderson writes that on the way back to Marion from one of his trips to the textile mills of the Deep South he saw a Marion man at a gas station and rejoiced to hear the man call to him, "Hello, Buck." On the other hand, the testimony of Joe Stephenson, the linotypist on the papers since World War I, is that the townspeople "knew and they didn't know." The men in the print shop never let on, Stephenson affirms, and when people would ask Anderson directly whether he were Buck, he would say, "Sure," in a way that would leave them still wondering. Whatever people knew, however, the important matter is the author's own conception of the relationship existing between himself and his created character. The relationship was an intimate one, but it can be summarized in a statement: in Anderson's real-life situation Buck was for his creator quite seriously a kind of *persona*, was, indeed, an actual psychological necessity.

The best way to get at this point is to describe a half-length figure of Buck Fever carved out of wood by Anderson's close friend, the artist, Wharton Esherick, which now perches in the main downstairs bedroom at Ripshin. Esherick had already done a beautifully balanced line drawing of Buck, which was made into a newspaper cut for the "Buck Fever Says" column, and, according to Joe Stephenson, had suggested in the lazily sprawled sitting posture of the mountain man one of Anderson's own favorite positions. Now out of a short wooden log, the limits of size reinforcing the artist's conception, he carved Buck from head to waist with arms tightly crossed over his chest, one hand covering a cheek in a symbolic gesture of concealment, the other holding to the nose of the slyly averted face a thumb and four spread fingers. Just as Esherick had caught in the line drawing of Buck a sense of Anderson the relaxed teller of endless tales, so he caught in the carving the notion both of concealment and of mocking amusement. To Anderson, one realizes, Buck must have been a mask, molded close to the features of his creator, but covering them and allowing him to speak out more completely his complicated feelings toward his position as editor of the newspapers and therefore a leading town citizen. These feelings, it turns out, were rather complicated.

Although the "educational experiment" of editorship kept the black dog off Anderson's back for about a year, it put him in a position that he felt strongly to be anomalous. Essentially he was living a paradox. As a lover of small towns and of human beings, Anderson desired community; as an intensely individualistic artist, one, moreover, who had dared break with many conventions, he rebelled against community. As early as the second issue of the *Smyth County News*, he described in his "What Say!" column the conflict in him between his love of privacy and his need for "group feeling." But, as he suggests in other numbers of the paper, the public-private conflict is complicated by the fact that, though he likes both "good" and "bad" people, his quickest sympathies are with "The Despised and Neglected," and he cannot help identifying himself with even the most wretched criminals. In one issue he writes that he would like to set all the prisoners in the county jail free at Christmas time. Granted society must be protected, still the townspeople should never elect him to an office of public trust, because he is always on the side of the criminal. And in the issue of the *News* for January 3, 1929, he specifically summarizes the conflict and suggests its psychic cost.

> There are always two men struggling in me. One of the men appears to want to lead a plain, common-sense life. I am to be a good steady man, pay my debts, be moral.
> The other is a wild fellow. He roves restlessly over the world. He would as soon consort with thieves or prostitutes as good respectable people.
> These two men fighting in me. They exhaust me with the fight.

The antagonists are evenly matched, one notes, and the conflict continues.

Here was Anderson, then, both in the community and not in it, even against it, given status by his editorship, liking that status, yet at the same time distrustful and scornful of it. While he edited the papers, the conflict could not be resolved, but it could be alleviated by certain psychological devices; and Buck Fever was one of the most important of these devices. Taking Buck with him, Anderson could attend the weekly Kiwanis Club meeting or the wedding of two members of Marion's highest society—either event was, as a matter of fact, enjoyable in its way—and then Buck could write the event up afterwards, poking fun at the entire proceedings. Sometimes Buck and his employer could, and did, publish two different versions of the same event on the same page, one comic, one straightforwardly factual. It was with considerable help from Buck, as the evidence of the papers makes clear, that Anderson could continue to function despite the conflict within him between "the good steady man" and the restless "wild fellow."

One final generalization and an illustration of it can be made. The ambivalence toward society shown by Anderson in his brief experience as country editor, his acceptance mixed with rebellion, seems to have been an important and always-present part, not only of his psychology as a person, but also of his psychology as a writer. Although his novels and stories are not autobiographical in any exact sense, they nevertheless can be read illuminatingly as the projection of this one among other deep personal ambivalences. Such a reading helps to clarify, for example, the novel *Poor White* or an apparently simple short story like "I'm a Fool"; yet *Winesburg, Ohio* affords the quickest illustration.

George Willard, to repeat, is not an autobiographical figure. Like Anderson, editor of the Marion papers, however, George Willard, reporter for the Winesburg *Eagle,* simultaneously accepts and rejects his town. He enjoys the status which this position provides and he runs around "like an excited dog" collecting local news items, but at the same time he is dissatisfied with the gospel of worldly success preached by his ironically unsuccessful father, who had secured him the position on the newspaper. His yearning, uncommunicative mother, on the other hand, wants him to be a writer and to avoid entrapment in the town. George too, confusedly, wishes to become a writer and to leave for the city; yet it is the various individuals in the town itself, many of them "the despised and neglected," who unwittingly teach him what he most needs to know as a writer, the value in simply comprehending, behind the house fronts and the personal facades, the real interiority of lives. Eventually, of course, George does leave the town, rejecting it in that sense. But when the train pulls out, he is not thinking of where he is going or of anything "big or dramatic." Rather he is recollecting intensely the "little things" he had seen in Winesburg; and his life in the town, though it has physically passed, does remain in his memory as "a background on which to paint the dreams of his manhood."

So young George Willard left Winesburg, and years later a middle-aged Sherwood Anderson came to Marion, Virginia, a town, he notes, much like the one he grew up in, Clyde, Ohio, the Winesburg of the book. Moving toward "the adventure of life," toward the fresh and unknown future, George Willard could travel alone. Moving out of the first phase of a dark depression and, unknowingly, toward the second and even deeper phase of emotional depression that succeeded his year and a half as editor, Sherwood Anderson needed a companion besides those of the flesh. It was Buck Fever, on the surface nothing but an extended joke, who was that companion, who mediated the subtle conflict between Anderson and his community, and who helped to keep his creator brave before the slow, inexorable loss of the storyteller's talent.

JAMES SCHEVILL

published the first modern biography of Sherwood Anderson in 1951, ten years after the author's death. Through his access to the Anderson papers and his associations with friends of the author, Schevill produced a study that is valuable for including otherwise unpublished documents from Anderson's life. In discussing that life, there is no area that requires the writer's own comment more than his brief association with the socialist movement of the early 1930's. This selection from Schevill's Sherwood Anderson is the best treatment of that relationship.

THE GLITTER OF COMMUNISM

James Schevill

In the early 1930's, parallel with the growth of the depression, the sympathy of many liberals for communism was increasing. As unemployment mounted, the moral failure of a society devoted mainly to business ends seemed more and more apparent. Karl Marx was cast in the role of the wise prophet of capitalism's downfall. Few critics questioned what would happen under the promised dictatorship of the proletariat. They considered the end worthy of the means. The one immediate issue was the obvious, terrible living conditions of the working class. Communism promised action to relieve this suffering. No other political doctrine seemed so dynamic. All considerations of Marxist political theory were bypassed and the sole issue seemed to be the necessity of a new system of government and a new way of life.

It was in this mood that Anderson found himself swept along with the surge of left wing sympathy. In January, 1931, he was living with his son, Bob, in a small apartment above the print shop in Marion. His love for Eleanor [1] had rejuvenated him. As he wrote to her father, she was the direct cause of his recovery from his siege with the "black dog." Eager once more to work, he impatiently told his lecture agent that he wanted to speak only on "Industries and Modern Machinery." "Speaking about writing," he said, "is a little bit too much like speaking

1. Eleanor Copenhaver of Marion, Virginia, whom Anderson married in 1933. (Ed.)

publicly of the lady with whom you are in love." At first this transfer of interest to the labor movement was more personal than political. He was fascinated by the effect of the machine upon man. It was a new concern only in the sense that he now respected and accepted the machine. In his previous books, *Winesburg, Ohio* and *Poor White,* he had been concerned with the industrial energy that had destroyed an agricultural way of life. With the acceptance of the machine, he began to think of it as having its own beauty of function. He became devoted to his automobile and liked to drive it as fast as he could along the mountain roads. Then the Danville strike gave him his first real consciousness of the political implications of the labor movement. He grew curious about the various groups fighting for control of the workers. Most of March, 1931, he spent in the mills and factories of Georgia, speaking eagerly to laborers and employers, or standing quietly in the background watching the huge machines at work. In April he had to give several lectures on country journalism at Northwestern University and the University of Chicago. As the news of his Danville talk spread through labor circles, he was solicited for more speeches. Requests to endorse various social action groups poured in. He found himself torn between his natural sympathy for labor and his obligations to his own writing. In May the latter impulse triumphed temporarily and he hid out in Elizabeth, New Jersey. The compulsion to write had returned and he said to his brother, Karl, on May 16: "I have been avoiding people in New York because I do not want to get involved in a lot of social obligations, as right now I want to put all the energy I have into the work."

His experience in the factories and the Danville strike had begun to coalesce in the shape of a novel about mill workers. At home in Marion he exulted to Burton and Mary Emmett that "I have been on a writing drunk since I have come and believe if it will last I may be on the road of a big novel that will satisfy me."

In June he also corrected the proofs of his little book of essays, *Perhaps Women,* which contained the first results of his venture into the factories and mills. If the main thesis of the book, the idea that women might provide a solution to the evils of the industrial age, was neither clearly nor convincingly stated, the essays were nevertheless a step forward after the long period of frustration. Under the stimulus of the machine his sense of language had revived, even though he was still groping in the short, curt, impressionistic style that he had experimented with since *Dark Laughter.* But if this style had its limitations, he was putting a revived energy and freshness into it. This was evident

in such pieces as "Lift Up Thine Eyes," a clever satire about an
assembly plant that turns out the "Bogel" car, and "Loom Dance," a fine
experimental sketch about a "minute man," an efficiency expert brought
to a southern mill.

The sense of renewed vigor in his writing increased his desire to
work. At the same time he was torn by the continuous requests for him
to speak to and endorse different workers' meetings. In June he received
a telegram asking him to address a group of miners in Charleston. A
general strike was threatening. After much hesitation he decided not to
accept. He was struggling to make up his mind about his position in
regard to the labor movement and to communism. On June 23 he
explained to Eleanor why he had not gone to Charleston:

> My real reason for not wanting to go lies deeper. I do feel
> myself, dear, in a transition stage. I may conceivably go to
> communism. There is something about the whole labor thing
> about which I am too uncertain. It is too easy to encourage men to
> strike. . . .
> If I had made up my mind to go stay with these people through
> everything, through the aftermath of defeat, etc., live their lives
> afterward, etc., that would be different. . . .
> Perhaps after all I should remain in the artist's position. I may
> be able to do more there. If for example I can really pull off this
> present story. I think it is of more importance. Do you? Am I
> right? . . . It [the novel] is in some way more important, even to
> those miners, than me talking, perhaps nonsense, on the court-
> house steps at Charleston.

The conflict in his mind was clear. Reading the newspapers closely,
the strikes, the rising unemployment, the menacing figure in Germany
with the vaudeville mustache awaiting the downfall of the Weimar
Republic, he sympathized intuitively with the necessity for social
action. Throughout Europe the forces of reaction were gaining power.
In the United States the depression was growing worse. Millions of
men had lost their jobs and were becoming more bitter about the
promise of democracy each day. In the midst of the world crisis the
Utopian pledges of communism seemed the only optimistic voices.
Anderson had appreciated the quality of some of the Communists he
had met. They seemed to be fighting hard for greater racial and
economic equality. The one thing that had disturbed him was that
these men and women had often been too dogmatic in their statements.
For the moment, however, he could attribute this belligerence to their
underdog position. He had read little Communist doctrine and his

sympathy was based almost completely on talks with friends and direct observation of working conditions. Still, he put aside the many political entreaties and stuck to his novel.

During the autumn he halted his writing only for several lectures. Chief among them was an amusing debate in New York with the philosopher, Bertrand Russell, on the subject "Shall the State Rear Our Children?" Before the lecture Anderson met his daughter in New York and told her the subject of the debate. She looked at him sceptically and asked which side he was on. He said that he was going to uphold the negative side, in favor of children being reared by their families.

"What, you?" said his daughter with a grin.[2]

Another story that Anderson liked to tell about the debate was that he forgot to change his socks and, as a result, appeared in evening clothes with bright red socks. Despite this oversight, the publicity was considerable and his lecture agent was asked whether he would be willing to debate with Margaret Sanger in New Orleans on birth control!

Christmas found him back in Marion enjoying the holidays with Eleanor. Although he was negotiating for a divorce from Elizabeth,[3] he was uneasy about the relationship between Eleanor and himself. He wondered if he could ever settle down to a happy marriage. The image of love provoked his words, "A man ought to keep loving—never stop—it's the only way." An idea came to him of how he could prove the depth of his feelings for Eleanor. Beginning with the first day of January, 1932, he would write her a letter every day. Instead of sending her the letters, they would be available to her after his death. They would form a diary of a year and reveal him as he was with all his faults. If the idea was romantic, he planned the contents of the letters to show a mind in conflict, with all his doubts and turmoils and yet his sincere devotion.

The Letter A Day series begins in Marion. Anderson was still absorbed in his novel. He followed Eleanor to New York and spent several happy weeks there before returning to Marion at the end of January to prepare the papers for his divorce from Elizabeth. In New York he was besieged by pleas to participate in numerous political activities, but again declined pleading work on his novel. Back in Marion, however, the need for social action continued to disturb him and he wrote in the Letter A Day of February 13:

2. Anderson had abandoned his wife and their children in 1913 in order to go to Chicago "to write." (Ed.)

3. Elizabeth Prall Anderson, whom Sherwood had married in 1924. (Ed.)

Is democracy as an idea then sacred? No—it must go. It has already gone. There is no American democracy. America is already controlled by a small group of men.

Controlled without altruism, with no hope, by entirely cynical men.

The spirit is out of the masses.

With such thoughts in his Letter A Day series, he was growing closer to an acceptance of communism. It was a negative approach at best. In the factories he had seen the terrible working conditions and recently in New York he had surveyed the tragic poverty of the unemployed. When he wrote that "democracy was dead," he meant that the nation had reached a crisis where a drastic change was necessary. Just what kind of a change, whether communism or something else, he was not yet prepared to say. In the meantime he continued to write and to grow indignant over such a symbolic social manifestation as a letter which he received from a publicity firm:

You are mentioned by newspapers less frequently than several others whose attainments are inferior to your own. This is not an accident. You can correct this condition if you will. . . . Whether you want local, state, or national publicity, once or fifty times a year, you can enjoy the full benefits of a personal publicity staff on terms based strictly on the nature and amount of service required.

Below this he scrawled angrily, "A perfect example of the vulgarity of our times."

Staying in Marion, he rewrote the end of his novel several times. He was hurrying to finish it because he planned to leave on a long lecture tour which would take him to the west coast. Eleanor was on her way to San Francisco for an unemployment conference and he had arranged his schedule to meet her there. No longer was he involved with the newspapers. In January he had sold them to his son, Bob. In a way he had become a little impatient with life in Marion. He was tired of the quiet routine and wanted to join Eleanor and see more of the factory world. By March 12 he was on the train, feeling better, riding to Detroit for a lecture and reading "for perhaps the twentieth time," Turgenev's *Annals of a Sportsman*. He arrived in Detroit only a few days after the hunger march. When the marchers had reached the suburb of Dearborn, they had been shot at and four had been killed. Anderson saw the funeral march for these men and described it in the Letter A Day of March 13:

. . . thousands marching in the streets with revolutionary power—thus the revolution will come some day—a little more cruelty—

More and more—

And then at last.

I spoke at night making my speech as ominous and threatening as I could. I was ashamed of the well-dressed audience.

Whenever he returned to the industrial centers and witnessed the conditions there after a rest in tranquil Marion, his sympathies were aroused and he felt closer to the idea of communism. This instinctive sympathy would then fade into doubts about the sincerity of mixing his writing with politics. That writing should reflect social problems, he believed with all his heart. What he could not justify was the thought that a writer could transform himself into the situation of the worker.

By the first of April he was in Los Angeles, "a false tinpan civilization," as he called it. In the Letter A Day of April 8 he left his impression of the Metro Goldwyn Mayer studio where he lunched and spent the afternoon visiting the sets:

Here thrown upon a great open field were fragments of Russian villages, a college campus—the street of a small middle-western town, the entrance to a large hotel, the prow of a ship, half a street car, a jungle village, a mine, a street in the suburb of a city, an armory—

These but a fragment of what I saw—all artificial, all paper maché.

Here in this place you get again the envious thing about American life. I talked to a writer. . . . What about the people? The nice people, he said, are the mechanics . . . in other words the workers.

On April 10 he arrived in San Francisco. He had a happy reunion with Eleanor, even though she was busy drawing up a report on the unemployment situation and could only see him occasionally. After a short trip to Portland for another lecture, he settled down in San Francisco and began to work hard. The Letter A Day of April 22 noted: "Very tired. A fever of writing—on Red—has been on me for three or four days, all I have going into it." The reference to Red, the main character of his novel, indicated that he was still revising the end. The spell of writing was interrupted only for visits with Eleanor when they talked excitedly of the social crisis and she told him of the tragic unemployment problems she was encountering. Towards the end of April the fleet sailed into the bay and he wrote indignantly in the Letter A Day of April 24:

> There was the city with hundreds of thousands of unemployed, all of these terrible modern social problems and before them strutting this queer neurotic thing—the imperialistic war strength of America—costing more each year than all education in America.
>
> Costing each year enough to feed all the hungry, house all our people comfortably, build great roads—make a new and a real civilization. . . .

The fleet and the close contact with the unemployment situation through Eleanor disturbed his concentration, and he swerved from his novel to a passionate indictment of "all our crowd—writers, painters, educators, scientists, intellectuals in general—in a time when the world so needs leadership into revolution." This indictment, which he called "I Accuse!" after Zola, revealed once more the continuous clash in his mind between the function of the writer and the function of the revolutionary. He was looking into the mirror and declaring "Mea Culpa," but the sight was not convincing and he later put the manuscript away to return to the novel.

In May, the edge of the writing streak worn off, he began to go out more. He seized an opportunity to visit San Quentin and meet the imprisoned hero of the labor movement, Tom Mooney. While he was convinced of Mooney's innocence, he was disappointed in the personality of the famous prisoner, feeling that he had become too self-righteous and bombastic in his martyr role. He also went with high expectations to hear Lincoln Steffens lecture. Steffens asked to see him after the meeting and invited him down to his home in Carmel. Anderson immediately liked the journalist, but argued about his idea that a business man would lead America into communism. Finally, Steffens smiled and admitted that he was not sure.

Towards the end of Anderson's San Francisco visit, the fleet steamed out of the bay. He bade it a fond farewell in the Letter A Day of May 13, calling it a "majestic funeral procession."

A few days later, Eleanor and he were on the train going to visit some of her relatives in Minnesota. As usual when leaving a big city for the relative quiet of a small town, his thoughts slipped back to writing and he observed:

Thinking all day of a new style into which my writing has fallen lately. It is broken, jagged, fragmentary. Often a word is made to carry the burden of a sentence. It all hurries forward. Often sentences have no beginning and no end.

But this broken fragmentary kind of writing seems to be natural to me now. I have tried to reject it, get rid of it. I seem unable to do it.

Now I shall try to let it flow on as it comes, so naturally—to see if it becomes, say in a long piece, intelligible. It is the only thing I can do now.

Actually, this "new style" was in the same vein as the short impressionistic manner he had been experimenting with since *Dark Laughter*. That it seemed to him even more broken and fragmentary was due to the recent turmoil in his life, on a personal level with Eleanor, and on a social scale with his involvement in political problems.

When he returned to Marion at the end of May, his sympathy towards communism had deepened. His leftward swing came from the disillusioned spirit that he had felt in people throughout the country. In the May 27 Letter A Day he mused: "It is strange and sad that all the celebrations in America—so young a country too . . . are always in celebration of the past."

This attitude led him to a definite commitment towards communism. Late in the spring he received a copy of a manifesto drawn up by Edmund Wilson, Waldo Frank, and Lewis Mumford. The manifesto declared the world predicament "a crisis of human culture," and called for "a new human order." To achieve this goal the following aims were prescribed:

a. The ruling castes hopelessly corrupted by the very conditions of their emergence, must be expelled from their present position.

b. A temporary dictatorship of the class-conscious workers must be set up, as the necessary instrument for abolishing all classes based on material wealth.

c. A new order must be established, as swiftly as can be, in which economic rivalry and private profit are barred; and in which competition will be lifted from the animal plane of acquisition to the human plane of cultural creation. . . .

. . . We believe that in imaginative works, in philosophic thought, in concrete activities and groups, the nucleus and the framework of the new society must be created now.

6. Wherefore in our function as writers:

a. We declare ourselves supporters of the social-economic revolution—such revolution being an immediate step toward the creation in the United States of a new human culture based on common material possession, which shall release the energies of men to spiritual and intellectual endeavor.

b. We recognize the fundamental identity of our interests with those of the workers and of the nation.

c. We call on our fellow writers, artists, teachers, scholars, engineers, and intellectuals of every kind, to identify their cause with that of the workers, in whose ultimate capacity to rise and to rule rests the destiny of America and mankind.

Despite the illusions, the basic idealism of the manifesto cannot be doubted. The men who drew it up sincerely believed that America had come to a dead end. In a similar spirit of defiance against existing conditions, Anderson signed the document. As for the political jargon, the "temporary dictatorship of the class-conscious workers," he had an instinctive doubt about such doctrine and it was this feeling of uneasiness that kept him from joining the party. More than most of the other serious writers in the country, he knew the working people and was dubious both of their "class-consciousness" and their ability to control a "dictatorship."

Publication of the manifesto containing the endorsement of such writers as Lincoln Steffens, John Dos Passos, Theodore Dreiser, Newton Arvin, Matthew Josephson, Malcolm Cowley, Sidney Hook, and others, caused a furore. Whispers of the impending "revolution" floated about the centers of gossip. In an article in *Scribners,* Paul Rosenfeld attacked the signers of the document. For a moment, Anderson and Rosenfeld grew a little apart, each feeling that the other was taking an extreme position.

The same sympathy for the plight of the workers led Anderson into another affiliation with a Communist group. In the June 9 Letter A Day he wrote: "Agreed with Robert Dunn to give my name to the communist organization for relief of political prisoners . . . to be shirt front for the real workers." The purpose of the Prisoner's Relief Fund, as stated on its letterhead, was to "raise money for all workers now in prison because of their activities in the labor movement." In the face of the treatment of the strikers he had observed, Anderson was convinced that the only humanitarian gesture he could make was to join such a group. For a time he even served as "dummy" chairman of the Fund, but soon resigned this role when he discovered that his name was being used on documents that he knew nothing about.

During June he was again deep in his writing to the exclusion of all political activity. He had begun to experiment with dictation and found it worked successfully. First he prepared an outline and then dictated from the notes. In the evenings he liked to talk with Eleanor's mother, Mrs. Copenhaver, a vital and intelligent woman for whom he had conceived an instant admiration. One evening, sitting on the porch of her home, they tried for the fun of it to name the five greatest Americans. Anderson came up with Jefferson, Lincoln, Henry Adams, Whitman, and Emerson. Then by mutual agreement they included Melville and Jane Addams. The choice is significant in that it pictures once more the duality in Anderson's mind, the faith in the popular tradition of Jefferson, Lincoln, Whitman, and Emerson, yet at the same time his instinctive attempt to balance the social optimism of that group with the deeper sense of individual tragedy in Henry Adams and Melville.

By July 1 he was able to write exultantly in the Letter A Day, "I got down the last of *Beyond Desire*. I felt like celebrating." With an intense satisfaction at having completed his first novel in seven years, he departed for New York to deliver the manuscript to his publisher. He stayed at the Emmetts' house as they were away in the country for the summer. Eleanor was in town, working, and he spent the evenings with her. During the days, when he was not going over the novel with the Liveright editors, he went to baseball games and listened to the soap-box political activity. The July 23 Letter A Day noted: "The parks are full of men—some of them well-dressed, sleeping out at night on benches—all looking tired and in the meantime the street in which I am living temporarily is filled with empty rooms . . . the people having gone off for the summer." Listening to the young Communists speaking on the corners, he was impressed with their passion and energy and wrote, "I am convinced that the future will be in the hands of the proletariat."

This preoccupation with politics led to arguments with Burton Emmett when he went to visit over the weekends. Emmett accused him of hating the business man. With a smile Anderson denied the accusation, trying to explain that what he hated was "immaturity." He argued that many business men never made the effort "to feel or think the way down into the roots of things."

In the turmoil of New York, with his novel completed, he could no longer resist the pressure to participate in political activity. The immediate cause was the presence of the Bonus Army in Washington. When the thousands of the Bonus Expeditionary Force, as it was called, had marched to Washington in the early summer, they had been led out to the Anacostia flats, four miles from the Capitol. There they had built crude shelters and erected tents. When their somewhat distant siege continued, President Hoover finally recommended to Congress a $100,000 appropriation to feed the men and send them home. Less than ten per cent of the veterans accepted the offer. Just before Congress adjourned without acting on the demands for a bonus, the date of the loans for transportation was extended to July 25. Still most of the ex-soldiers refused to accept the money and remained in Washington. When a riot took place over the Treasury's attempt to reoccupy government property on which members of the Bonus Army had been living, several veterans were killed. The three District of Columbia Commissioners immediately asked President Hoover to call out the federal troops. Hoover consented, and General MacArthur, immaculate in full uniform, directed the operation. What happened was a grim display of force. The troops marched directly into the unorganized ranks of the Bonus Army. With fixed bayonets prodding those unwilling to retreat and tear gas ripping through the crowds, the veterans were driven out of Washington. The worst was still to come. The troops advanced to the Anacostia bridge, beyond which, on the mudflats, lay the shambles of Bonus City. The camp commander was given an hour's grace to evacuate the women and children. Then the infantry marched into the wretched city, gassing and firing each shack. By midnight, the site where 10,000 unemployed men and women had lived was a lurid glow of flames. The next day the rationalizations began. President Hoover said righteously, "Many of the Bonus marchers are communists and persons with criminal records. . . . The government cannot be coerced by mob rule." General MacArthur called the Bonus Army "a bad looking mob animated by the essence of revolution." Meanwhile, the Communists, gleeful over drawing the arrows of both Hoover and MacArthur, began to claim the credit for the action in Washington even though they were only a small minority of the veterans.

Shocked by what he considered an obvious injustice, Anderson consented to lead a group of writers to make a personal protest to President Hoover. The group included Waldo Frank and several lesser known authors. When they reached Washington, Hoover refused to see them and they were shunted off to a secretary, Theodore Joslin. Joslin proceeded to lecture them severely, saying, according to an Associated Press dispatch:

> I want to give you my personal view as a fellow craftsman. It is your duty to spread the truth. If you do so you will relate that from 3,000 to 4,000 men, turning from their own leaders to the leadership of radicals and communists, made an organized attack on the police of the District of Columbia. . . . The first duty of the President of the United States is to maintain order . . . this republic is founded on order, not upon attack on the police. If you do your duty, you will tell these indisputable facts to the American people.

If the writers would have liked to dispute the idea that the first duty of the President was to "maintain order," nevertheless they listened sceptically, left their protest, and departed. City police had been instructed to keep an eye on them. According to an Associated Press dispatch, the police "later reported to the White House that the delegation upon leaving there went to a communist headquarters." This was a complete fabrication which Anderson indignantly denied. Going to Norfolk, Virginia, for a day, he reflected on the episode and then wrote his well-known open letter to President Hoover, stating his belief that the Bonus Army had been badly mistreated.

After dispatching the open letter, he went to Marion for a few days' rest and then returned to New York. A hurried trip to Europe had suddenly become a prospect. Earlier that year he had planned to go to Russia to see for himself whether the claims for communism were justified. Until he did see for himself he did not intend to join the party. But another European venture was offered to him and he felt he should go. In September, the leftwing "World's Congress Against War" was scheduled to meet in Amsterdam. The tense situation in Germany was rising to a climax, and the international peace meeting, even if controlled by Communists, promised to be an important one. Furthermore, a wealthy New York woman in sympathy with the aims of the Congress offered to pay Anderson's passage if he would become a member of the American delegation. Anxious to see whether such an assembly would have any effect on the world situation, he accepted.

The American delegates sailed from New York on August 18. Anderson tried to stay in the background as much as possible. He didn't want to push himself merely on the strength of his literary reputation.

The Congress started ominously when the Russian group, including Maxim Gorky, was refused entry into Holland. On Sunday, August 28, Anderson noted in the Letter A Day:

The opening was not good. The intellectuals were too intellectual. The French, Barbusse and Rolland, were too flowery. It was
impossible to hear the speakers. The crowd milled about in the
great hall. When the crowds sang everything became clear and
fine.

But the next day the meeting gathered force and he became more
impressed:

The Americans sit with the English. The great body of
delegates are French and German who sit close together. . . .
There is a tenseness broken by song, by cries, by thousands of fists
raised—
The Red Front
The Red Front
The Red Front
The International is sung in many languages. The very
building shakes with it. . . .
It is a real international meeting, the largest, the most
determined ever held. . . .
An end to the old meaningless pacifism is the universal cry
here. . . . The best speakers are the workers. What a contrast to
the eloquence of the intellectuals. . . .

Twenty-seven countries with 2,195 delegates participated in the
Congress. While the Communists were a majority, the Social Demo-
crats and the trade unions were also strongly represented. The theory of
the "Popular Front" was at its highest pitch of enthusiasm and most left
wing groups still believed it possible to cooperate with the Communists.
On Monday, August 29, the big hall was filled with men in their shirt
sleeves. French and German workers jostled together, smiling and
shouting at each other in their different languages. Whenever a well-
known speaker arose, the crowd stood up and cheered. The atmosphere
was infectious. Clenched fists shook the air in the Communist salute.
The International was sung again and again, the many languages
blending together with the fervent notes of the music. The next day,
Tuesday, August 30, Anderson witnessed the episode which he
considered the most dramatic of the entire conference. A sailor from an
Italian warship, dressed in his uniform, was brought to the rostrum. He
spoke out passionately against Mussolini and the war fever in Italy and
was then hustled away. On the same day Anderson gave a short one
minute talk on the problem of the writer in America. He hurried

through his speech, almost mumbling the words, as he thought it insignificant in comparison with the other speakers. After more speeches the conference ended. The result was a document called *Manifest—War Congress Against The Imperialist War*. As the "manifest" is typical of the many resolutions adopted by "Popular Front" groups in the early thirties, it is pertinent to list its main points:

. . . The Congress, without consideration of the ideological and political nuances which might separate the various elements of which it is composed, is considering the facts and only the facts. . . .
. . . The Congress denounces the attitude of the big newspapers . . . because of servility to profit. . . .
. . . It denounces capitalist politics.
. . . It calls attention to the tireless and systematic peace policy followed by the Soviet Union and repudiates the legend of Red Imperialism. . . .
. . . Each one of us makes here a sort of pledge. . . .
We swear that we will never again allow the unity which has been established here among the multitudes of exploited and victimized persons to be broken.
We swear to struggle . . . against capitalism which is the purveyor of slaughter.
We swear to dedicate ourselves . . .
against armaments . . .
against chauvinism and nationalist propaganda, against fascism . . .
against the propaganda campaigns and the lies against the Soviet Union . . .
against the partition of China. . . .

It was in the same emotional fervor of the Congress, in the belief that it was possible to work with the Communists against fascism, in the belief that the workers could bring about peace, that Anderson felt the meeting to be an enormous success. His judgment, like that of many other liberals of the period, was based on the feverish enthusiasm of the moment, rather than any rational view. The future was forming quietly behind the scenes.

Ironically, on the day the Amsterdam conference ended, the new Reichstag, already doomed, met in Berlin. The session opened with a speech by the aged Clara Zetkin. Hunched and sick, the Communist was carried to the tribune and sank into the chair of the Reichstag President. She delivered a violent attack on the government, the Nazis, and the Socialists. At the end of her speech she had to propose that the House elect its president. Captain Goering, the Nazi candidate, received 367 votes out of 583 and with a grim smile answered "Jawohl" to Frau Zetkin's reluctant question as to whether he accepted election. The peace had already been betrayed.

CHARLES CHILD WALCUTT

has provided in his American Literary Naturalism: A Divided Stream *the most acceptable history of naturalistic fiction in America. Walcutt traces the rise of naturalism in the United States to the division in the stream of Transcendentalism that resulted in the appeal to intuition and the appeal to science. These approaches to man's nature must not be seen as mutually exclusive in any one writer, as the work of Sherwood Anderson demonstrates.*

Anderson has traditionally been criticized as a "naturalist," a label that the writer disliked. And the traditional criterion of mechanistic determinism does seem to fail when applied to Anderson's fiction. Yet, if the intuitional insights of Anderson into human nature are considered revelations of deterministic force, Sherwood Anderson is seen as perhaps America's most satisfying writer in the tradition of naturalism.

SHERWOOD ANDERSON: IMPRESSIONISM AND THE BURIED LIFE

Charles Child Walcutt

Sherwood Anderson (1876–1941) was less than ten years younger than Stephen Crane, but his productive period came a generation later than Crane's. Whereas Crane wrote in the 1890s and died in 1900, Anderson began writing after 1915 and published his first outstanding work, *Winesburg, Ohio,* in 1919. I mention them together because I believe Anderson's work shows what Crane's might have developed into if he had lived another twenty-five years. It also shows how a certain quality of the naturalistic impulse finds expression after twenty years of literary experimentation have altered and enriched the technical resources upon which it can draw.

In an earlier chapter I called Stephen Crane an impressionist—a writer particularly concerned to render with a new vividness the feel and flavor of experience. He uses fantastic metaphors to convey the incredibleness of being under fire; he communicates shock, outrage, and fright with a sensuous density that was brand-new to American literature in 1895. He takes bold strides, furthermore, along the way of altering the Victorian notions of character and personality. His people are not types; nor are they presented to us as a collection of moral traits (loyalty, honesty, thrift) by which they can be judged. Crane takes us inside his people and shows the impingement of experience upon their minds. This is impressionism. This is writing that is particularly concerned with the life of the mind—particularly but not exclusively, for Crane has definite moral convictions around which his stories are constructed. *Maggie* asserts that a girl of the streets is spiritually too poor to be capable of moral conduct. "The Blue Hotel" asserts that responsibility is so intricate a matter that it is in fact impossible to hold any single individual responsible for an event. *The Red Badge of Courage* asserts that bravery is not a characteristic that one has or has not and for which one can be praised or blamed; bravery is nothing, but a man can know something of himself through a series of battle experiences, learn a sort of discipline, and if he survives emerge with some knowledge of his capacities and limitations. *The Red Badge* asserts the futility of "judging" a "coward," although it does not deny that there may be rich satisfaction in achieving what is called courage.

This inwardness of experience cannot be reached by a writer who recognizes conventional standards and judges his characters according to them. But in Crane's day these traditional norms could not be ignored. To question them in the America of 1895 was to defy the orthodox (if not *épater les bourgeois*), and much of Crane's work includes a conscious and formal attack upon the accuracy and validity of the accepted measuring stick. "The Blue Hotel," as I have suggested, takes its shape around a formal attack on the notion of responsibility. *Maggie* likewise attacks the norms that measure sexual morality. *The Red Badge* is as concerned with attacking the Fourth-of-July idea of bravery as it is with exploring the inwardness of fear and hysteria. Crane's attacks on these problems imply a philosophical position which can be defined as anti-supernaturalism, anti-abstractionism, and anti-orthodoxy.

If we took the genius and the energy that Crane devoted to these social and philosophical considerations and used them instead on his explorations of the inwardness of the mind we might approach perhaps the quality of Sherwood Anderson's exquisite insight. Writing a generation later and therefore freed from the compulsion to fight ideological battles, Anderson renders qualities of personality and dimensions of experience beyond anything in the work of Crane, Norris, London, or Dreiser. He is far freer from taboos than they; he works on smaller areas; he does not condescend to his characters nor does he feel obliged to defend them. As a result he has laid bare an American heart which had not been known until it was caught and felt in his stories. Whereas by the severest standards Dreiser is ponderous, Norris turgid, Crane staccato and tense, and London often close to ridiculous, Anderson is mellow, lyrical, controlled, and glowing with sonorous warmth. Paul Rosenfeld, who has written the best apprecia- tion of Anderson's work,[1] likens it to field-flowers: "Flowing rhythmi- cally as it does, made like them with zest, it has the freshness of clover, buttercups, black-eyed Susans. It has their modesty, their innocence. . . . No personal interest, neither desire for display or prestige, money or applause, motivated these writings. They are the uninduced, naive consequences of a simple need for understanding and the communi- cation of that understanding, fulfilled by an extraordinary imagina- tion."

1.

Anderson's naturalism may be considered on three planes: his explora- tion of character without reference to the orthodox moral yardsticks; his questionings, and his quiet, suppressed conclusions as to what orders our cosmos and what is man's place in it; and his social attitudes, which are left-wing and increasingly critical, as the years pass, of American business enterprise. After briefly discussing these aspects of Anderson's work, I shall try to show how his naturalism, while making possible his exquisite insights into personality, confronts him with a later version of the problem of structure that baffled Hamlin Garland: Anderson's medium is the short story or sketch; in the novel he is baffled by the problem of form.

Understanding naturalism as a result of the divided stream of American transcendentalism enables us to account for many confusions and contradictions which appear in the tradition. Does the appeal to nature, for example, commit us to reason or unreason? Is truth to be found in the study of the scientist, the insight of the mystic, or the simple reactions of the folk? In short, is reason or impulse to be more respected? These are old questions, indeed, but they seem no less confusing now than they have ever been, for never have the poles of order and frenzy whirled more bewilderingly around an unknown center. Respect for reason seems to be a part of modern naturalistic thinking, but so does respect for instinct. How can it be that these two contrary notions exist in the same general pattern of ideas? The answer is that the dichotomy between order and frenzy, between reason and instinct, is not the important or major one. In a larger scheme, Authority goes at one pole, and at the other stands Nature whose two children are order (or reason) and instinct. Under the orthodox

1. *The Sherwood Anderson Reader* (Boston, 1947), p. viii.

dispensation man was to be enlightened by revelation and controlled by the rule of Authority. Under the new, he is to find the truth in himself. Since the emotions have been most severely distrusted under the aegis of orthodoxy, it is natural that, in the revolt against it, the rationalism of the eighteenth century should precede the emotionalism of the nineteenth, and that the scientific materialism of the late nineteenth century should precede the second return to emotion that we see in the psychology of Freud and the fiction of Sherwood Anderson. In each trend the return to reason comes as the first rebellion against orthodoxy, the return to emotion the second. Anderson, in almost everything he writes, searches out the emotional values involved in an experience. He seeks to render the actual flow of life to people in small towns and on farms who are struggling with all their *natural* ardor against the confines of tradition or the inhibitions of Puritanism.

Anderson explores two major themes. One is discovery, the other inhibition. These themes correspond with the demands of the two branches of the divided stream of transcendentalism. The theme of discovery is the recognition of spirit, the unfolding of the world and its perception by the intuition, the secret insight by which a man's life is suddenly revealed to him. It comes when George Willard sits in the dark over the fairground with Helen White; when the adolescent narrator of "The Man Who Became a Woman" (in *Horses and Men,* 1923) after a night of extraordinary adventures, culminating in the illusion that he has turned into a woman, breaks through the veil of ignorance and confusion and goes forth to a new life; when Rosalind Westcott of "Out of Nowhere into Nothing" (in *The Triumph of the Egg,* 1921), who has gone home from Chicago to ask her mother's advice and has found only a complete lack of sympathy, walking through the night comes into possession of a delicious confidence in her powers: "She found herself able to run, without stopping to rest and half-wished she might run on forever, through the land, through towns and cities, driving darkness away with her presence."

The theme of inhibition appears in almost every story of Anderson's, and it relates to three general areas of cause and experience. The first is the problem of growing up. Every youth finds himself baffled, inarticulate, frustrated because he does not know what he wants out of life. He wants to be loved, more than anything else, perhaps, but he also wants to express himself and to communicate with others, and these needs cannot be answered until they are clearly recognized. Childhood and youth are therefore characterized by bottled-up yearnings, unformed desires, and wild resentments. Second is the frustration which comes from the absence of a tradition of manners that could lend graciousness and ease instead of the rawness and harshness that grow when people express themselves through broad humor, scurrility, and cruel pranks. Third is the problem of social opportunity which becomes increasingly important in Anderson's later work. People without education, mill workers in *Beyond Desire,* all the countless Americans who have not even a meager share of the opportunities which constitute the democratic dream of a full life for all—these live in endless spiritual privation, and passages which appear with increasing frequency in the later books suggest that Anderson shared the hatred of the oppressed for the vapid plutocrats who deprive them. This theme of inhibition obviously reflects the materialistic branch of the transcendental stream when it identifies spiritual and material privation. If Anderson ever suggested that all we need in America is a tradition of manners and devout observances to control the wildness of the yokel, he would be returning to orthodoxy and dualism. This he never does.

Rather he evolves the concept of the *grotesque* to indicate what small-town life has done to its people. The grotesque is the person who has become obsessed by a mannerism, an idea, or an interest to the point where he ceases to be Man in the ideal sense. This condition is not the single defect referred to by Hamlet:

> these men
> *Carrying, I say, the stamp of one defect,*
> *Being Nature's livery, or Fortune's star—*
> *Their virtues else—be they as pure as grace,*
> *As infinite as man may undergo—*
> *Shall in the general censure take corruption*
> *From that particular fault.*

It is, rather, the state wherein the defect has become the man, while his potentialities have remained undeveloped. Anderson describes it thus:

> That in the beginning when the world was young there were a great many thoughts but no such thing as a truth. Man made the truths himself and each truth was a composite of a great many vague thoughts. . . .
>
> And then the people came along. Each as he appeared snatched up one of the truths and some who were quite strong snatched up a dozen of them.
>
> It was the truths that made the people grotesques. The old man had quite an elaborate theory concerning the matter. It was his notion that the moment one of the people took one of the truths

to himself, called it his truth, and tried to live his life by it, he became a grotesque and the truth he embraced became a falsehood.[2]

Again and again the stories of Anderson are marked by a union of surprise and insight. What was apt to be merely shocking or horrendous or sensational in the work of Zola and Norris acts in Anderson's stories as a key to a fuller grasp of the extraordinary range of "normal" reality. He has got into the heart of bizarre, even fantastic experiences which are nevertheless also universal.

"Godliness: A Tale in Four Parts," in *Winesburg, Ohio,* presents the effects on children and grandchildren of the zeal for possessions and godliness that dominates the simple heart of Jesse Bentley. Jesse has the simplicity and power of a prophet; with these go the blindness of a fanatic and the pitiful ignorance of a bigot. When his grandson, David, is twelve, he takes him into the forest and terrifies him by praying to God for a sign. The boy runs, falls, and is knocked unconscious on a root, while the old man, oblivious to the boy's terror, thinks only that God has frowned upon him. When David is fifteen, he is out with the old man recovering a strayed lamb when Jesse conceives the notion that, like Abraham, he should sacrifice the lamb and daub the boy's head with its blood. Terrified beyond measure, the boy releases the lamb, hits Jesse in the head with a stone from his sling, and, believing he has killed the old man, leaves that part of the country for good. As for old Jesse, "It happened because I was too greedy for glory," he declared, and would have no more to say on the matter. Here Anderson is, on the surface, studiously objective, presenting only the cold facts; but the delicacy and sweetness of his style invest this harsh tale with a rare quality of understanding and love. The hidden life has never been more effectively searched out. Here there is no judgment either of the fanatical old man or of the terrified boy whose life he nearly ruins. Pity, understanding, and insight there are, made possible by the naturalistic impulse to seek into the heart of experience without reference to the limits or prepossessions of convention.

Winesburg, Ohio is full of insights into the buried life, into the thoughts of the repressed, the inarticulate, the misunderstood. Most frequently frustrated is the desire to establish some degree of intimacy with another person. A tradition of manners would accomplish just this by providing a medium through which acquaintance could ripen into

2. *Winesburg, Ohio* (New York, 1919), pp. 4–5. There is no collected edition of Anderson's writings.

intimacy. Small-town America has wanted such a tradition. In place of
it, it has had joking, back-slapping, and buffooning which irk the
sensitive spirit and make him draw ever more secretly into himself. The
concluding paragraph of "The Thinker" shows these confused and
constricted emotions working at a critical moment in the life of a boy
who wants to get away. He has told a girl whom he has long known
rather at a distance that he plans to leave Winesburg, and she has
offered to kiss him:

> Seth hesitated and, as he stood waiting, the girl turned and ran
> away through the hedge. A desire to run after her came to him,
> but he only stood staring, perplexed and puzzled by her action as
> he had been perplexed and puzzled by all of the life of the town
> out of which she had come. Walking slowly toward the house, he
> stopped in the shadow of a large tree and looked at his mother
> sitting by a lighted window busily sewing. The feeling of
> loneliness that had visited him earlier in the evening returned and
> colored his thoughts of the adventure through which he had just
> passed. "Huh!" he exclaimed, turning and staring in the direction
> taken by Helen White. "That's how things'll turn out. She'll be
> like the rest. I suppose she'll begin now to look at me in a funny
> way." He looked at the ground and pondered this thought. "She'll
> be embarrassed and feel strange when I'm around," he whispered
> to himself. "That's how it'll be. That's how everything'll turn out.
> When it comes to loving some one, it won't never be me. It'll be
> some one else—some fool—some one who talks a lot—some one
> like that George Willard."

In another story he speaks of "the quality of being strong to be loved" as
if it were the key to America's need.

These ideas are all in the naturalistic tradition in that they are
motivated by the feeling of need for their expression of the "inner
man." Anderson assumes that this inner man exists and is good and
"should" be permitted to fulfill itself through love and experience. The
need is alive and eager; it is the social order that prevents its
satisfaction.

Patterns emerge in *Winesburg, Ohio* through the growth of George
Willard, who may be considered the protagonist of what connected
story there is. George appears frequently, sometimes in an experience
and sometimes hearing about another's. An extraordinary pattern
emerges when George receives, late at night in the newspaper office
where he works, a hint he cannot yet interpret from the minister, who

enters brandishing a bloody fist, exclaiming that he has been "delivered." "God," he says, "has appeared to me in the person of Kate Swift, the school teacher, kneeling naked on a bed." The minister has been peeping at her through a small hole in the colored window of his study. This night as his lustful thoughts were running wild, Kate, naked, beat the pillow of her bed and wept, and then knelt to pray, and the minister was moved to smash the window with his fist so that the glass would be replaced and he would no longer be tempted. The turmoil in the schoolteacher's bosom resulted from a mixture of interest, desire, enthusiasm, and love. Earlier the same evening she had been thinking of George Willard, whom she wanted to become a writer, and became so excited that she went to see him in the newspaper office, and for a moment allowed him to take her in his arms. George was only a youth at this point, and the schoolteacher's interest in his talents was perfectly genuine and unselfish. But she was also a passionate and unsatisfied woman in whom interest and desire interacted. When George put his arms around her she struck his face with her fists and ran out into the night again. Some time later the minister burst in, and it seemed to George that all Winesburg had gone crazy. George goes to bed later, fitting these puzzling incidents together and thinking that he has missed something Kate Swift was trying to tell him.

All the gropings and cross-purposes of these grotesques and semi-grotesques reveal the failure of communication in Winesburg. The mores impose a set of standards and taboos that are utterly incapable of serving the pent-up needs in the hearts of the people. They regard themselves with wonder and contempt while they study their neighbors with fear and suspicion. And the trouble, which begins with the gap between public morality and private reality, extends finally into the personality of a rich and good person like Kate Swift. Because her emotions are inhibited she acts confusedly toward George; is desperate, frightened, and ashamed; and fails to help him as she had wanted to do.

The climax (perhaps it should only be called the high point in George's life to then) of the book occurs when George Willard and Helen White reach a complete understanding one autumn evening, sitting up in the old grandstand on the fairgrounds, rapt and wordless. "With all his strength he tried to hold and to understand the mood that had come upon him. In that high place in the darkness the two oddly sensitive human atoms held each other tightly and waited. In the mind of each was the same thought. 'I have come to this lonely place and here is this other,' was the substance of the thing felt." It is most significant that this experience is almost entirely wordless. The shared feeling, indeed, is of seeking and wondering. It is inarticulate because it occurs in a world without meaning. Such incidents suggest that men's instincts are good but that conventional morality has warped and stifled them. Interpreted in terms of the divided stream of transcendentalism, they show that the spirit is misdirected because its physical house is mistreated. When Whitman wrote

> *Logic and sermons never convince,*
> *The damp of the night drives deeper into my soul*
> *Only what proves itself to every man and woman is so*

he was making the same plea for the liberation of body and spirit together that we infer from *Winesburg, Ohio.* I say infer, because Anderson does not precisely declare this; one might indeed infer that he regards these repressions as inseparable from life—that he takes the tragic view of man—but I think not entirely so. The pains of growth are probably inevitable, but the whole world is not as confining as Winesburg, and Anderson seems to say that people *should* be able to grow up less painfully to more abundant lives. His protagonist does, and gets away from Winesburg, though he endures torments of misunderstanding and unsatisfied love which cannot be laid to Winesburg so much as to the condition of youth in this world.

But George Willard, who will escape, is different from Elmer Cowley, who is literally inarticulate with frustration and the conviction that everyone in Winesburg considers him "queer"; from old Ray Pearson, who runs sobbing across a rough field through the beauty of an autumn evening in order to catch Hal Winters and tell him not to marry the girl whom he has got in trouble—not marry like himself and be trapped into having more children than he can support and living in a tumble-down shack by the creek, working as a hired hand, bent with labor, all his dreams come to naught. Those buried lives are disclosed with heartbreaking insight. And as we reflect upon them we sense the aptness of the "naturalistic" view of life that the author puts into the mind of George Willard and also presents as his own thought. "One shudders at the thought of the meaninglessness of life while at the same instant . . . one loves life so intensely that tears come into the eyes."

If the universe here seems meaningless, the needs and emotions of men are intensely meaningful. Anderson feels love for them and pity for their desperate and usually fruitless questing. It is not therefore surprising that he should turn increasingly in his later works toward emphasis on the social and institutional causes of their frustration. Like

Hamlin Garland, however, Anderson does not master the structure of the novel. His poignant sketches, which contain some of the best and most memorable writing in our literature, do not "connect" naturally into the sustained expression of the longer form. Perhaps the scale is too narrow or the feeling too intense and special. Perhaps Anderson could not achieve the necessary objectivity. Certainly the patterns of protest and socialism do not provide the sort of frame upon which he could weave.

2.

Impressionism involves two or three attitudes and literary modes which can be related to naturalism only by careful definition. To begin with, impressionism attempts to render the *quality* of experience more closely, more colorfully, more delicately than it has been rendered. To this end it presents the mind of a character *receiving* impressions rather than judging, classifying, or speculating; and because it attempts to catch the experience as it is received, that experience will not have a reasonable order but a chronological or associational one. The order in Anderson's work is one of its most striking qualities, for he shows people thinking of several things at once, combining incidents in the past with present experience which now makes those incidents relevant, and having at the same time emotions which they cannot understand while they entertain thoughts which do not do any sort of justice to their emotional states. As a device of presentation he tells his stories through the minds of ignorant—or certainly unstudied—narrators who have no sense of selection and arrangement and so give a story that has the tone and flavor of free association. Here in the mixture of impressionist rendering of experience and the device of the story told by a disorderly narrator we find the heart of Anderson's form. He makes a virtue of beginning a story at the end and ending it at the middle. He gives away information which would create suspense of the conventional sort and yet contrives to produce a surprise and a satisfaction at the end of his story by a psychological revelation or a sharing of experience that suddenly becomes coherent out of the chaos of the narrator's apparently objectless rambling. Often what begins as incoherence emerges as the disorder caused by emotion which the story discloses and which indeed turns out to be the cause of its telling.

Such a story is "I'm a Fool," in *Horses and Men* (1923). Its indignant narrator, who is all mixed up about money, horses, and girls, tells about a day at the races and his meeting with a truly nice girl who is strongly attracted to him. He tells her a pack of fantastic lies in order to impress her and of course comes too late to the realization that he loves her and can never go back to her and endure the shame of admitting to all the lies he has told. The rambling story represents the ignorant and disorganized character of the narrator. It reveals his naïveté and his ludicrous confusion of values. It also shows a fundamental goodhearted sincerity in a fellow who keeps repeating that he is a fool. It shows how the absence of "manners" makes it impossible for him to establish an easy intimacy with the girl. And finally it represents the universal in this provincial story—the tendency of all young men to brag before girls and be ashamed of themselves afterwards. The "disorderly" arrangement of the details in the story finally appears quite orderly, for it is perfectly suited to the kind of experience that it renders.

In addition to identifying new flavors of experience and providing a new order for storytelling, Anderson's impressionism quite obviously questions the established social and moral orders. It asks, "What *is* reality?" and repeatedly shows that the telling experience, the thing at the heart of life, is not what is ordinarily represented. Things do not make the kind of sense they are "supposed" to make. They are more complicated and more subtle than the public moralists have heart to see or words to express. This is the theme of *Winesburg, Ohio* and *The Triumph of the Egg*: what appears on the surface, what is commonly described, is not the true and inward reality. But what the true reality is remains a mystery. Characters continually discover that the world is complex, that evil and good are inseparable, and that their simple ideals are inadequate. But this discovery is pathetic because its bewilderment does not pass.

3.

The theme of *Beyond Desire* (1932) is, still, inhibition, but the attempt to make a novel out of the same materials and the same attitudes that were so successfully integrated into *Winesburg, Ohio* does not come off. *Beyond Desire* is bare of movement. Instead of an action or plot it flows in and out of the sensibilities of various characters and develops their feelings about life, the incidents which have shaped or scarred them, and the ways in which they are dominated by the forces of American social inequality. Now in Winesburg the people are so boldly and so poignantly dealt with that the reader is made vividly aware of their privations, of the way they are fenced in by ignorance, fear, and insecurity. When Anderson reaches out into the dimension of the novel in *Beyond Desire*, he accumulates his added material by dealing with somewhat more complicated characters and, instead of contenting himself with their *plights,* showing how their minds react in a variety of situations.

A long opening section presents the character of Red Oliver, a member of the better class of people in Langdon. He has been north to college, has thought about socialism, and yearns for a woman. He differs from other townspeople in being less sensitive to the differences between whites and Negroes, and in being willing to work in the cotton mills on terms of equality with the "lint-heads." He is presented almost entirely in terms of his strange poetical thoughts, his feeling of strangeness in Langdon, and his confusion as to the meaning or purpose of life.

The second part takes us into the twilight minds of the mill girls. Some of these girls have imagination and spirit, whereas others are ill and work at the edge of exhaustion; but all of them are terribly deprived, so that a day at the fair ranks as a major event in their lives. Some marry, but they can hardly be said to have homes, because both girl and husband will have to work long hours in the mill, and there will be no energy left for home. In this smothered life there always remains the dimension of inwardness, where the secret heart lives:

> There are days when nothing can touch you. If you are just a mill girl in a Southern cotton mill it doesn't matter. Something lives inside you that looks and sees. What does anything matter to you? It is queer about such days. The machinery in the mill gets on your nerves terribly some days, but on such days it doesn't. On such days you are far away from people. It's odd, sometimes then you are most attractive to them.[3]

A great deal of this part of the story flows in and out of the thoughts of the girls, in this manner.

Part Three presents Ethel, the town librarian, who has always lived on the edge of life, feeling that she is missing the great experiences; firm and formidable, she frightens the people she would like to attract; she does not find the love for which she yearns. All is misunderstanding until, after a disappointing affair one evening with Red Oliver, she marries an older man—for security. Her life has been, then, a struggle for expression and love which she has never found, and we leave her trapped.

The last part returns to Red Oliver, shows him, as a result of working in the mills, drawn to the poor people who are enslaved by the

3. *Beyond Desire* (New York, 1932), pp. 92–93.

machine, reveals his confused thoughts about communism, and has him, at the end, uselessly and almost accidentally killed by an officer of the state militia. The book plays with the idea of communism, but I think without conviction—and certainly without much persuasiveness. Passages like the following reveal Anderson's fundamental sympathy with the working masses, his belief that there is in them more essential human goodness than in their exploiters:

> The point was . . . that you have to work in a place to know. People on the outside didn't know. They couldn't. You feel things. People from the outside don't know how you feel. You have got to work in a place to know. You have got to be there through long hours, day after day, year after year. You've got to be there at work when you aren't well, when your head aches.

Here is the primitivist echo, the notion of man struggling for self-hood but lacking the means of expression. Thinking of such suppressed and inarticulate people, Red Oliver exclaims, "Oh, hell, it's true. Those who are always getting it in the neck are the nicest people. I wonder why." But although the people are good, it appears doubtful whether communist agitation will lead to anything but more misery. These speculations are turned over so often in the mind of the leading character that they create the impression of volitional paralysis: everything is so uncertain, so balanced between alternatives, that action when it comes springs from whim or accident rather than reason, and the results are tragic or futile. Red Oliver is among a group of strikers, but he is not one of them; yet his anger at the moment is such that when the officer of the militia announces that he will shoot the first man who dares to step forward onto the bridge, Red steps forward and is shot. Through the mind of the man shot and the man shooting runs the same thought: "What the hell . . . I'm a silly ass."

The technique of impressionism leads into (as it springs from) the belief that reality is illusory and phantasmagoric. The impressionistic technique of *Beyond Desire* has made this idea finally dominate the book. The minds of the characters are detached from reality; they grope always without ever finding themselves or defining their relation to society. Red Oliver's death is a grisly mistake, for Red acts in confusion and anger. It accomplishes nothing; it does not serve to focus a revolutionary spirit.

Thus the impact of the method which Anderson developed for his short stories has carried over into his novel and imposed upon it an effect which I suspect he did not intend. It is not necessary to labor this point through other books, although it would be instructive to see how impressionism dominated *Dark Laughter*. Let us see how a similar pattern of loose, groping, baffled inquiry appears in *Kit Brandon*.

Kit Brandon (1936) combines Anderson's themes of discovery and social protest into a loosely chronological-associational-autobiographical narrative of a girl who comes "up" from a southern hill farm to a mill town where she works until the yearning to escape is satisfied by her marrying the worthless son of a big-time bootlegger. For a time she spends money greedily, indulging her flair for clothes and becoming a stylish figure. Then she separates from her husband and, partly as a sort of compensation to his father and partly for excitement, becomes a driver of liquor cars, racing across state lines, dodging federal agents, acting as decoy. From this life she escapes, too, when the bootlegging gang is broken up and its members jailed. The book ends with Kit having eluded the chase, a warm young woman of thirty, stimulated to go into a way of life, whatever it might be, that would not isolate her from society as her illegal rum-running had done. "There might be some one other puzzled and baffled young one with whom she could make a real partnership in living." [4]

This thin thread of narrative emerges piecemeal as Kit confides to the author. It comes out with no particular shape. Rather the emphasis is on two or three themes that are reiterated tiresomely through the girl's rambling discourse. One is the old Anderson theme of discovery: an utterly unsophisticated, illiterate young girl comes down from the hills and begins to know life through the society of the mill in which she works. Naturalistic primitivism saturates this "discovery," for Kit is presented as having finer sensibilities and a more decent heart than the rich people by whom she is exploited. Through Kit's personal development Anderson works in the theme of isolation, dwelling constantly on the loneliness, the spiritual poverty, the yearning and groping of young people who do not have the intellectual equipment to communicate with each other or the financial and social status to work their way into the great grasping hypocritical world of American opulence. Kit's situation as a rum-driver becomes a symbol of this isolation. Going by night from town to town, living under aliases, spending days in hotel rooms with nothing to do but read and look out at the people on the streets, she represents the plight of the individual in a society given over to the soul-hardening rapacities of American industrial materialism. The following passages of reverie show how this theme is presented (hiatus dots are in the text):

4. *Kit Brandon* (New York, 1936), p. 373.

She had a terrible need . . . it growing in her . . . of something . . . a relationship . . . some man or some woman, to whom she could feel close. Just at that time she had . . . it was she felt the strongest thing in her . . . the hunger to give.

Loneliness.
The loneliness, so pronounced in Kit at that time, was not so unlike the loneliness of many Americans.
Loneliness of the radical in a capitalistic society, of the man who wants to fight it, who does feel in himself a kind of social call . . .
Immediately the thing called "respectability" gone. Such a one, a Eugene Debs for example, may be the most gentle of men. He becomes in the public mind something dangerous, is pictured as Kit had been pictured, as a dangerous one.
. . . The life of the artist in any society.
. . . Life of the labor leader and for that matter loneliness also of the lives of successful Americans, even the very rich, the leaders of a capitalistic society.

And so on, through other applications that so isolated a person as Kit Brandon, with her meager background, would not be able to make.

But the question here is not so much that Kit would not be capable of this order of abstraction, but that the method in which this and a hundred other passages are presented displays an endpoint of naturalistic unform. It is experience recorded without commentary, without adequate selection, and without the saving grace of being organically related to an action. It is indeed related to an action, but as I have said it is a very thin thread of narrative, and when it has worked itself out enough has not happened to justify the amount of idle reverie accompanying it. The pretense of completeness—the appearance of giving all the unselected facts—which I have elsewhere identified as the secret of successful naturalism, has here become what it pretended. Here indeed we have a random and repetitious gathering of reverie that seems to say again and again, "This is the way life feels. How dreary and cheated it is!" Only once or twice during the book does it take the shape of a statement like the following: "What a queer mixed-up thing life was, people always being driven here and there by forces they themselves couldn't understand, some being hurt, sold-out by life, others apparently lifted up." This could be a quotation from *Sister Carrie*, but whereas it is an idea that is woven into the form of that novel, it enters without breathing life into the body of *Kit Brandon*. The early ideal of appearing to give a complete circumstantial account of an area of reality has been replaced by the unhappy fact of random and uninteresting repetition. The massive documentation of *An American Tragedy* is sustained and informed by an idea; here the vague themes of loneliness, discovery, and inhibition appear in dozens of static reveries.

Nor does the form here do anything with Anderson's later theme of social protest. The naturalist-primitivist assumption that the underprivileged are essentially kinder and wiser than their exploiters is not made credible by reiteration alone; but the action that would dramatize this idea is not here. What has happened to Anderson's later books closely resembles what appears in the three latest novels of James T. Farrell about Bernard Clare (or Carr), although the differences are as illuminating as the similarities.

FREDERICK J. HOFFMAN

led literary historians in the attempt to explain the overwhelming effects of Freudian thought on modern writers and critics. His Freudianism and the Literary Mind, *which appeared in 1945 and in a slightly revised version in 1957, is a masterful treatment of the direct and indirect influence of the new psychology on James Joyce, D. H. Lawrence, Waldo Frank, Franz Kafka, Thomas Mann, F. Scott Fitzgerald, and Sherwood Anderson.*

In this selection from Freudianism and the Literary Mind, *Hoffman discusses Sherwood Anderson's indirect acquaintance with Freudian theory through his early associates in the Chicago Renaissance and the lasting effects of that knowledge on his writing. This essay, entitled "Anderson—Psychologist by Default" in the 1945 edition of* Freudianism and the Literary Mind, *is here reprinted as it appears in the 1957 edition of that work.*

From *FREUDIANISM AND THE LITERARY MIND*

Frederick J. Hoffman

I.

At the peak of his career, in the mid-twenties, critics hailed Sherwood Anderson as the "American Freudian," the one American writer who knew his psychology and possessed a rich fund of knowledge and experience to which it could best be applied. Anderson had spoken of the repressed villager, the frustrated American businessman; he appeared to be admirably equipped to portray both, for he himself had had personal knowledge of both types. To the critic of the twenties, the villager or townsman, suffering from the hindering conventionalities of his time and place, and the businessman, deliberately shutting out life so that he might importune the goddess of success, were ideal patients for a psychoanalyst; and a writer who dealt intimately with them must have noticed the remarkable opportunity for the literary use of the new psychology.

This was, at any rate, the nature of Anderson's critical reputation. For one thing, the critics, determined to find influences, were scarcely willing to grant him a native talent, which was founded on personal experience and nurtured by a native sympathy for his subject matter. Was Anderson his own psychoanalyst? Did he proceed utterly unmindful of this influence? In order to answer these questions, it is necessary to determine the antecedent, local influences which affected Anderson's style and attitude. There is no lack of autobiographical material—for, besides the two admittedly autobiographical stories, *A Story Teller's Story* (1924) and *Sherwood Anderson's Memoirs* (1942), there are the two autobiographical novels, *Windy McPherson's Son* (1916) and *Tar* (1926). In these, and in other sources, there is a mass of contradictory material, which has for some time since his death made the biographer's task difficult. We can at best hope only to settle upon certain recurrent themes which, if they are not drawn from life, can at least be regarded as matters with which Anderson's mind was preoccupied.

One of these important themes is Anderson's relationship with his parents. He calls his father a "ruined dandy from the South . . ." who was "made for romance. For him there was no such thing as a fact." [1] He describes his own initiation into the world of letters as a rebirth: "And if you have read Freud you will find it of additional interest that, in my fanciful rebirth, I have retained the very form and substance of my earthly mother while getting an entirely new father, whom I set up —making anything but a hero of him—only to sling mud at him. . . ." [2]

This father is portrayed in Anderson's first published novel as "a confirmed liar and braggart." [3] He describes a pathetic scene in which Windy McPherson offered to blow the bugle for a Fourth-of-July celebration, then, in a critical moment, revealed his utter incompetence with the instrument. In these and many other references to his father [*sic*]. [4] In Anderson's image, the father possessed the same quality of vivid imagination that Sherwood was to exploit in himself, and there is a closer tie between the two men than one would gather from the citations made. In *Memoirs* Anderson devotes a chapter to explaining this ambiguous relationship. His father was "always showing off"; yet Anderson admits that there was a hidden bond of sympathy and common interest. Among the incidents which reveal this bond to him is a common adventure at a near-by lake: "For the first time I knew that I was the son of my father. He was a story teller as I was to be. It may be that I even laughed a little softly there in the darkness. If I did, I laughed knowing that I would never again be wanting another father." [5] This is a last, considered view, a recognition of the fact that, in the field of literary art, Anderson was himself to demonstrate his father's skill in story telling.

1. *A Story Teller's Story* (New York, 1924), 3, 4.
2. *Ibid.*, 114. His portrait of his mother seemed equally imaginative, for his brothers did not recognize in it any resemblance to the actual mother.
3. Sherwood Anderson, *Windy McPherson's Son* (New York, 1922), 22. First published, New York, 1916.
4. Anderson's methods were such that the father of the autobiographical books is as fully colored as is the father-image of the fiction.
5. *Sherwood Anderson's Memoirs* (New York, 1942), 49.

For his mother Anderson felt great sympathy and love. His desire to romanticize her, to show her a heroine who struggled boldly and patiently with poverty and loved silently but sincerely, results in several idealized portraits in his early works. "It is so wonderfully comforting to think of one's mother as a dark, beautiful and somewhat mysterious woman. . . . When she spoke her words were filled with strange wisdom . . . but often she commanded all of us by the strength of her silences." [6] In his imagination he is always championing her cause against an irresponsible villain, usually some imaginative replica of his father. This devotion to his mother, though it has ample justification in fact, is part of Anderson's rationalization of his life—the "mother image" pursues him through his later years, and the fear that he may be like his father in his treatment of women colors much of his self-criticism.

These are obviously native influences, and he needed no textbook psychology to appreciate their weight or value. Aside from that, Anderson lived his own theory of the imagination, altogether separate from the world of fact. From the childhood which he describes in *Tar*, Anderson is forever shifting from the world of fact to the "larger world of fancy"; standards of honesty and intellectual integrity are presumably rigid in this latter world, though they can not be evaluated by direct reference to the facts of the real world. The artist's deliberate entrance into the life of the fancy serves to free him of the restrictions of "Philistia," and secures his work against any tendencies he may have had toward prostituting his talents.

> There are no Puritans in that life. The dry sisters of Philistia do not come in at the door. They cannot breathe in the life of fancy. The Puritan, the reformer who scolds at the Puritans, the dry intellectuals, all who desire to uplift, to remake life on some definite plan conceived within the human brain die of a disease of the lungs. They would do better to stay in the world of fact. . . . (*Story Teller's Story*, 77)

The world of fancy was often the real world—Anderson entertained the idea that the people of his dreams and visions might have more reality than his own physical self and the men and women who populated the ostensible world. His constant reading served apparently to feed his dream mind, or to give him "a background upon which I can construct new dreams." (156) This world of fancy is the half-conscious state of daydream, supplemented by dreams and visions, for the most part elaborated upon by the dreamer. Dreams are for Anderson the most

6. Anderson, *A Story Teller's Story*, 7, 8.

coherent expression of his other world. Dream fragments are the facts of the world of fancy. They are the means by which Anderson flees reality; most often, they are simply wish-fulfillments, with the artist playing a heroic role and gaining in fancy what he has failed to get in actual life.[7] Yet they are not always this; he sometimes reports a dream which one may, with some misgiving, accredit as having actually been experienced:

> Thoughts flitting, an effort to awaken out of dreams, voices heard, voices talking somewhere in the distance, the figures of men and women I have known flashing in and out of darkness.
>
> . . . . . .
>
> Again the great empty place. I cannot breathe. There is a great black bell without a tongue, swinging silently in darkness. It swings and swings, making a great arch and I await silent and frightened. Now it stops and descends slowly. I am terrified. Can nothing stop the great descending iron bell? It stops and hangs for a moment and now it drops suddenly and I am a prisoner under the great bell.
>
> With a frantic effort I am awake. . . . (189–91)

This follows the pattern of an anxiety dream, with all its distortion and complicated symbolism. Yet Anderson regards the dream as the artist's birthright, an image of the fancy which he may treat as he pleases. He will retreat into it as a means of indirect expression of social criticism; in many respects his trances appear to be deliberately made, though their eventual effect may be genuine enough.

So, in Elyria, as he has pictured the incident in *A Story Teller's Story* and elsewhere, he walks out of his place of business and his home, bound for the adventurous nowhere. To his astonished stenographer he says: " 'My feet are cold and wet and heavy from long wading in a river. Now I shall go walk on dry land. . . .' " (313) [8] This dramatic renunciation of the business world, while it demonstrates a lively imagination, scarcely accords with the facts. According to newspaper dispatches of the time, Anderson was discovered on December 2, 1912, wandering about the streets of Cleveland, and was taken to a near-by hospital, to which his wife came immediately. The case was described as a "nervous breakdown," caused evidently by overwork. While he was still in the hospital, Anderson contemplated writing a book "of the sensations he experienced while he wandered over the country as a

7. Cf. "The Relation of the Poet to Day-Dreaming," 173–83. The writer "creates a world of phantasy which he takes very seriously."
8. This incident is described more briefly in *Memoirs*, 194.

nomad. 'It is dangerous, but it will be a good story, and the money will always be welcome,' he said." [9] Upon his return from Cleveland, he spent two more months in Elyria and there made plans for his life in Chicago. The drama of the episode subsides considerably, in the light of these facts. These quotations suggest at best a tenuous relationship between two kinds of experience. He is not willing that these statements be criticized for inaccuracy; often they are imaginative reconstructions of the past, only major themes running through them, the details derived from the moment of composition. "When I had been working well," he says in his *Notebook*, "there was a kind of insanity of consciousness. There may be little nerves in the body that, if we could bear having them sensitive enough, would tell us everything about every person we meet." [10] The hidden thoughts are dangerous and had best be glossed over by the fancy. As for the dreams which he is always reporting, "One feels sensuality, wonder, interest, quite naturally—is unashamed, does not try to be logical. . . . As for myself, I leave the fact that I have such dreams to the psychoanalysts." (*Notebooks* [sic], 224)

With the help of Floyd Dell, whom he first met in 1913, Anderson was soon associating with the Chicago intellectuals in their "Greenwich Village." Anderson rarely participated in discussions of ideas, but was always ready to tell a story. (*Memoirs*, 241–43) Nevertheless, he was present when his friends discussed Freud eagerly as a new thing, and he agreed to an amateur analysis:

> Freud had been discovered at the time and all the young intellectuals were busy analyzing each other and everyone they met. Floyd Dell was hot at it. We had gathered in the evening in somebody's rooms. Well, I hadn't read Freud (in fact, I never did read him) and was rather ashamed of my ignorance. . . .
> And now [Dell] had begun psyching us. Not Floyd alone but others in the group did it. They psyched me. They psyched men passing in the street. It was a time when it was well for a man to be somewhat guarded in the remarks he made, what he did with his hands. (*Memoirs*, 243) [11]

Anderson had come to Chicago with his mind as yet only vaguely made up about the life of the artist. He was very timid about admitting

9. Elyria (Ohio) *Evening Telegram*, December 6, 1912. This information was supplied by William Sutton.

10. *Sherwood Anderson's Notebook* (New York, 1926), 183.

11. This amateur psyching ordinarily followed one of two patterns: (1) experiments with word associations, a technique which Freud and Jung recommend as part of the analytic procedure; (2) vague generalizations about a

that he was interested in writing. Whether or not he had found a parallel in the psychoanalytic approach to human behavior, he denied having actually read Freud or exploited him in his writing. He was in the habit of reading widely, with no more deliberate purpose than to add to his dreams; his reading was unsystematic and diffuse; and he was perhaps jealous of his own originality. It was his habit to search out a man's works, once they had been referred to him, or he had seen some similarity to his own way of thinking. When the critics pointed to a Russian influence, "I began to read the Russians, to find out if the statement, so often made concerning me and my work, could be true." (*Story Teller's Story,* 48) Sometimes he and his brother would get a copy of a book and read aloud from it; about the work of Gertrude Stein he reports: "My brother had been at some sort of a gathering of literary people on the evening before and someone had read aloud from Miss Stein's new book . . . he bought *Tender Buttons* and he brought it to me, and we sat for a time reading the strange sentences." [12]

Whatever Anderson's reactions were to psychoanalysis, they were scarcely professional. With Dr. Trigant Burrow, the New York psychologist whose work had been approved by both Lawrence and Frank, Anderson held a long discussion of the matter. The argument concerned the ability of any one man successfully to enter into other lives. Burrow ended it by saying: "You think you understand but you don't understand. What you say can't be done can be done." [13] The conversation demonstrates the conflict of two opposing minds concerning a central problem:

> As with the psychiatrist who has kept himself out of the mess and the psychoanalyst who has got himself into it, the result of our differing inquiries seems to me merely to have left us both on conflicting sides of the dilemma. We were both the unconscious instruments of private improvisations. In both, the theme we used owed itself, though unacknowledged, to the personal equation that secretly actuated our separate positions. [14]

---

person's "complexes" and "repressions," and popular analysis of symptomatic acts, following roughly the suggestions given in Freud's *Psychopathology of Everyday Life,* and referring, if the group was well enough read, to parts of the *Three Contributions to a Theory of Sex.*

12. Sherwood Anderson, Preface to Gertrude Stein's *Geography and Plays* (Boston, 1922), 5.

13. Trigant Burrow, "Psychoanalytic Improvisations and the Personal Equation," *Psychoanalytic Review,* XIII (1926), 174. Burrow uses the words reported by Anderson in "Seeds," in *The Triumph of the Egg* (New York, 1921), 23. The incident, says Burrow, occurred "ten years ago," in 1916.

14. Burrow, *loc. cit.*

Anderson's opposition to psychoanalysis appears here to be founded upon a personal conviction that the "universal illness" of which he speaks in "Seeds" cannot be remedied by science, though it can be described by the artist. It is another assertion of his independence of the psychologists, and is this time supported by an accurate reference to it by the psychologist in question. In a letter Trigant Burrow has reaffirmed his opinion regarding Anderson's intellectual independence:

> My feeling is that Sherwood Anderson was, like Freud, a genius in his own right. Anderson was a man of amazing intuitive flashes but again, like Freud, the chief source of his material was his own uncanny insight.
>
> I can say very definitely that Anderson did not read Freud, nor did he draw any material from what he knew of Freud through others. Don't you think that all schools like to lay claim to an apt scholar? I think this largely accounts for the psychoanalysts' quite unwarranted adoption of Anderson. Of Anderson I would say that socially he was one of the healthiest men I have ever known. His counter-offensive in "Seeds" amply testifies to this. Indeed on this score many orthodox psychoanalysts might very profitably take a leaf from his book.[15]

There is internal evidence, however slight, that leads us to suspect that Anderson was aware of the intellectual version of Freud and that he did not altogether dismiss it from his mind. The classic reference to Freud in Anderson's writings is the line given to Bruce Dudley: "If there is anything you do not understand in human life, consult the works of Doctor Freud." [16] Nothing further seems to have been done with this reference; it appears to be casual and of little consequence.

Elsewhere, when he deals with such matters as dreams, Anderson submits them to the psychoanalysts for further consideration, but he refuses to label his experience with any of their terms. Occasionally the language appears in his novels. In *Poor White* he refers to Clara Butterworth's vision on the train: "So strong was it that it affected her deeply buried unconscious self and made her terribly afraid." [17] When he describes the dreams of Ben Peeler, Bidwell carpenter, he uses language not dissimilar to that analyst—though there is nothing in this description which Anderson could not have written without the aid of

15. Trigant Burrow to Frederick J. Hoffman, October 2, 1942.
16. *Dark Laughter* (New York, 1925), 230.
17. Sherwood Anderson, *Poor White* (New York. n.d.), 181; first published, New York, 1920.

psychoanalysis. Ben's night is taken up with two dreams. In the first, he kills a man, or thinks that he has killed him. Then, "With the inconsistency common to the physical aspect of dreams, the darkness passed away and it was daylight." (206) This is not without some significance, for it indicates a knowledge of the phenomenon of distortion in dreams (as the second dream itself does) and may imply either a deep personal interest in dreams, or a study of Freud's dream-interpretation, or even both.

This is slender evidence indeed for the critics' extravagant claims. Rebecca West, for example, says that Anderson's "excessive preoccupation with the new psychology strikes deeply at the root of his talent." Contrasting his *The Triumph of the Egg* with another American work, Miss West calls Anderson's book infinitely more valuable precisely because its author is saturated with the new psychology, "to an extraordinary degree. It dictates his subjects. His stories are monotonously full of young girls coming back to their home towns with a suitcase and a psychosis, of middle-aged men corked by inhibitions." [18] Reviewing *Winesburg, Ohio*, H. W. Boynton links psychoanalysis with Russian realism as the principal influences upon Anderson: "At worst he seems in this book like a man who has too freely imbibed the doctrine of the psychoanalysts, and fares thereafter with eyes slightly 'set' along the path of fiction." [19]

In 1931 a volume of essays was published by Regis Michaud, whose task was primarily to oppose the assumptions of psychoanalysis to the inhibitions of Puritanism in American literature. His two chapters on Anderson call him "the Freudian novelist *par excellence*." [20] Anderson, above all, devoted his literary career to proving and justifying psychoanalytic theory, and to testing it in literary works. The value of *Poor White* "resides in the Freudian sketches aside from the main plot, and in the analysis of the pathological forms of sensibility." *Winesburg* is likewise a "first-rate psychological document . . . entirely in harmony with the most recent contributions of American literature to psychoanalysis." (182) In his enthusiasm for this single preoccupation, Michaud indulges in extremes of commentary; speaking of "The New Englander," he refers to a scene in that story as "literarily beautiful and al-

18. Rebecca West, "Notes on Novels," in *New Statesman*, XVIII (1922), 564–66. See also "An Exponent of the New Psychology," in *Literary Digest*, LXXIII (1922), 33.

19. Henry W. Boynton, "All Over the Lot," in *Bookman*, XLIX (1919), 729.

20. Regis Michaud, *The American Novel To-day: A Social and Psychological Study* (Boston, 1931), 156.

most technically Freudian. . . . The tortures of inhibition have rarely been so dramatically and scientifically described." (188–91) Anderson, says Michaud, cooperates with the Freudian psychologist in advocating the release of inhibitions and repressions. He will preach the doctrine, and life will empty the prisons. "It will raise the lid of the 'well' where the Freudian monsters are asleep, these monsters which the Puritan felt groping within himself, and which he carefully and wisely held in chains." (195–96) [21]

One other example of such criticism comes from the pen of Camille J. McCole, who uses psychoanalysis to prove that Anderson's writings are evil. If we cannot follow Anderson, he says, we shall have to go to Freud for explanation; "One must know the master before he can comprehend the pupil." McCole's method is to argue by analogy, but to confuse the reader so that he is led to believe that the parallel activity actually means direct influence. Anderson commits two of the Freudian fallacies: he looks only "on one side of Main Street and that side the very shady one up which slinks the stream of day-dreamers, perverts, the 'inhibited,' the morally atrophied, the erotics, and the eccentrics that infest his pages." Secondly, Anderson, like Freud, believes that the method of free association, as employed in psychoanalysis, is a good model for the novelist to follow. His characters should "speak freely" and hold nothing back that might be either "shameful or painful." In so following the Freudian method of "telling all," Anderson has violated both good taste and morality. Anderson's preoccupation with sex is not only just *like* Freud's; it is *derived from* psychoanalysis. The cure, for Anderson's patients as well as for Freud's, is to have them give up all restraints, "surrender themselves to the particular impulse or passion which is disturbing their lives. . . ." [22]

These are extreme cases of critical misjudgment. Those who were closest to Anderson during his life in Chicago and New York, either do

21. This seemingly apt quotation is derived from John Webster's stream of consciousness, *Many Marriages* (New York, 1923), 217. But Michaud distorts the reference, and introduces the term "Freudian monsters" of his own accord. It must be admitted, however, that this description of the unconscious "well" resembles closely other metaphors which popularizers or opponents of psychoanalysis used to describe the unconscious.

22. "Sherwood Anderson, Congenital Freudian," *Catholic World*, CXXX (1929), 131, 132, 133. McCole quotes from Eduard Hitschmann, *Freud's Theories of the Neuroses* (New York, 1917), 195, as he acknowledges in a footnote; but the quotations appear to be coming from Anderson, and stand, to the reader, for Anderson's theory of fiction.

not refer to Freud at all [23] or suggest moderately that Anderson and Freud are working along parallel lines.[24] There seems little hesitancy, however, in associating the two men; and the temptation to ascribe an actual influence is easily indulged. The reasons for this easy ascription are not obscure. Most important, of course, was the recognition that Freud had contributed to American criticism the term *repression,* which acquired new significance, almost immediately, for the fields of sociology, history, biography, and literary criticism. Anderson was hailed as the leader in the American fight against conventional repression; his novels appeared coincidentally with the beginning of the interest in the new psychology. He dealt with frustration, in many cases with the frustration of normal sex expression. His dedication of *Winesburg, Ohio* to his mother is explained on the grounds that she first awoke in him "the hunger to see beneath the surface of lives." Had not the "new wisdom" been here clearly applied to the field of fiction? Anderson's use of dream symbolism, and of the vision appeared also to play a role in influencing his critics. Not the least important, however, was the fact that Anderson hesitated himself to acknowledge any influence; that is, he never committed himself fully, in answer to his critics. Though in many other cases, such as the influence of Gertrude Stein, George Borrow, and James Joyce, he was ready enough to admit influences, and in some cases to embrace his "mentors" enthusiastically, he was oddly silent about Freud and psychoanalysis. The exaggeration of the critics was, therefore, pardonably easy to make.

(1) Anderson's early life in Ohio towns had much to do with his fundamental attitude toward his writing. Certainly he needed no handbook of psychoanalysis as a guide to using his eyes, his ears, or his imagination.

(2) When he came to Chicago for the third time in 1913, anx-

23. See, for example, Robert Morss Lovett, "Sherwood Anderson, American," in *Virginia Quarterly Review,* XVII (1941), 384: "Many of Anderson's stories are concerned with the frustration of human life that comes from isolation, the inability of one being to come near another, to enter into understanding with another."

24. Among the more moderate critical references to Anderson, one may note John Crowe Ransom's "Freud and Literature," 161; Leo A. Speigel's "The New Jargon: Psychology in Literature," 478 (reference to Bruce's affair in *Dark Laughter*); Maxwell Bodenheim's "Psychoanalysis and American Fiction," 684; Henry Seidel Canby's *Definitions: Essays in Contemporary Criticism,* second series (New York, 1924), 242–48, which links Anderson's *Many Marriages* with the morals of the new age; John Farrar's "Sex Psychology in Modern Fiction," 669; Alyse Gregory's "Sherwood Anderson," in *Dial,* LXXV (1923), 246.

ious to begin a writer's life, he had not as yet heard of psychoanalysis. The ideas in two of his earliest books, *Windy McPherson's Son* (1916) and *Winesburg, Ohio* (1919), so far as we can determine from internal evidence or from a consideration of the facts of Anderson's early "Chicago period," may safely be said to be his own.

(3) In Chicago, with Floyd Dell, the Lucian Carys, and Margaret Anderson, he participated in literary discussions, and it was here that he first became acquainted with the ideas and terms comprehended under the phrase "the new psychology." He noted the similarity in subject matter, remarked upon the popular habit of "psyching," but claims not to have gone any further than that.

(4) Beginning with *Poor White* (1920), though he did not alter radically his point of view, he noted that his field was also being explored by psychoanalysis, whose researches bore many of the same marks which characterized his fictional approach. *Many Marriages* (1923) and *Dark Laughter* (1925), together with several shorter stories in *The Triumph of the Egg* (1921) and *Horses and Men* (1923), reflect this interest in frustrations and repressions, as they affect families, or unmarried women.

(5) Anderson developed his themes quite independently of Freudian influence, but with such a startling likeness of approach that critics fell into the most excusable error of their times; it seemed an absolute certainty that Anderson should have been influenced directly by Freud.

Throughout all of this Anderson maintains a skeptical attitude toward the new psychology; sometimes the reaction is simply humorous; [25] At other times, as in the case of Trigant Burrow, he becomes actively insistent upon his independent position. That psychoanalysis encouraged hostility to the social sources of repression, especially in America, cannot be denied; but the Freudian deals only with the *individual problem* of neurosis, and has always hesitated to suggest changes in the social system which is in part responsible either for a neurosis or for its imperfect cure. Many writers of the twenties thought otherwise, however; to them psychoanalysis suggested a weapon for fighting the sources of repression, or an excuse for fleeing from them. Further, Anderson's frequent reference to the sex problems of his

25. As, for example: "Only a few weeks ago I dined with a lady who spoke of 'spiral evolution.' My head snapped back. . . . Perhaps I am trying to escape the age of words. I have a dreadful fear of being psychoanalyzed by a psychoanalyst. On some nights I dream of these birds. One has got me cornered on West 8th street in New York. I squirm and squirm but cannot escape. I tore a bed sheet to pieces trying to get away from one. She was a female psychoanalyst, too. . . ." Sherwood Anderson, "Let's Go Somewhere," in *Outlook*, CLI (1929), 247.

characters was likely to convince the critics more readily. They hesitated to distinguish between the clinical study of neurosis and the literary study of frustration.

2.

The Andersonian village is examined "from within." Anderson bothers little with the placid and deceptive exteriors of village life, but is concerned primarily with the feelings of those who live within the narrow confines of village society. The energy of the villager has only infrequent opportunity for expression; most often it fails to appear at all, except in violent explosions of emotion, affective orgies, which erupt and disturb mightily the calm surface of appearances.[26] The forces that keep emotional expression imprisoned are often the conventions of the village, and the tendency to misunderstand pure for impure motives; not unusually, however, it is the timidity of the villager himself, who permits the curtailment of his emotional life because he is afraid of his strength. Hatred of the conventions or hatred of persons serves to deflect the energies of men from what might be their normal outlets. Escape from boredom, or from a worse fate, disgrace in the eyes of the community, is manifested in little, symptomatic acts—such as Doc Reefy's "paper pills"[27] or Adolph Myers's nervous gestures with his hands[28]—or in symbolic substitutes for actual sensual gratification. The revelation to the Reverend Curtis Hartman, for example, satisfies him because he has observed the hand of God laid on the "immoral" naked form of a woman. For Anderson's villagers the body is fundamentally a medium of expression; no force can effectively silence the body without making it ugly. The desire for wealth has caused Tom Butterworth to neglect the life of the body, makes him a servant of industrial masters; all of his relationships with his wife and daughter are distorted and twisted as a consequence. Clara's "coming of age" temporarily arouses his interest in the body: "As in the days of his courtship of her mother

26. As, for example, in the case of Michael McCarthy, who shouts his prayer from the jail: "Oh Father! Send down to men a new Christ. . . . Let him go into churches and into courthouses, into cities, and into towns like this, shouting 'Be Ashamed! Be ashamed of your cowardly concern over your snivelling souls!' " Anderson, *Windy McPherson's Son*.

27. "In the office he wore also a linen duster with huge pockets into which he continually stuffed scraps of paper. After some weeks the scraps of paper became little hard round balls, and when the pockets were filled he dumped them out upon the floor." Sherwood Anderson, *Winesburg, Ohio* (New York, n.d.), 19.

28. "The slender expressive fingers, forever active, forever striving to conceal themselves in his pockets or behind his back, came forth and became the piston rods of his machinery of expression." *Ibid.*, 9.

and before the possessive passion in him destroyed his ability to love, he began to feel vaguely that life about him was full of significance." (*Poor White*, 143–44) But this new interest is soon counteracted by suspicion of his daughter's actions; he refuses to allow her any normal outlets for her newly awakened passion, and ships her off to the state university at the earliest opportunity.

Are not these examples evidences of "neurosis through repression"? Not altogether—and in some respects, not at all. For Anderson has another explanation for many of these acts—the native inarticulateness of the Middle Westerner. The valiant soul of which Anderson speaks [29] will rebel against conformity and defeat it; but the average, all-too-human townsman suppresses the beauty or the yearning in his soul, and appears inarticulate and weak in his community. To Anderson the forces which deprived man of the simple, beautiful life are sometimes social and economic; but it is man's inherent timidity, his unwillingness or his inability to circumvent the laws and restrictions of the "just" which account mainly for his conformity. The life within him is stilled for lack of courage; if it is ever revealed, the realization comes in moments of poignant sorrow, or violent, deathly revolt. Mary Cochran, for example, has hated her father to the day of his death—hated him for what he has done to her mother. Only a moment before he dies of a heart attack does the truth come to her; the wall between him and her has been built solely by his inarticulateness.[30] Not infrequently this inarticulateness arises from an enforced taciturnity regarding matters of sex. Rosalind Wescott confesses to her mother her intention to go to her Chicago lover; her mother breaks a lifelong silence on the subject: love is a male-made fiction, she says; sex is dirty and a sin.[31]

Frustration has two causes: external pressures against an active search for normal happiness—that is, conventionality and "the morality of the average"; and the timidity and weakness of the individual. The plight of May Edgley has been brought about by both of these agents. She is a strict and severe person, the sole hope of a family of village

29. "Knowing that all about him in the world are men and women striving to fasten upon him their own insanity of conformity, the young and valiant soul will find here a constant demand upon his resources that will be to him a tonic against the insidious poison of association with the weak." Anderson, *Notebook*, 23. This remark was first printed in 1916.

30. Sherwood Anderson, "Unlighted Lamps," in *The Triumph of the Egg*, 92.

31. Anderson, "Out of Nowhere into Nothing," in *The Triumph of the Egg*, 260–61. An effective portrait of these small town attitudes is also found in Carl Van Vechten's *The Tattooed Countess: A Romantic Novel with a Happy Ending* (New York, 1924).

scoundrels. Her studies in the high school, her determination to become respectable against the odds of village opinion, enjoy a temporary success, but eventually she yields to the importunities of Jerome Hadley, and the tongues begin to wag:

> There was a very tender delicate thing within her many people had wanted to kill—that was certain. To kill the delicate thing within was a passion that obsessed mankind. All men and women tried to do it. First the man or woman killed the thing within himself, and then tried to kill it in others. Men and women were afraid to let the thing live.[32]

The sin had temporarily released her from the respect of her fellows, but for several reasons it did not point the way to full happiness. The accusing finger of her society forced her into a lie—the work of fantasy, which elaborated as elaboration was needed, until she herself believed and lived it. This projection of her one sin against conventional morality was absorbed in the world of fancy, until that world alone existed for her, dictated its laws, and demanded its own kind of conformity. It was eventually to demand suicide of her. There are psychoanalytic terms for all of this experience—repression, projection, "defense mechanism," "substitutive gratification"—but they are not needed. Had a psychoanalyst come upon May Edgley before the coroner was yet needed, he might have heard her story and interpreted it in much the same way as Anderson did. For the psychoanalyst the study of her problem might have led to a cure—a redirection of interests, or a more wholesome and sensible sublimation of her instinctive life; for Anderson, the result was tragic death.

Anderson regarded the Puritan world of fact a hard and cruel master of many of his characters; here too he is speaking of the phenomenon of repression, as his American contemporaries had used that term. Anderson considers the conflict one between nature itself and the world of power, wealth, and religion. The contrast is symbolized on several occasions by a natural world in which the character hides from the artificial. In the cornfields the heroine of "The New Englander" finds the source of life, so long ignored by her New England world. In answer to an obscure impulse, she rushes into the cornfield, exposes herself, and, in a frantic effort to find recompense for thirty-five years of repression, kisses the cornstalks. This wild, impetuous act is her answer to the stifling world of the Puritan; it is as though the earth itself could

32. "Unused," in *Horses and Men* (New York, 1923), 76–77.

serve to point out the folly of excessive inhibition. In his *Memoirs,* Anderson speaks of the cornfield symbol with tenderness and affection: "I could lie on the warm earth under the corn and see the life of insects, hear the soft sound of broad green leaves rubbing across each other as the summer winds blew over the fields. It was a place for lovely thoughts. . . . I even fancied that the rustling leaves of the corn were whispering to me." (33)

Anderson was sympathetically aware of the mute, inglorious midwesterner, and felt that men failed most of all to find adequate sex orientation. The solution of many of the problems posed in his stories (if it can actually be called a solution) lies in sex understanding, just as much of the frustration is discovered in misunderstanding, or mismating. In "The Other Woman," man finds the key to happiness by spending the night before his wedding with a strange woman.[33]

Many Marriages is Anderson's most thorough study of this problem. This novel, one of the first to come from his newly awakened interest in D. H. Lawrence, is indebted to an imperfect understanding of such novels as *Women in Love* much more than to any other source. It is one of the most self-conscious developments of a "thesis," or a documented feeling, that Anderson was ever to be guilty of. In the Preface Anderson says that "If one seek love and go towards it directly, or as directly as one may in the midst of the perplexities of modern life, one is perhaps insane." The thing to do, as his hero decides, is to accept one's insanity. "Nothing either animate or inanimate can be beautiful that is not loved." (27) This need, so strong in him, is almost entirely disregarded by his wife: "She thought, or believed she thought, that even in marriage a man and woman should not be lovers except for the purpose of bringing children into the world." (64) This is the Puritan attitude toward sex—the practical regard for the continuance of the race: "Even when, after long preparation, talk, prayer, and the acquiring of a little wisdom, a kind of abandon is acquired, as one would acquire a new language, one has still achieved something quite foreign to the flowers, the trees, and the life and carrying on of life among what is called the lower animals." It is amazing that life can be perpetuated at all under such conditions; it "proves, as nothing else could, the cold determination of nature not to be defeated." (65)

John Webster decides to leave this false world, but before he does he must explain to his wife and daughter the real secret of his revolt. He purchases an image of the virgin, sets it up in his bedroom, and begins

---

33. "The Other Woman," in *The Triumph of the Egg,* 33–45.

his private ritual of the body. Stripping himself, he walks before the image, in a room lighted only by two candles. This is insanity; he will accept it as such: "I accept the notion that I am at present insane and only hope I shall remain so." (86) It is, at any rate, a free surrender to the impulse within himself. Webster tells his daughter the story of his life; he has had "cause to remember" his wife's body, but she has denied the sacred life of the flesh through her own fear of it.

> . . . a thing people called shame, had come between her and the getting of that glad cry past her lips.
>
> .   .   .   .   .   .
>
> Outside voices cried "Shame! Shame!" . . . Should one listen to the voices or should one close the ears, close the eyes? (157, 163)

They are living in a world already dead; the only hope for a rebirth lies in a new awakening of the senses, a world unafraid to live intuitively and sensually. There is a constant struggle between the forces of life (the life of the senses and of sex harmony) and the forces of death (rigid conformity to a mechanical social pattern). "There was a deep well within every man and woman and when life came in at the door of that house, that was the body, it reached down and tore the heavy iron lid off the well. Dark hidden things, festering in the well, came out and found expression for themselves, and the miracle was that, expressed, they became often very beautiful." (217)

This study of Webster's conflict and of his solution has an intensity of analysis which does not characterize Anderson's earlier books. This added intensity, though it has not helped his narrative style at all, may be said to indicate an attempt on the part of Anderson to understand more fully the problem of frustration which he considered but fragmentarily in *Winesburg, Ohio* and *The Triumph of the Egg.* Unlike *Windy McPherson's Son,* the economic problem is thrown into the background, and the nature of the inner conflict is considered as basically psychological. *Many Marriages* shows Anderson attempting to "intellectualize" his feelings, in the manner of what he at least thought was Lawrence's analysis.

Under Lawrence's influence, Anderson tried to assert a "thesis": that the primitive mind "understood" more fully and more easily the basic secrets of man. Wyndham Lewis has pointed the parallel between Anderson's primitivism and that of Lawrence: the Negresses in *Dark Laughter* "are in the role of the *parrots* in Mr. Lawrence's book." Anderson, Lewis suggests, ". . . is a poor, henpecked, beFreuded, bewildered White, with a brand new 'inferiority complex.' " [34] In *Dark Laughter* Anderson offers a contrast between the embattled, imprisoned white, who has sacrificed almost everything for the dead values of money, power, and social prestige, and the uninhibited Negro consciousness. John Stockton, who has left his Chicago wife and changed his name to Bruce Dudley, meets the wife of his employer; she arranges to escape with him from her husband. In the background the laughter of the Negro servants helps to remind us that Negroes order these matters more gracefully. In this study Anderson reiterates the doctrine of *Many Marriages:* that man (white man, of course) has suffered the life forces to atrophy, and that nature will have its revenge. The ironic chorus of Negresses points to the essential primitiveness and simplicity of Anderson's solution. The figure of Sponge Martin, a kind of imitation of Lawrence's Mellors, represents the ideal triumph over civilization; not at all reconciled with the industrial ingenuity which has threatened his love of craftsmanship, he succeeds in forcing a belligerent compromise upon the enemy. His answer is a vigorous and healthy animalism.[35]

Anderson's themes are primarily bound by his search for the causes of man's frustration. What makes men more decent and moral, than healthy and sensual beings? The figures of *Winesburg, Ohio,* and of *Poor White* are victims of both external restrictions and of their own timidity—a sort of perverted gentleness. The source of much impotence lies in basic repressions of society—the business world, industrialism, middle-class decorum. Anderson is anxious to point out that primitive life is unimpeded by such barriers to happiness. He offers a variety of suggestions to imprisoned man: the totalitarian, rhythmic discipline preached by Beaut McGregor in *Marching Men;* simple repudiation, as practised by John Webster in *Many Marriages* and by Aline Grey in *Dark Laughter;* the communism of *Beyond Desire.* Fundamentally, Anderson offers no real solution to the problems he raises.

Anderson himself admits the power of dreams and visions in the creative life. It is as though he deliberately constructed a world whose particulars and relationships would be valid only in the imagination. He is rarely content with simple realism; he abhors the world of fact—

34. Wyndham Lewis, "Paleface," in *Enemy,* II (1927), 61, 65. The reference to Lawrence is to *Mornings in Mexico,* 3–20. The most thorough study of Anderson and Lawrence is in Irving Howe's *Sherwood Anderson* (New York, 1951), 179–96.

35. Anderson's failure to make this kind of thesis convincing is at least partly testified to in Hemingway's parody of it in *The Torrents of Spring* (New York, 1926).

the world of the Puritan, he calls it. His frame of reference is almost always the psychic center of personal experience. One may say that the realistic novel seeks to display the physical causality of events. To supplement this type of realism, in many respects to replace it, postwar writers went to psychology for a new form of characterization and description. Hence, in the case of the narrative portrait of the village, in place of the sentimental realism of Eggleston and the drab realistic pessimism of Ed[gar] Howe, the twenties offered the psychic realism of Sherwood Anderson. Anderson's characters are real, but in a peculiar sense; they become real to us only if and when we suspend ordinary judgment and accept them—not for what they appear—but for what they think and feel. His method is to approach a character in terms of his psychic life, and to consider external acts as either symptomatic or symbolic expressions of it.

The author's critical judgment which ordinarily manifests itself in selection of judgments stated or implied, is replaced in Anderson by *sympathy*—that is, in the etymological sense of that word, a "suffering with." This is especially true, since there is an autobiographical fragment in almost every one of his creations—they are creatures both of his imagination and of his temperament. This preoccupation with the soul of himself, as one critic has put it, demands recognition of Anderson as a writer whose explorations of the psyche are peculiar to him.[36]

The gentleness and vagueness of Anderson's sympathy are important factors in considering the legitimacy of his village characters as fictional personalities. Violence—and there is much of it in Anderson's novels— is always tempered by the fact that both the act and the actor are at least in part excused by elaborate and advance explanations of the event. Witness the character of Joe Wainsworth, harness-maker of Bidwell. The ultimate succession of acts is demoniac, extravagant. Yet the first of them is preceded by Wainsworth's weeping; the weeping climaxes, as it symbolizes, the defeat of Wainsworth's purpose in life. Anderson proceeded originally from a recognition that "something was wrong"; the *bête noire* was not clearly known. It is referred to variously as industrialism, the business mind, the sophistication of the civilized man, the white fear of wholesome impulses.

36. Rachel Smith, "Sherwood Anderson: Some Entirely Arbitrary Reactions," in *Sewanee Review*, XXXVII (1929), 163. Anderson himself admits that his theory of writing is based upon the autobiographical projection of the writer. Cf.: "In every man or woman dwell dozens of men and women, and the highly imaginative will lead fifty lives." Sherwood Anderson, "Some More about the 'New Note,'" in *Little Review*, I (1914), 16.

Were the critics altogether wrong in calling Anderson the "American Freudian"? There is no evidence that he wrote with Freud's works, or a psychoanalytic dictionary, at his elbow. The critics labeled Anderson as they did for this reason: almost any one of his characters could, at a certain stage of his career, have walked into an analyst's office and been justified in asking for treatment. May Edgley, Jesse Bentley, Fred Grey, Bruce Dudley, Hugh McVey, Mrs. Willard—each in his or her own way suffered, not physical, but psychic pain. For each the accepted way of life did not accord well with the inner, psychically motivated wish. In all cases the clinical report and Anderson's narrative report would have had a different conclusion. There is some justification in noting the parallel courses of psychoanalysis and Anderson's fiction, but there seems little evidence to prove that those two courses intersected at any vital points. It is as though Anderson were thrusting upon Freud the burden of clarifying the artist's analysis: "Men who have passed the age of thirty and who have intelligence understand such things. A German scientist can explain perfectly. If there is anything you do not understand in human life consult the works of Dr. Freud." (*Dark Laughter*, 230) If you have been unable to follow with me into the lives of these characters, Anderson seems to be saying; if they still seem queer to you—if their acts are merely violent and inexplicably so—Dr. Freud has studied these matters calmly and scientifically, and he will aid you. But if you do go to him, you will have failed to understand much of what I wish to say to you.

WILLIAM FAULKNER

waited until 1953 to express his gratitude to Sherwood Anderson for persuading Horace Liveright to publish Soldiers' Pay in 1926. When Faulkner and Anderson met in New Orleans in 1924, the older writer had already published his greatest work, while the younger man was yet to create the books that would earn him the Nobel Prize for Literature for 1949. William Faulkner here describes his relationship to Sherwood Anderson.

SHERWOOD ANDERSON:
AN APPRECIATION

William Faulkner

I.

One day during the months while we walked and talked in New Orleans—or Anderson talked and I listened—I found him sitting on a bench in Jackson Square, laughing with himself. I got the impression that he had been there like that for some time, just sitting alone on the bench laughing with himself. This was not our usual meeting place. We had none. He lived above the Square, and without any especial prearrangement, after I had had something to eat at noon and knew that he had finished his lunch too, I would walk in that direction and if I did not meet him already strolling or sitting in the Square, I myself would simply sit down on the curb where I could see his doorway and wait until he came out of it in his bright, half-racetrack, half-Bohemian clothes.

This time he was already sitting on the bench, laughing. He told me what it was at once: a dream: he had dreamed the night before that he was walking for miles along country roads, leading a horse which he was trying to swap for a night's sleep—not for a simple bed for the night, but for the sleep itself; and with me to listen now, went on from there, elaborating it, building it into a work of art with the same tedious (it had the appearance of fumbling but actually it wasn't: it was seeking, hunting) almost excruciating patience and humility with which he did all his writing, me listening and believing no word of it: that is, that it had been any dream dreamed in sleep. Because I knew better. I knew that he had invented it, made it; he had made most of it or at least some of it while I was there watching and listening to him. He didn't know why he had been compelled, or anyway needed, to claim it had been a dream, why there had to be that connection with dream and sleep, but I did. It was because he had written his whole biography into an anecdote or perhaps a parable: the horse (it had been a racehorse at first, but now it was a working horse, plow carriage and saddle, sound and strong and valuable, but without recorded pedigree) representing the vast rich strong docile sweep of the Mississippi Valley, his own America, which he in his bright blue racetrack shirt and vermilion-mottled Bohemian Windsor tie, was offering with humor and patience and humility, but mostly with patience and humility, to swap for his own dream of purity and integrity and hard and unremitting work and accomplishment, of which *Winesburg, Ohio* and *The Triumph of the Egg* had been symptoms and symbols.

He would never have said this, put it into words, himself. He may never have been able to see it even, and he certainly would have denied it, probably pretty violently, if I had tried to point it out to him. But this would not have been for the reason that it might not have been true, nor for the reason that, true or not, he would not have believed it. In fact, it would have made little difference whether it was true or not or whether he believed it or not. He would have repudiated it for the reason which was the great tragedy of his character. He expected people to make fun of, ridicule him. He expected people nowhere near his equal in stature or accomplishment or wit or anything else, to be capable of making him appear ridiculous.

That was why he worked so laboriously and tediously and indefatigably at everything he wrote. It was as if he said to himself: "This anyway will, shall, must be invulnerable." It was as though he wrote not even out of the consuming unsleeping appeaseless thirst for glory for which any normal artist would destroy his aged mother, but for what to him was more important and urgent: not even for mere truth, but for purity, the exactitude of purity. His was not the power and rush of Melville, who was his grandfather, nor the lusty humor for living of Twain, who was his father; he had nothing of the heavy-handed disregard for nuances of his older brother, Dreiser. His was that fumbling for exactitude, the exact word and phrase within the limited scope of a vocabulary controlled and even repressed by what was in him almost a fetish of simplicity, to milk them both dry, to seek always to penetrate to thought's uttermost end. He worked so hard at this that it finally became just style: an end instead of a means: so that he presently came to believe that, provided he kept the style pure and intact and unchanged and inviolate, what the style contained would have to be first rate: it couldn't help but be first rate, and therefore himself too.

At this time in his life, he had to believe this. His mother had been a bound girl, his father a day laborer; this background had taught him that the amount of security and material success which he had attained was, must be, the answer and end to life. Yet he gave this up, repudiated and discarded it at a later age, when older in years than most men and women who make that decision, to dedicate himself to art, writing. Yet, when he made the decision, he found himself to be only a one- or two-book man. He had to believe that, if only he kept that style pure, then what the style contained would be pure too, the best. That was why he had to defend the style. That was the reason for his hurt and anger at Hemingway about Hemingway's *The Torrents of Spring*, and at me in a lesser degree since my fault was not full book-length but instead was merely a privately-printed and -subscribed volume which few people outside our small New Orleans group would ever see or hear about, because of the book of [William Philip] Spratling's caricatures which we titled *Sherwood Anderson and Other Famous Creoles* and to which I wrote an introduction in Anderson's primer-like style. Neither of us—Hemingway or I—could have touched, ridiculed, his work itself. But we had made his style look ridiculous; and by that time, after *Dark Laughter*, when he had reached the point where he should have stopped writing, he had to defend that style at all costs because he too must have known by then in his heart that there was nothing else left.

2.

The exactitude of purity, or the purity of exactitude: whichever you like. He was a sentimentalist in his attitude toward people, and quite often incorrect about them. He believed in people, but it was as though only in theory. He expected the worst from them, even while each time he was prepared again to be disappointed or even hurt, as if it had never happened before, as though the only people he could really trust, let himself go with, were the ones of his own invention, the figments and symbols of his own fumbling dream. And he was sometimes a sentimentalist in his writing (so was Shakespeare sometimes) but he was never impure in it. He never scanted it, cheapened it, took the easy way; never failed to approach writing except with humility and an almost religious, almost abject faith and patience and willingness to surrender, relinquish himself to and into it. He hated glibness; if it were quick, he believed it was false too. He told me once: "You've got too much talent. You can do it too easy, in too many different ways. If you're not careful, you'll never write anything." During those afternoons when we would walk about the old quarter, I listening while he talked to me or to people—anyone, anywhere—whom we would meet on the streets or the docks, or the evenings while we sat somewhere over a bottle, he, with a little help from me, invented other fantastic characters like the sleepless man with the horse. One of them was supposed to be a descendant of Andrew Jackson, left in that Louisiana swamp after the Battle of Chalmette, no longer half-horse half-alligator but by now half-man half-sheep and presently half-shark, who—it, the whole fable—at last got so unwieldy and (so we thought) so funny, that we decided to get it onto paper by writing letters to one another such as two temporarily separated members of an exploring-zoological expedition might. I brought him my first reply to his first letter. He read it. He said:—

"Does it satisfy you?"

I said, "Sir?"

"Are you satisfied with it?"

"Why not?" I said. "I'll put whatever I left out into the next one." Then I realized that he was more than displeased: he was short, stern, almost angry. He said:—

"Either throw it away, and we'll quit, or take it back and do it over." I took the letter. I worked three days over it before I carried it back to him. He read it again, quite slowly, as he always did, and said, "Are you satisfied now?"

"No sir," I said. "But it's the best I know how to do."

"Then we'll pass it," he said, putting the letter into his pocket, his voice once more warm, rich, burly with laughter, ready to believe, ready to be hurt again.

I learned more than that from him, whether or not I always practised the rest of it any more than I have that. I learned that, to be a writer, one has first got to be what he is, what he was born; that to be an American and a writer, one does not necessarily have to pay lip-service to any conventional American image such as his and Dreiser's own aching Indiana or Ohio or Iowa corn or Sandburg's stockyards or Mark Twain's frog. You had only to remember what you were. "You have to have somewhere to start from: then you begin to learn," he told me. "It dont matter where it was, just so you remember it and aint ashamed of it. Because one place to start from is just as important as any other. You're a country boy; all you know is that little patch up there in Mississippi where you started from. But that's all right too. It's America too; pull it out, as little and unknown as it is, and the whole thing will collapse, like when you prize a brick out of a wall."

"Not a cemented, plastered wall," I said.

"Yes, but America aint cemented and plastered yet. They're still building it. That's why a man with ink in his veins not only still can but sometimes has still got to keep on moving around in it, keeping moving around and listening and looking and learning. That's why ignorant unschooled fellows like you and me not only have a chance to write, they must write. All America asks is to look at it and listen to it and understand it if you can. Only the understanding aint important either: the important thing is to believe in it even if you dont understand it, and then try to tell it, put it down. It wont ever be quite right, but there is always next time; there's always more ink and paper, and something else to try to understand and tell. And that one probably wont be exactly right either, but there is a next time to that one, too. Because tomorrow America is going to be something different, something more and new to watch and listen to and try to understand; and, even if you cant understand, believe."

To believe, to believe in the value of purity, and to believe more. To believe not in just the value, but the necessity for fidelity and integrity; lucky is that man whom the vocation of art elected and chose to be faithful to it, because the reward for art does not wait on the postman. He carried this to extremes. That of course is impossible on the face of it. I mean that, in the later years when he finally probably admitted to himself that only the style was left, he worked so hard and so laboriously and so self-sacrificingly at this, that at times he stood a little bigger, a little taller than it was. He was warm, generous, merry and fond of laughing, without pettiness and jealous only of the integrity which he believed to be absolutely necessary in anyone who approached his craft; he was ready to be generous to anyone, once he was convinced that that one approached his craft with his own humility and respect for it. During those New Orleans days and weeks, I gradually became aware that here was a man who would be in seclusion all forenoon— working. Then in the afternoon he would appear and we would walk about the city, talking. Then in the evening we would meet again, with a bottle now, and now he would really talk; the world in minuscule would be there in whatever shadowy courtyard where glass and bottle clinked and the palms hissed like dry sand in whatever moving air. Then tomorrow forenoon and he would be secluded again—working; whereupon I said to myself, "If this is what it takes to be a novelist, then that's the life for me."

So I began a novel, *Soldiers' Pay*. I had known Mrs. Anderson before I knew him. I had not seen them in some time when I met her on the street. She commented on my absence. I said I was writing a novel. She asked if I wanted Sherwood to see it. I answered, I dont remember exactly what, but to the effect that it would be all right with me if he wanted to. She told me to bring it to her when I finished it, which I did, in about two months. A few days later, she sent for me. She said, "Sherwood says he'll make a swap with you. He says that if he doesn't have to read it, he'll tell Liveright (Horace Liveright: his own publisher then) to take it."

"Done," I said, and that was all. Liveright published the book and I saw Anderson only once more, because the unhappy caricature affair had happened in the meantime and he declined to see me, for several years, until one afternoon at a cocktail party in New York; and again there was that moment when he appeared taller, bigger than anything he ever wrote. Then I remembered *Winesburg, Ohio* and *The Triumph of the Egg* and some of the pieces in *Horses and Men,* and I knew that I had seen, was looking at, a giant in an earth populated to a great—too great—extent by pygmies, even if he did make but the two or perhaps three gestures commensurate with gianthood.

WILLIAM L. PHILLIPS

wrote this account of the relationship of Sherwood Anderson to William Faulkner and Ernest Hemingway in 1954, when the lack of success given to the Letters of Sherwood Anderson seemed a disappointment to students of Anderson's work. Phillips did not recognize the coming increase of popular and scholarly interest in Anderson and other writers of the 1920's, and he perhaps erred in repeating the judgment that Anderson is, ultimately, more important as an influence than as a creator of great literature. Yet "Sherwood Anderson's Two Prize Pupils," which appeared in The University of Chicago Magazine in January, 1955, supplies valuable information on the role played by Sherwood Anderson in the careers of William Faulkner and Ernest Hemingway.

SHERWOOD ANDERSON'S
TWO PRIZE PUPILS

William L. Phillips

Since Sherwood Anderson's death in 1941 his literary reputation has continued to describe the slow decline which it had taken almost since his early success with *Winesburg, Ohio* and *The Triumph of the Egg*. Academic critics have dismissed him as "the poor man's Gide," and most of the reviews of the excellent collection of Anderson's letters published a year ago were content to consign him to a minor, though permanent, place in the history of American fiction.

Indeed, Anderson is out of fashion. But, ironically, Anderson's place as hero has been taken by two writers who owe him a great debt: Ernest Hemingway, the recipient of this year's Nobel Prize for literature and the 1953 Pulitzer Prize, and William Faulkner, by general agreement our most distinguished writer of fiction, awarded the Nobel Prize in 1950. The development of these two prize pupils forms a curious pattern; in each case Anderson helped the younger man break out of anonymity and into print, lent him important parts of his art, watched the novice refine his craft and exceed Anderson's own work in quantity and quality, and finally found himself rejected as mentor and friend.

Hemingway was the first to meet Anderson, in Chicago in the early fall of 1920. Returning from his service on the Italian front, limping on a shrapnel scarred leg and nursing a psychic wound which was reopened with every experience of the middle-class complacency of his native Oak Park, Hemingway had been searching for a way to make his living while he practiced the craft of writing. After six months of newspaper work in Toronto, he had taken a position as associate editor of *Co-operative Commonwealth,* the monthly house organ of the notorious Co-operative Society of America, and had settled among the Bohemians of Chicago's near North Side. The "Chicago Renaissance," that short-lived but vigorous flowering of letters in the Midwest, was already showing signs of dissolution, although several of the products of the movement were still in Chicago, some of them supplementing the returns from their books by writing for the *Daily News* or by turning out advertising copy.

Anderson was the leader of a group of writers loosely associated with the Critchfield Company, an advertising agency, and since Hemingway shared an apartment with two Critchfield writers, the two soon became friends. Anderson had already published two novels, a book of free verse, and his Winesburg stories, a body of work which seemed like an immense achievement to a young writer whose sketches had as yet appeared only in newspaper Sunday supplements.

As person, Anderson with his devotion to the craft of fiction and his rejection of the conventional life of a businessman (his Chicago associates still talked with awe of his leaving his Elyria, Ohio paint factory) seemed like a literary hero to the young apprentice who had already learned in Italy to distrust heroics. As artist, the older man was almost as appealing; he had shown that it was possible to write as one really felt and still find a substantial following, that it was possible to take for material the lives of race-track swipes, adolescent boys, or degenerate old men, and write about them with lyric intensity, and that it was possible to create a style, stripped clean of "literary" mannerisms, capable of evoking intense emotion from simple incidents. Anderson's only short-coming, as Hemingway saw it, was the theory of unconscious, instinctive creation under which, unknown to many of his friends, Anderson hid his laborious rewriting and revising. Hemingway was finding that "the greatest difficulty, aside from knowing truly what you felt, rather than what you were supposed to feel, and had been taught to feel, was to put down what really happened in action," and later he was to build his whole moral framework from a self-imposed aesthetic discipline; Anderson's profession of automatic writing must have seemed to be a mark of shallowness or dishonesty in his literary method.

During the year that Hemingway stayed in Chicago, however,

Anderson's reputation continued to grow. He published another book
of short stories, *The Triumph of the Egg,* and his best novel, *Poor
White;* he spent the summer of 1921 in Europe, where he met James
Joyce, Ezra Pound, Ford Madox Ford, and Gertrude Stein and arranged
for the translation of his books into French; and, a month before
Hemingway left Chicago, Anderson received the *Dial* prize of two
thousand dollars for "service to letters." Nevertheless, when Anderson
discovered that Hemingway was leaving Chicago in December, 1921, to
become a European correspondent for the *Toronto Star,* he offered him
letters of introduction to Gertrude Stein and others of the Paris literati,
a generous gesture toward a young writer made by one who had
"arrived."

By the next March Hemingway was writing enthusiastic letters back
to Anderson from Paris—letters full of gossip about his fellow expa-
triates but also full of admiration for the work of Gertrude Stein.
Gertrude Stein, herself a great admirer of Anderson's work, had taken
Hemingway as pupil and with Ezra Pound was subjecting him to an
artistic discipline which Anderson had been unable or unwilling to
undertake. Despite the attractiveness of his new mentors Hemingway
still showed a strong attraction toward Anderson's style and material;
wherever he went during 1922 he talked of Anderson.

Thus it should have surprised no one who knew the relationship of
the two men to find that of the three stories in Hemingway's first book,
Three Stories and Ten Poems, printed in Dijon in the summer of 1923,
two should have been Andersonian in material and style. One of them,
My Old Man, told by a boy who is forced to redefine his simple moral
code when he discovers that his jockey father is crooked, was so similar
to Anderson's *I Want to Know Why* that it appeared to be a conscious
imitation. The second, *Up In Michigan,* concerned the adolescent
discovery of sex, a situation which formed the basis for dozens of
Anderson stories, and was written in a clipped, brittle prose which
suggested a ruthlessly blue-penciled *Winesburg, Ohio.* The third, *Out
of Season,* bore only the slightest resemblance to Anderson; indeed the
"Hemingway style," itself to be imitated shamelessly during the next
thirty years, may be said to have first appeared in *Out of Season.* These
three stories, marked by a progression away from the plainly imitative
My Old Man toward the controlled, self-sufficient prose of *Out of
Season,* date the end of Anderson's direct influence on Hemingway's
work, except for Hemingway's use of the growth of young Nick Adams
as the organizing principle of his second book, *In Our Time,* possibly a

vestige of a similar use of the boy George Willard in Anderson's Winesburg stories. (There may, of course, have been other fiction in the vein of *My Old Man* among the eighteen stories and the novel in the briefcase full of Hemingway's manuscripts stolen from a train in the Gare du Lyons in December, 1922, and never recovered.)

Unfortunately, just when Hemingway had developed his own idiom, the critics began to remark the Andersonian influence in his work, and he was stung into contradictory denials. Although he told F. Scott Fitzgerald that *Winesburg, Ohio* was his first model, he wrote Edmund Wilson that *My Old Man* wasn't "anything like" Anderson's stories, and he even told his friend Louis Cohn that the story was written before he had read "anything by Anderson." Since the story shows an intimate knowledge of Paris and the French racetracks which Hemingway could not have had until the summer of 1922, this last remark seems absurd. Yet it indicates the compulsion which Hemingway was beginning to feel to cut the ties which held him to his literary adolescence; Anderson was of another generation and place. Hemingway's favorite lines from the dramatist Webster, "but that was in another country, and besides the wench is dead," seemed applicable to Anderson; for Anderson's abilities *did* seem to be dying, as his experiments with stream of consciousness writing (he was trying to imitate *Ulysses* in *Dark Laughter*) led him into the excesses of sentimentality and subjectivity in static, pseudo-psychological studies like *Many Marriages* and *Dark Laughter*.

Despite the fact that his own gropings toward a new manner (he called *Dark Laughter* a "fantasy" rather than a novel) were taking his writing in exactly the opposite direction from Hemingway's continuing emphasis upon a translucent style describing "what really happened in action," Anderson continued to praise the work of his young friend. Primarily as a result of Anderson's intervention, in early 1925 Horace Liveright offered Hemingway a contract for publication of *In Our Time,* a collection of short stories and his first book to be published in the United States. Although another publisher, at the urging of F. Scott Fitzgerald, was beginning to make inquiries about taking Hemingway's book and although it is probable that a writer of Hemingway's ability would not have had to wait much longer for public recognition in any case, Hemingway was properly grateful for Anderson's help, and he wrote to Anderson in May, 1925, giving him full credit for "having put my book over with Liveright." Yet in that same letter Hemingway indicated that his opinions of Anderson as friend and as artist were distinctly separated; he told Anderson of his dislike for *Many Marriages,* although he insisted that no one really knew anything about a writer's work except the writer himself.

Anderson may have recalled this last remark, expressing an attitude toward literary criticism which Hemingway was to hold for many years, when almost exactly a year later he read Hemingway's critical attack upon his work. The dust jacket of *The Torrents of Spring* announced that "Ernest Hemingway . . . here departs for a time from his own characteristic style, joins the so-called 'Chicago School of Literature,' allows himself to fall under the influence of Sherwood Anderson, *et al.,* and shows that he can do it too." This novel length parody, dashed off in a week, was Hemingway's declaration of literary independence from Anderson, and to a lesser extent Gertrude Stein; only moderately witty, it probably would have remained in manuscript as something to be read to friends in the Cafe du Dome had it not become a part of a battle between two publishers for Hemingway's contract. Indeed it was not reprinted for twenty-five years, most of the writers on Hemingway's work ignored it, and a generation of Hemingway admirers grew up hardly having heard of it.

Some criticisms of Anderson's work implied in the book were justifiable; in the parodies of the crude symbolism in *Dark Laughter* and *Many Marriages,* of the sentimentality into which Anderson's earnest attempts to capture human moods often led him, of his willingness to allow his insights into his characters to remain unstated or clearly suggested, and of his preoccupations with vague sex longings poked fun at elements of Anderson's fiction which embarrassed his most ardent admirers. The scene in which Scripps O'Neill, Hemingway's mock-hero, has his Harvard-trained sensibilities shaken by the sight of an Indian squaw walking into Browns Beanery in Petoskey, Michigan, dressed only in a pair of moccasins, is a hilarious condensation of many Anderson mannerisms ("Scripps O'Neill was feeling faint and shaken. Something had stirred inside him, some vague primordial feeling, as the squaw had come into the room.")

Much less justifiable were Hemingway's frontal assaults upon Anderson's daring in *Dark Laughter* to write about a returned war veteran without having himself served in the infantry at the front and his somewhat inconsistent scorn for the Midwestern subjects (not their literary treatment) of Anderson's fiction. These criticisms seemed to be directed toward Anderson personally, and the two conciliatory letters which Hemingway wrote Anderson soon after his parody was published did little to raise the attack to the level of impersonality. The letters seemed "patronizing" to Anderson, probably because Hemingway continually slipped into the analogy, which he has often indulged since, between the literary scene and the world of professional sports. Anderson was, it seemed, an aging middle-weight champion who was slipping and who needed a talented young challenger for a sparring partner; if writers could not honestly exchange punches at each other's weaknesses, the United States would produce nothing (and here the analogy shifted to the racetrack) but "Great American Writers, i.e. apprentice allowance claimed."

Despite the fact that its writing took valuable time away from the completion of *The Sun Also Rises, The Torrents of Spring* seemed to be a necessary public act of renunciation for Hemingway, who had chosen for himself the long road of private struggle which was to lead from *My Old Man* to *The Old Man and the Sea.* If we see Hemingway's parody as an inflated *My Old Man* in which the young man retraces his disillusionment with the integrity of his literary father, Anderson's last function for Hemingway becomes clear; Anderson was erected as a symbol of failure, failure to accept the obligations of his chosen craft and to undergo the aesthetic discipline which alone brings order into the world.

Two years before *The Torrents of Spring* marked the end of the Anderson-Hemingway relationship, Anderson had formed an attachment with another young war veteran who wanted to be a writer, this time not in the bustling Bohemia of Chicago's ad-writers but in the leisurely Bohemia of the Vieux Carre in New Orleans. It was William Faulkner, who had come down from his native Oxford, Mississippi, to associate himself with the writers who had gathered around the *Times-Picayune* and *The Double Dealer,* a little magazine which had published several of his poems (and, incidentally, Hemingway's first magazine story). The two had met through Anderson's wife, Elizabeth Prall Anderson, who had been Faulkner's employer in the New York book shop where Faulkner had worked for a short time two years before. Through the winter and spring of 1925 Anderson and Faulkner walked almost daily through the French Quarter talking about the task of the writer.

Anderson's sketch *A Meeting South,* which concerned a young returned aviator, limping, living in "the black house of pain," and eager to "write like Shelley" shows the strength of the impression which the young Faulkner made on Anderson at that time. Anderson's impression upon Faulkner was equally intense; he saw him as a writer dedicated to purity and "exactitude" in his art but still capable of commanding a

large popular audience (the romantic fantasy of *Many Marriages*
seemed not to alienate the young poet who imitated Shelley and
Swinburne.) Anderson's secluded mornings of writing and his afternoons and evenings of walking and talking with friends seemed to
Faulkner to approach the ideal life for a writer, although Faulkner
could hardly have known that Anderson's two years in New Orleans, so
unlike the harried year in Chicago that Hemingway had seen, were the
only ones in his life in which he was able to achieve the leisurely
existence which the younger man so envied.

Encouraged by Anderson, Faulkner turned to the writing of novels.
In two months he had written *Soldiers' Pay*, a "lost generation" novel
filled with bitterness at the black house of physical and psychic pain
into which the war had thrust him. When he took his manuscript to
Anderson, Anderson is supposed to have said that he would recommend
it to his new publisher, Horace Liveright, if he "didn't have to read it."
Although it is not impossible that Anderson should have neglected to
read *Soldiers' Pay* before he recommended it (Liveright's immediate
acceptance of Hemingway's first book only two months before would
have given him confidence in the power of his recommendation), the
story has, as several critics have pointed out, all the marks of the literary
tall tale in which both Anderson and Faulkner delighted. Certainly
there is objective evidence that Anderson read parts of Faulkner's next
novel, *Mosquitoes;* during one afternoon in Jackson Square the two
men began a joint elaboration of a yarn about the descendants of
Andrew Jackson who herded half-sheep-half-alligators in the Tchu-
functa river swamp, the yarn being continued in letters that they wrote
to each other as they "discovered" the Jacksons. Two of Faulkner's
letters survive as parts of *Mosquitoes,* told in the novel as impromptu
tales spun by Dawson Fairchild, the Midwestern Mark Rampion of this
minor New Orleans *Point Counter Point*. Dawson Fairchild is a thinly
disguised Sherwood Anderson, who emerges from the book comparatively unscathed by the satirical barbs which Faulkner throws at the
New Orleans literati. More important, Dawson Fairchild's stories mark
the first signs of Faulkner's interest in the folk materials of his native
Mississippi and the exaggerated humor of physical discomfort developed seventy-five years before by Crockett, Harris, and Thorpe of the
old Southwest. It is only a short step from Anderson's Flu Balsam, one
of Al Jackson's "fishherders" who lost his horse by trading it to "an easygoing restful Texan" for a night's sleep, to Faulkner's Flem Snopes in
The Hamlet who sells his spotted Texas horses to his cousins who
spend the night chasing them without success.

But *Mosquitoes* is more important as an end than as a beginning; for in that novel and the one preceding it Faulkner had written away the immediate, personal irritants of his post-war return and his life in the New Orleans Bohemia. His next five novels, coming in a burst of genius not to be matched anywhere in the history of the novel—*Sartoris* and *The Sound and the Fury* in 1929, *As I Lay Dying* in 1930, *Sanctuary* in 1931, and *Light in August* in 1932—brought into being, almost fully elaborated, the mythical framework within which Faulkner worked out his tragic vision of the world. Balzac's *Comedie Humaine* has been suggested as the model from which Faulkner took the Yoknapatawpha framework which encompasses all of his major novels (except the recent *Fable*), since he admired Balzac's concentration on the *local*, which became "eternal and timeless despite him." But a more immediate model was *Winesburg, Ohio*.

In *Winesburg, Ohio* Anderson had constructed an Ohio community, complete down to the last livery barn and peopled by characters whose twisted lives interlock to form a tangled myth of the grotesque. Anderson's characters acquire their special poignance from being cut off from the love and peaceful order which they associate, rightly or not, with the pastoral world of Winesburg; each is driven back into the recesses of himself where his efforts at individual realization most often lead him to distorted and largely ineffectual gestures. The abnormalities resulting from this isolation function in two ways; occasionally they point back to a desirable norm of values from which the grotesque is cut off; religious awe, for example, of which Jesse Bentley's sacrifice of his grandson is a horrible perversion. Often, however, they suggest qualities which the community itself seems incapable of achieving: Wing Biddlebaum, the frightened little man in "Hands," becomes a visionary unable to express adequately the overpowering sense of love toward which his persecution by the community has led him.

The method of Faulkner's Yoknapatawpha novels is an elaboration of the *Winesburg* method. Extend the town of Winesburg in space and time and one has Yoknapatawpha County; develop Jesse Bentley and Wing Biddlebaum of *Winesburg* throughout a long novel and one has Doc Hines and Gail Hightower of *Light in August*; further into Belle Carpenter's vanished soul and one has Temple Drake of *Sanctuary* or Caddie Compson of *The Sound and the Fury*; extend Anderson's *Winesburg* almost infinitely in time, space, and depth and one has the massive body of Faulkner's novels. Faulkner's recognition of Anderson's role in directing him toward his new method may be seen in his dedication of the first of the Yoknapatawpha novels to "Sherwood

Anderson through whose kindness I was first published, with the belief that *this* book will give him no reason to regret that fact" (italics mine); and he continued to admire Anderson and *Winesburg,* in spite of a series of petty quarrels which marred the friendship of the two men.

Faulkner and Hemingway have become two of the world's leading novelists, no longer requiring apprentice allowances for novels like *The Fable* and *The Old Man and the Sea.* Nor can any discovery of indebtedness to another writer detract from the honor due the two most recent Americans to earn the Nobel Prize for literature. Yet the success which they have achieved is a tribute to the man under whom each worked as an apprentice, and an indication of the lasting debt which we all owe, beyond proper recognition for his own books, to Sherwood Anderson.

LIONEL TRILLING

finds that the work of Sherwood Anderson is ultimately unsatisfying. This is the reasoned opinion of not a few critics who find greater satisfaction in the more intellectually tough writers of later years. To Trilling, Sherwood Anderson is apparently best when read in adolescence, for the era that concerned Anderson was the adolescent period of American culture. Using the writer's own theory of the "grotesque," Trilling argues that Anderson became warped by his particular truth—the truth of emotion. Anderson's fiction is thus sometimes well crafted, but it lacks genuine people and true emotion.

Lionel Trilling himself may have answered these charges of artistic failure by saying of Sherwood Anderson that "he spoke in visions." There is no persuasion that American society has "matured" since Sherwood Anderson wrote or that the lonely individuals whom Anderson described are less lonely today. Anderson in his vision never found answers that remained satisfying to him, but to have spoken his visions is more an accomplishment than Trilling would grant.

SHERWOOD ANDERSON

Lionel Trilling

I find it hard, and I think it would be false, to write about Sherwood
Anderson without speaking of him personally and even emotionally. I
did not know him; I was in his company only twice and on neither
occasion did I talk with him. The first time I saw him was when he was
at the height of his fame; I had, I recall, just been reading *A Story-
Teller's Story* and *Tar,* and these autobiographical works had made me
fully aware of the change that had taken place in my feelings since a
few years before when almost anything that Anderson wrote had
seemed a sort of revelation. The second time was about two years before
his death; he had by then not figured in my own thought about
literature for many years, and I believe that most people were no longer
aware of him as an immediate force in their lives. His last two novels
(*Beyond Desire* in 1932 and *Kit Brandon* in 1936) had not been good;
they were all too clearly an attempt to catch up with the world, but the
world had moved too fast; it was not that Anderson was not aware of
the state of things but rather that he had suffered the fate of the writer
who at one short past moment has had a success with a simple idea
which he allowed to remain simple and to become fixed. On both
occasions—the first being a gathering, after one of Anderson's lectures,
of eager Wisconsin graduate students and of young instructors who
were a little worried that they would be thought stuffy and academic by
this Odysseus, the first famous man of letters most of us had ever seen;

the second being a crowded New York party—I was much taken by Anderson's human quality, by a certain serious interest he would have in the person he was shaking hands with or talking to for a brief, formal moment, by a certain graciousness or gracefulness which seemed to arise from an innocence of heart.

I mention this very tenuous personal impression because it must really have arisen not at all from my observation of the moment but rather have been projected from some unconscious residue of admiration I had for Anderson's books even after I had made all my adverse judgments upon them. It existed when I undertook this notice of Anderson on the occasion of his death, or else I should not have undertaken it. And now that I have gone back to his books again and have found that I like them even less than I remembered, I find too that the residue of admiration still remains; it is quite vague, yet it requires to be articulated with the clearer feelings of dissatisfaction; and it needs to be spoken of, as it has been, first.

There is a special poignancy in the failure of Anderson's later career. According to the artistic morality to which he and his friends subscribed —Robert Browning seems to have played a large if anonymous part in shaping it—Anderson should have been forever protected against artistic failure by the facts of his biography. At the age of forty-five [sic for thirty-one], as everyone knows, he found himself the manager of a small paint factory in Elyria, Ohio; one day, in the very middle of a sentence he was dictating, he walked out of the factory and gave himself to literature and truth. From the wonder of that escape he seems never to have recovered, and his continued pleasure in it did him harm, for it seems to have made him feel that the problem of the artist was defined wholly by the struggle between sincerity on the one hand and commercialism and gentility on the other. He did indeed say that the artist needed not only courage but craft, yet it was surely the courage by which he set the most store. And we must sometimes feel that he had dared too much for his art and therefore expected too much merely from his boldness, believing that right opinion must necessarily result from it. Anderson was deeply concerned with the idea of justification; there was an odd, quirky, undisciplined religious strain in him that took this form; and he expected that although Philistia might condemn him, he would have an eventual justification in the way of art and truth. He was justified in some personal way, as I have tried to say, and no doubt his great escape had something to do with this, but it also had the effect of fatally fixing the character of his artistic life.

Anderson's greatest influence was probably upon those who read him

in adolescence, the age when we find the books we give up but do not
get over. And it now needs a little fortitude to pick up again, as many
must have done upon the news of his death, the one book of his we are
all sure to have read, for *Winesburg, Ohio* is not just a book, it is a
personal souvenir. It is commonly owned in the Modern Library
edition, very likely in the most primitive format of that series, even
before it was tricked out with its vulgar little ballet-Prometheus; and
the brown oilcloth binding, the coarse paper, the bold type crooked on
the page, are dreadfully evocative. Even the introduction by Ernest
Boyd is rank with the odor of the past, of the day when criticism existed
in heroic practical simplicity, when it was all truth against hypocrisy,
idealism against philistinism, and the opposite of "romanticism" was not
"classicism" but "realism," which—it now seems odd—negated both. As
for the Winesburg stories themselves, they are as dangerous to read
again, as paining and as puzzling, as if they were old letters we had
written or received.

It is not surprising that Anderson should have made his strongest
appeal, although by no means his only one, to adolescents. For one
thing, he wrote of young people with a special tenderness; one of his
best-known stories is called "I Want To Know Why": it is the great
adolescent question, and the world Anderson saw is essentially, and
even when it is inhabited by adults, the world of the sensitive young
person. It is a world that does not "understand," a world of solitude, of
running away from home, of present dullness and far-off joy and
eventual fulfillment; it is a world seen as suffused by one's own
personality and yet—and therefore—felt as indifferent to one's own
personality. And Anderson used what seems to a young person the very
language to penetrate to the heart of the world's mystery, what with its
rural or primeval willingness to say things thrice over, its reiterated
"Well . . ." which suggests the groping of boyhood, its "Eh?" which
implies the inward-turning wisdom of old age.

Most of us will feel now that this world of Anderson's is a pretty
inadequate representation of reality and probably always was. But we
cannot be sure that it was not a necessary event in our history, like
adolescence itself; and no one has the adolescence he would have liked
to have had. But an adolescence must not continue beyond its natural
term, and as we read through Anderson's canon what exasperates us is
his stubborn, satisfied continuance in his earliest attitudes. There is
something undeniably impressive about the period of Anderson's work
in which he was formulating his characteristic notions. We can take,
especially if we have a modifying consciousness of its historical

moment, *Windy MacPherson's* [*sic*] *Son,* despite its last part which is so curiously like a commercial magazine story of the time; *Marching Men* has power even though its political mysticism is repellent; *Winesburg, Ohio* has its touch of greatness; *Poor White* is heavy-handed but not without its force; and some of the stories in *The Triumph of the Egg* have the kind of grim quaintness which is, I think, Anderson's most successful mood, the mood that he occasionally achieves now and then in his later short pieces, such as "Death in the Woods." But after 1921, in *Dark Laughter* and *Many Marriages,* the books that made the greatest critical stir, there emerges in Anderson's work the compulsive, obsessive, repetitive quality which finally impresses itself on us as his characteristic quality.

Anderson is connected with the tradition of the men who maintain a standing quarrel with respectable society and have a perpetual bone to pick with the rational intellect. It is a very old tradition, for the Essenes, the early Franciscans, as well as the early Hasidim, may be said to belong to it. In modern times it has been continued by Blake and Whitman and D. H. Lawrence. Those who belong to the tradition usually do something more about the wrong way the world goes than merely to denounce it—they *act out* their denunciations and assume a role and a way of life. Typically they take up their packs and leave the doomed respectable city, just as Anderson did. But Anderson lacked what his spiritual colleagues have always notably had. We may call it *mind,* but *energy* and *spiritedness,* in their relation to mind, will serve just as well. Anderson never understood that the moment of enlightenment and conversion—the walking out—cannot be merely celebrated but must be developed, so that what begins as an act of will grows to be an act of intelligence. The men of the anti-rationalist tradition mock the mind's pretensions and denounce its restrictiveness; but they are themselves the agents of the most powerful thought. They do not of course really reject mind at all, but only mind as it is conceived by respectable society. "I learned the Torah from all the limbs of my teacher," said one of the Hasidim. They think with their sensations, their emotions, and, some of them, with their sex. While denouncing intellect, they shine forth in a mental blaze of energy which manifests itself in syntax, epigram, and true discovery.

Anderson is not like them in this regard. He did not become a "wise" man. He did not have the gift of being able to throw out a sentence or a metaphor which suddenly illuminates some dark corner of life—his role implied that he should be full of "sayings" and specific insights, yet he never was. But in the preface to *Winesburg, Ohio* he utters one of the few really "wise" things in his work, and, by a kind of irony, it explains something of his own inadequacy. The preface consists of a little story about an old man who is writing what he calls "The Book of the Grotesque." This is the old man's ruling idea:

> That in the beginning when the world was young there were a great many thoughts but no such thing as a truth. Man made the truths himself and each truth was a composite of a great many vague thoughts. All about in the world were truths and they were all beautiful.
>
> The old man listed hundreds of the truths in his book. I will not try to tell you all of them. There was the truth of virginity and the truth of passion, the truth of wealth and of poverty, of thrift and of profligacy, of carelessness and abandon. Hundreds and hundreds were the truths and they were all beautiful.
>
> And then the people came along. Each as he appeared snatched up one of the truths and some who were quite strong snatched up a dozen of them.
>
> It was the truths that made the people grotesques. The old man had quite an elaborate theory concerning the matter. It was his notion that the moment one of the people took one of the truths to himself, called it his truth, and tried to live his life by it, he became a grotesque and the truth he embraced became a falsehood.

Anderson snatched but a single one of the truths and it made him, in his own gentle and affectionate meaning of the word, a "grotesque"; eventually the truth itself became a kind of falsehood. It was the truth— or perhaps we must call it a simple complex of truths—of love-passion-freedom, and it was made up of these "vague thoughts": that each individual is a precious secret essence, often discordant with all other essences; that society, and more particularly the industrial society, threatens these essences; that the old good values of life have been destroyed by the industrial dispensation; that people have been cut off from each other and even from themselves. That these thoughts make a truth is certain; and its importance is equally certain. In what way could it have become a falsehood and its possessor a "grotesque"?

The nature of the falsehood seems to lie in this—that Anderson's affirmation of life by love, passion, and freedom had, paradoxically enough, the effect of quite negating life, making it gray, empty, and devoid of meaning. We are quite used to hearing that this is what excessive intellection can do; we are not so often warned that emotion, if it is of a certain kind, can be similarly destructive. Yet when feeling is understood as an answer, a therapeutic, when it becomes a sort of critical tool and is conceived of as excluding other activities of life, it can indeed make the world abstract and empty. Love and passion, when considered as they are by Anderson as a means of attack upon the order of the respectable world, can contrive a world which is actually without love and passion and not worth being "free" in.[1]

In Anderson's world there are many emotions, or rather many instances of a few emotions, but there are very few sights, sounds, and smells, very little of the stuff of actuality. The very things to which he gives moral value because they are living and real and opposed in their organic nature to the insensate abstractness of an industrial culture become, as he writes about them, themselves abstract and without life. His praise of the racehorses he said he loved gives us no sense of a horse; his Mississippi does not flow; his tall corn grows out of the soil in his dominating subjectivity. The beautiful organic things of the world are made to be admirable not for themselves but only for their moral superiority to men and machines. There are many similarities of theme between Anderson and D. H. Lawrence, but Lawrence's far stronger and more sensitive mind kept his faculty of vision fresh and true; Lawrence had eyes for the substantial and even at his most doctrinaire he knew the world of appearance.

And just as there is no real sensory experience in Anderson's writing, there is also no real social experience. His people do not really go to church or vote or work for money, although it is often said of them that they do these things. In his desire for better social relationships Anderson could never quite see the social relationships that do in fact exist, however inadequate they may be. He often spoke, for example, of unhappy, desperate marriages and seemed to suggest that they ought to

1. In the preface of *The Sherwood Anderson Reader*, Paul Rosenfeld, Anderson's friend and admirer, has summarized in a remarkable way the vision of life which Anderson's work suggests: "Almost, it seems, we touch an absolute existence, a curious semi-animal, semi-divine life. Its chronic state is banality, prostration, dismemberment, unconsciousness; tensity with indefinite yearning and infinitely stretching desire. Its manifestation: the non-community of cranky or otherwise asocial solitaries, dispersed, impotent and imprisoned. . . . Its wonders—the wonders of its chaos—are fugitive heroes and heroines, mutilated like the dismembered Osiris, the dismembered Dionysius. . . . Painfully the absolute comes to itself in consciousness of universal feeling and helplessness. . . . It realizes itself as feeling, sincerity, understanding, as connection and unity; sometimes at the cost of the death of its creatures. It triumphs in anyone aware of its existence even in its sullen state. The moment of realization is tragically brief. Feeling, understanding, unity pass. The divine life sinks back again, dismembered and unconscious."

be quickly dissolved, but he never understood that marriages are often unsatisfactory for the very reasons that make it impossible to dissolve them.

His people have passion without body, and sexuality without gaiety and joy, although it is often through sex that they are supposed to find their salvation. John Jay Chapman said of Emerson that, great as he was, a visitor from Mars would learn less about life on earth from him than from Italian opera, for the opera at least suggested that there were two sexes. When Anderson was at the height of his reputation, it seemed that his report on the existence of two sexes was the great thing about him, the thing that made his work an advance over the literature of New England. But although the visitor from Mars might be instructed by Anderson in the mere fact of bisexuality, he would still be advised to go to the Italian opera if he seeks fuller information. For from the opera, as never from Anderson, he will acquire some of the knowledge which is normally in the possession of natives of the planet, such as that sex has certain manifestations which are socially quite complex, that it is involved with religion, politics, and the fate of nations, above all that it is frequently marked by the liveliest sort of energy.

In their speech his people have not only no wit, but no idiom. To say that they are not "real" would be to introduce all sorts of useless quibbles about the art of character creation; they are simply not *there*. This is not a failure of art; rather, it would seem to have been part of Anderson's intention that they should be not there. His narrative prose is contrived to that end; it is not really a colloquial idiom, although it has certain colloquial tricks; it approaches in effect the inadequate use of a foreign language; old slang persists in it and elegant archaisms are consciously used, so that people are constantly having the "fantods," girls are frequently referred to as "maidens," and things are "like unto" other things. These mannerisms, although they remind us of some of Dreiser's, are not the result, as Dreiser's are, of an effort to be literary and impressive. Anderson's prose has a purpose to which these mannerisms are essential—it has the intention of making us doubt our familiarity with our own world, and not, we must note, in order to make things fresher for us but only in order to make them seem puzzling to us and remote from us. When a man whose name we know is frequently referred to as "the plowmaker," when we hear again and again of "a kind of candy called Milky Way" long after we have learned, if we did not already know, that Milky Way is a candy, when we are told of someone that "He became a radical. He had radical thoughts," it becomes clear that we are being asked by this false naïveté to give up our usual and on the whole useful conceptual grasp of the world we get around in.

Anderson liked to catch people with their single human secret, their essence, but the more he looks for their essence the more his characters vanish into the vast limbo of meaningless life, the less they are human beings. His great American heroes were Mark Twain and Lincoln, but when he writes of these two shrewd, enduring men, he robs them of all their savor and masculinity, of all their bitter resisting mind; they become little more than a pair of sensitive, suffering happy-go-luckies. The more Anderson says about people, the less alive they become—and the less lovable. Is it strange that, with all Anderson's expressed affection for them, we ourselves can never love the people he writes about? But of course we do not love people for their essence or their souls, but for their having a certain body, or wit, or idiom, certain specific relationships with things and other people, and for a dependable continuity of existence: we love them for being there.

We can even for a moment entertain the thought that Anderson himself did not love his characters, else he would not have so thoroughly robbed them of substance and hustled them so quickly off the stage after their small essential moments of crisis. Anderson's love, however, was real enough; it is only that he loves under the aspect of his "truth"; it is love indeed but love become wholly abstract. Another way of putting it is that Anderson sees with the eyes of a religiosity of a very limited sort. No one, I think, has commented on the amount and quality of the mysticism that entered the thought of the writers of the twenties. We may leave Willa Cather aside, for her notion of Catholic order differentiates her; but in addition to Anderson himself, Dreiser, Waldo Frank, and Eugene O'Neill come to mind as men who had recourse to a strong but undeveloped sense of supernal powers.

It is easy enough to understand this crude mysticism as a protest against philosophical and moral materialism; easy enough, too, to forgive it, even when, as in Anderson, the second births and the large revelations seem often to point only to the bosom of a solemn bohemia, and almost always to a lowering rather than a heightening of energy. We forgive it because some part of the blame for its crudity must be borne by the culture of the time. In Europe a century before, Stendhal could execrate a bourgeois materialism and yet remain untempted by the dim religiosity which in America in the twenties seemed one of the likeliest of the few ways by which one might affirm the value of spirit; but then Stendhal could utter his denunciation of philistinism in the name of Mozart's music, the pictures of Cimabue, Masaccio, Giotto, Leonardo, and Michelangelo, the plays of Corneille, Racine, and Shakespeare. Of what is implied by these things Anderson seems never to have had a real intimation. His awareness of the past was limited, perhaps by his fighting faith in the "modern," and this, in a modern, is always a danger. His heroes in art and morality were few: Joyce, Lawrence, Dreiser, and Gertrude Stein, as fellow moderns: Cellini, Turgeniev; there is a long piece in praise of George Borrow; he spoke of Hawthorne with contempt, for he could not understand Hawthorne except as genteel, and he said of Henry James that he was "the novelist of those who hate," for mind seemed to him always a sort of malice. And he saw but faintly even those colleagues in art whom he did admire. His real heroes were the simple and unassuming, a few anonymous Negroes, a few craftsmen, for he gave to the idea of craftsmanship a value beyond the value which it actually does have—it is this as much as anything else that reminds us of Hemingway's relation to Anderson— and a few racing drivers of whom Pop Geers was chief. It is a charming hero worship, but it does not make an adequate antagonism to the culture which Anderson opposed, and in order to make it compelling and effective Anderson reinforced it with what is in effect the high language of religion, speaking of salvation, of the voice that will not be denied, of dropping the heavy burden of this world.

The salvation that Anderson was talking about was no doubt a real salvation, but it was small, and he used for it the language of the most strenuous religious experience. He spoke in visions and mysteries and raptures, but what he was speaking about after all was only the salvation of a small legitimate existence, of a quiet place in the sun and moments of leisurely peace, of not being nagged and shrew-ridden, nor deprived of one's due share of affection. What he wanted for himself and others was perhaps no more than what he got in his last years: a home, neighbors, a small daily work to do, and the right to say his say carelessly and loosely and without the sense of being strictly judged. But between this small, good life and the language which he used about it there is a discrepancy which may be thought of as a willful failure of taste, an intended lapse of the sense of how things fit. Wyndham Lewis, in his attack in *Paleface* on the early triumphant Anderson, speaks of Anderson's work as an assault on responsibility and thoughtful maturity, on the pleasures and uses of the mind, on decent human pride, on Socratic clarity and precision; and certainly when we think of the "marching men" of Anderson's second novel, their minds lost in their marching and singing, leaving to their leader the definitions of their aims, we have what might indeed be the political consequences of Anderson's attitudes if these were carried out to their ultimate implications. Certainly the precious essence of personality to which Anderson was so much committed could not be preserved by any of the people or any of the deeds his own books delight in.

But what hostile critics forget about Anderson is that the cultural situation from which his writing sprang was actually much as he described it. Anderson's truth may have become a falsehood in his hands by reason of limitations in himself or in the tradition of easy populism he chose as his own, but one has only to take it out of his hands to see again that it is indeed a truth. The small legitimate existence, so necessary for the majority of men to achieve, is in our age so very hard, so nearly impossible, for them to achieve. The language Anderson used was certainly not commensurate with the traditional value which literature gives to the things he wanted, but it is not incommensurate with the modern difficulty of attaining these things. And it is his unending consciousness of this difficulty that constitutes for me the residue of admiration for him that I find I still have.

MALCOLM COWLEY

told the story of the Lost Genera-
tion of the 1920's, in which Sherwood Anderson was at least
chronologically and temperamentally a participant, in his well-
known Exile's Return, *published in 1934. In later years, Cowley
came to see Anderson as basically separate from the Lost Generation and superior as an artist to many of the exiled writers. This re-
evaluation of Anderson's achievement, an eminently fair appraisal,
first appeared in the February 15, 1960, issue of* The New
Republic.

ANDERSON'S LOST DAYS OF INNOCENCE

Malcolm Cowley

Sherwood Anderson was the only story teller of his generation—he was born in 1876—who left his mark on the style and vision of the generation that followed. Hemingway, Faulkner, Wolfe, Steinbeck, Caldwell, Saroyan, Henry Miller . . . each of these owes him an unmistakable debt, and their names might stand for dozens of others. Thus, Hemingway was regarded as his disciple in 1920, when both men were living on the Near North Side of Chicago. Faulkner says of himself that he had written very little, "poems and just amateur things," before meeting Anderson in 1925 and becoming, for a time, his inseparable companion. Looking at Anderson he thought to himself, "being a writer must be a wonderful life." He set to work on his first novel, *Soldiers' Pay*, for which Anderson found a publisher after the two had ceased to be close friends.

Thomas Wolfe proclaimed in 1936 that Anderson was "the only man in America who ever taught me anything"; but they quarreled a year later, and Wolfe shouted to him at a party that Anderson had shot his bolt, that he was done as a writer. All the disciples left him sooner or later, so that his influence was chiefly on their early work, but still it was decisive. With Walt Whitman he might have said:

> *I am the teacher of athletes,*
> *He that by me spreads a wider breast than my own proves the*
>   *width of my own,*

*He most honors my style who learns under it to destroy the
teacher.*

What Anderson did for younger writers was to open vistas by finding
new depths or breadths of feeling in everyday American life. Again
with Whitman he might have boasted that he led each of them to a
knoll, from which he pointed to "landscapes of continents, and a plain
public road." He gave them each a moment of vision, and then the
younger writer trudged off toward his separate destiny, often without
looking back. Rereading Anderson's work after many years, one is
happy to find that its moments of vision are as fresh and moving as ever.
They are what James Joyce called "epiphanies"; that is, they are
moments at which a character, a landscape, or a personal relation stands
forth in its essential nature or "whatness," with its past and future
revealed as if by a flash of lightning. For Anderson each of the moments
was a story in itself. The problem he almost never solved was how to
link one moment with another in a pattern of causality, or how to
indicate the passage of time.

In his personal life there must have been many such moments, and
there was one in particular that has become an American legend. After
serving as a volunteer in the Spanish-American war, after supplementing his one year in high school with a much later year at Wittenberg
Academy, and after becoming a locally famous copywriter in a Chicago
advertising agency, Anderson had launched into business for himself;
by the age of 36 he had been for some years the chief owner and
general manager of a paint factory in Elyria, Ohio. The factory had
prospered for a time, chiefly because of Anderson's talent for writing
persuasive circulars, and he sometimes had visions of becoming a paint
baron or a duke of industry. He had other visions too, of being
sentenced to serve out his life as a businessman. At the time he was
already writing novels—in fact he had four of them under way—and he
began to feel that his advertising circulars were insulting to the dignity
of words.

"The impression got abroad—I perhaps encouraged it," Anderson
says, "—that I was overworking, was on the point of a nervous
breakdown." He wondered whether he mightn't take advantage of the
impression. If his neighbors thought he was a little insane, perhaps they
would forgive him for deserting the business in which they had
invested their money. Then came the moment to which he would
always return in his memoirs and in his fiction. He was dictating a

letter: "The goods about which you have inquired are the best of their kind in the—" when suddenly he stopped without completing the phrase. He looked at his secretary for a long time, and she looked at him until they both grew pale. Then he said with the American laugh that covers all sorts of meanings, "I have been wading in a long river and my feet are wet." He went out of the office for the last time and started walking eastward toward Cleveland along a railroad track. "There were," he says, "five or six dollars in my pocket."

So far I have been paraphrasing Anderson's account—or two of his many accounts, for he kept changing them—of an incident that his biographers have reconstructed from other sources. Those others give a different picture of what happened at the paint factory on November 27, 1912. Anderson had been struggling under an accumulation of marital, artistic, and business worries. Instead of pretending to be a little crazy so that investors could forgive him for losing their money, he was actually—so the medical records show—on the brink of nervous collapse. Instead of making a conscious decision to abandon his wife, his three children, and his business career, he acted as if in a trance. There was truly a decision, but it was made by something deeper than his conscious will; one feels that his whole being, psyche and some [*sic* for soma] together, was rejecting the life of a harried businessman. He had no plans, however, for leading a different life. After four days of aimless wandering, he was recognized in Cleveland and taken to a hospital, where he was found to be suffering from exhaustion and aphasia.

Much later, in telling the story time after time, Anderson forgot or concealed the painful details of his flight and presented it as a pattern of conduct for others to follow. What we need in America, he liked to say, is a new class of individuals who, "at any physical cost to themselves and others"—Anderson must have been thinking of his first wife—will "agree to quit working, to loaf, to refuse to be hurried or try to get on in the world." In the next generation there would be hundreds of young men, readers of Anderson, who rejected the dream of financial success and tried to live as artists and individuals. For them Anderson's flight from the paint factory became a heroic exploit, as memorable as the choice made by Ibsen's Nora when she walked out of her doll's house and slammed the door. For Anderson himself when writing his memoirs, it was the central moment of his career.

Yet the real effect of the moment on his personal life was less drastic or immediate than one would guess from the compulsive fashion in which he kept writing about it. His flight stopped short in Cleveland.

After being released from the hospital, he went back to Elyria, wound up his business affairs, then took the train for Chicago, where he talked himself into a job with the same advertising agency that had employed him before he went into business for himself. As soon as he had the job, he sent for his wife and children. He continued to write persuasive circulars—corrupting the language, as he said—and worked on his novels and stories chiefly at night, as he had done while running a factory. It would be nearly two years before he separated from his first wife. It would be ten years before he left the advertising business to support himself entirely by writing, and then the change would result from a gradual process of getting published and finding readers, instead of being the sequel to a moment of truth.

These moments at the center of Anderson's often marvelous stories were moments, in general, without a sequel; they existed separately and timelessly. That explains why none of his seven published novels was a unified work and why, with a single exception, he never even wrote a *book* in the strict sense of the word. A book should have a structure and a development, whereas for Anderson there was chiefly the flash of lightning that revealed a life without changing it.

The single exception, of course, is *Winesburg, Ohio,* and that became a true book for several reasons: because it was conceived as a whole, because Anderson had found a subject that released his buried emotions, and because most of it was written in what was almost the same burst of inspiration, so that it gathered force as it went along. It was started in the late autumn of 1915, when he was living alone in a rooming house at 735 Cass Street, on the Near North Side of Chicago, and working as always at the Critchfield Agency. Earlier that year he had read two books that set his mind to working. One was *Spoon River Anthology,* by Edgar Lee Masters, which may have suggested the notion of writing about the secret natures of people in another Midwestern town. The other was Gertrude Stein's *Three Lives,* which pointed the way toward a simpler style, closer to the rhythms of American speech than that of Anderson's first novels, *Windy McPherson's Son* and *Marching Men.*

Then came another of his incandescent moments, one that he called "the most absorbingly interesting and exciting moment in any writer's life . . . the moment when he, for the first time, knows that he is a real writer." Twenty years later he described the experience in a letter, probably changing the facts, as he had a weakness for doing, but remembering how he felt:

. . . I walked along a city street in the snow. I was working at work I hated. Already I had written several long novels. They were not really mine. I was ill, discouraged, broke. I was living in a cheap rooming house. I remember that I went upstairs and into the room. It was very shabby. I had no relative in the city and few enough friends. I remember how cold the room was. On that afternoon I had heard that I was to lose my job.

. . . There was some paper on a small kitchen table I had bought and brought up into the room. I turned on a light and began to write. I wrote, without looking up—I never changed a word of it afterwards—a story called "Hands." It was and is a very beautiful story.

I wrote the story and then got up from the table at which I had been sitting, I do not know how long, and went down into the city street, I thought that the snow had suddenly made the city very beautiful. . . . It must have been several hours before I got the courage to return to my room and read my own story.

It was all right. It was sound. It was real. I went to sit by my desk. A great many others have had such moments. I wonder what they did. For the moment I thought the world very wonderful, and I thought also that there was a great deal of wonder in me.

"Hands" is still sound and real; as Henry James said of *The Scarlet Letter,* "it has about it that charm, very hard to express, which we find in an artist's work the first time he has touched his highest mark." It was, however, the second of the Winesburg stories to be written, since the first was "The Book of the Grotesque," which serves as a general prologue. "Paper Pills" was the third, and the others followed in roughly the same order in which they appear in the published book. All the stories were written rapidly, with little need for revision, each of them being, as Anderson said, "an idea grasped whole as one would pick an apple in an orchard." He was dealing with material that was both fresh and familiar. The town of Winesburg was based on his memories of Clyde, Ohio, where he had spent most of his boyhood and where his mother had died at the same age as the hero's mother. The hero, George Willard, was the author in his late adolescence, and the other characters were either remembered from Clyde or else, in many cases, suggested by faces glimpsed in the Chicago streets. Each face revealed a moment, a mood, or a secret that lay deep in Anderson's life and for which he was finding the right words at last.

As the book went forward, more and more of the faces—as well as more streets, buildings, trades, and landscapes—were carried from one story to another, with the result that Winesburg itself acquired a physical and corporate life. Counting the four parts of "Godliness," each complete in itself, there would be 25 stories or chapters in all. None of them taken separately—not even "Hands" or "The Untold Lie" —is as effective as the best of Anderson's later work, but each of them contributes to all the others, as the stories in later volumes are not expected to do. There was a delay of some months before the last three chapters—"Death," "Sophistication," and "Departure"—were written with the obvious intention of rounding out the book. In the first of these George Willard is released from Winesburg by the death of his mother; then, in "Sophistication," he learns how it feels to be a grown man; then finally he leaves for the city on the early-morning train, and everything recedes as into a framed picture. "When he aroused himself and looked out of the car window," Anderson says, "the town of Winesburg had disappeared and his life there had become but a background on which to paint the dreams of his manhood."

In structure the book lies midway between the novel proper and the mere collection of stories. Like several famous books by more recent authors, all early readers of Anderson—like Faulkner's *The Unvanquished* and *Go Down, Moses,* like Steinbeck's *Tortilla Flat* and *The Pastures of Heaven,* like Caldwell's *Georgia Boy*—it is a cycle of stories with several unifying elements, including a single background, a prevailing tone, and a central character. In *Winesburg* the underlying plot or fable, though hard to recognize, is unmistakably present, and I think it might be summarized as follows:

George Willard is growing up in a friendly town full of solitary persons; the author calls them "grotesques." Their lives have been distorted not, as Anderson tells us in his prologue, by their each having seized upon a single truth, but rather by their inability to express themselves. Since they cannot truly communicate with others, they have all become emotional cripples. Most of the grotesques are attracted one by one to George Willard; they feel that he might be able to help them. They try to explain themselves to George, believing that he alone in Winesburg has an instinct for finding the right words and using them honestly. They urge him to preserve and develop his gift. "You must not become a mere peddler of words," Kate Swift the teacher insists, taking hold of his shoulders. "The thing to learn is to know what people are thinking about, not what they say." Dr. Parcival tells him, "If something happens perhaps you will be able to write the book I may never get written." All the grotesques hope that George Willard will some day speak what is in their hearts and thus re-establish their connection with mankind. George is too young to understand them at the time, but the book ends with what seems to be the promise that, after leaving Winesburg, he will become the voice of inarticulate men and women in all the forgotten towns.

If the promise is truly implied, and if Anderson felt that he was keeping it when writing "Hands" and the stories that followed, then *Winesburg, Ohio* is far from the pessimistic or destructive or morbidly sexual work it was once attacked for being. Instead it is a work of love, an attempt to break down the walls that divide one person from another. It is also, in its own fashion, a celebration of small-town life in the lost days of good will and innocence.

FREDERICK J. HOFFMAN

attempts in this essay to "position" Sherwood Anderson according to the roles which the writer played in the literary tradition of America. According to Hoffman, Anderson produced a very small amount of good work which, read with an understanding of the author's personality, gives authenticity to his many "voices." It is in these "voices" that Anderson speaks to the modern world—as tutor of writers better than himself, as interpreter of the creative process, as product of the national "immaturity," and as the supreme artist of loneliness.

THE VOICES OF SHERWOOD ANDERSON

Frederick J. Hoffman

I.

I begin this essay with the feeling that its subject belongs to an age so long past that he can scarcely any longer be called "modern." One does not usually have such doubts about the "great moderns"—Pound, Eliot, Stevens—even though they were roughly of the same generation. The fact is that Anderson's best work was published in a remarkably brief span of time. If we grant *Winesburg, Ohio* as the beginning, the time of true worth lasted only five years, from 1919 to 1923. He was forty-three years old when *Winesburg* appeared, a man of middle age, who had come from a rich, varied, and erratic past, and had fixed upon the role of the dedicated artist after having tried several other kinds of life, and rejected them.

I do not want to suggest that Anderson's creative life was limited to those few years. He had obviously spent years "annotating life" and scrupulously noting his discontents before he began his career as a writer. He lived a "life of the imagination" many years before the beginning of his public career and after his best work was published. It was a very special kind of life, an extraordinary one if the facts of it are examined. He spoke in several "voices," played several roles, and contributed to the appraisal of several important areas of American life.

As a "modern," Anderson was always uncomfortably and self-consciously a failure. He took to contemporary modes eagerly after *Winesburg* established him as a "literary hero." But except for Gertrude Stein, who harmed only those who tried literally to imitate her and was a blessing to those who did not, he scarcely profited from his enthusiasms. *Many Marriages* (1923) is a strange, and even a ludicrous attempt to "understand" both Freud and D. H. Lawrence. For *Dark Laughter* (1925) Anderson claims a great indebtedness to Joyce's *Ulysses:* "I think as a matter of prose experiment you will sense what Mr. Joyce was driving at when you read *Dark Laughter.* As I think I told you when you were here, I very frankly took his experiment as a starting place for the prose rhythm of the book. . . ." The perspective of more than three decades allows us to say that if *Dark Laughter* has virtues, they do not come from an imitation of Joyce's "prose rhythms."

Anderson was similarly bemused by the radical persuasions of the 1930s; he was even less a contemporary of his fellows in the decade of proletarian literature. As his style forced him to stand aside from the major tendencies of literature in the 1920s, his personal convictions separated him from the extremists of the following decade. He was deeply touched and profoundly dejected by the sufferings of the Depression, but he was even less susceptible to political doctrine than Dreiser. For all their appearance of offering "searching analyses" of the times, the novel *Beyond Desire* (1932) and the strange book-length editorial *Perhaps Women* (1931) are only incidentally "doctrinal" or social documents. In both cases Anderson was dealing with a human situation that grieved and puzzled him and prodded him with the demand to "do something" about it. "I am puzzled about Communism," he wrote to Dreiser in 1931, "as I am sure you must be."

> It may be the answer, and then it may only be a new sort of Puritanism, more deadly than the old Puritanism, a new kind of Puritanism at last got power in one place to push its rigid Puritanism home.

Without attempting either to defend his work or to label or classify it, I should like to consider the several roles of Anderson's "voices" in the American literary scene. He was, first of all, an advisor of his contemporaries, generous and often wise, and much abused by them. He was a "theorist of the imagination," who took down innumerable notes on the creative process and its several kinds of psychological *angst.* He was pre-eminently a literary analyst of the several variants of human loneliness, its causes and its relations to larger social dilemmas.

Finally, he was an important "historian" of the period of transition and change (roughly from 1870 to 1915) to American industrialized society. In each of these roles Anderson performed seriously and often wisely, but with only occasional and often indifferent success. Indeed, it is one of the curious paradoxes of modern literature that a man of whom one can say so many things in praise turns out after all to be the author of so little that is first-rate or enduring.

2.

As to the first role, we have the tribute of William Faulkner (*Atlantic Monthly*, June, 1953) to his friend of three decades earlier, who had walked and drunk with him, urging him to write and offering to find a publisher. In New Orleans in 1924, Anderson and Faulkner were often together, prodding each other's imagination into more and more derring-do. Anderson was the famous one, Faulkner the unknown. Like Hemingway two years later, Faulkner repaid him with a caricature of his style, this one in an introduction to *Sherwood Anderson and Other Famous Creoles* (1926), "Neither [Hemingway nor I] could have touched, ridiculed the work itself," Faulkner said in his *Atlantic* tribute. "But we had made his style look ridiculous; and by that time, after *Dark Laughter*, when he had reached the point where he should have stopped writing, he had to defend that style at all costs because he too must have known by then in his heart that there was nothing left."

There is enough truth in Faulkner's remark to have hurt Anderson seriously. He *was* concerned about style, about a style and "the" style; he had pricked and goaded his imagination on, to exert itself in new and different and "modern" ways. Sensitive to the critics' suggestion that he was a raw, untutored genius who spoiled more than he created, he went to one master after another, seeking both assistance and confirmation. It was when he was in this mood that he met and talked to Hemingway and Faulkner in the role of an achieved success who was nevertheless unhappily aware of not having yet produced the thoroughly satisfying work. He had long since settled upon *what* he should say, but was not sure that he was saying it well enough. The role of adviser to his celebrated contemporaries left him extremely vulnerable. He could help them; they could do little for him.

As for Faulkner, there is the fabulous yarn about Al Jackson, a descendant of the famous Andrew Jackson; it can be found in Faulkner's second novel, *Mosquitoes* (1927). It is the best thing in an otherwise second-rate novel, and it was almost entirely the product of

Anderson's fertile imagination. The story has the qualities and the wild excesses of his powerful fantasy, in the American tradition of the folk yarn, the hyperbole of the telescopic eye. This tale, for which Faulkner never truly gave Anderson credit, was only one of many contributions. Faulkner later came into his own, at a time when Anderson's letters showed him more and more sensitive to his failures. It was Anderson, for one, who suggested that he go back to his "own little postage stamp of native soil" and make what he could of his own country and his own experience. Whether Faulkner would have "gone back" on his own or not, there is no doubt that the advice was just what he needed. Yoknapatawpha County, as the private haunt of Faulkner's imagination, has a greater ring of authenticity than Anderson's Winesburg, perhaps because of the powerful concentration of creative effort Faulkner expended upon it. There are many different "voices" speaking in it. But it is like Winesburg in being an exploitation of native resources, both resources of place and of the imagination.

After the caricature of 1926, Anderson shied away from Faulkner, but he sensed in him the possibility of greatness. "I do not like the man personally," he wrote Horace Liveright in 1926, "but I have a hunch on that he is a man who will write the kind of novels that will sell. He is modern enough and not too modern; also he is smart. . . ." In many other cases as well, Anderson was the conscientious friend who survived personal offense and insult and seemed, as Faulkner said, "taller, bigger than anything he ever wrote." When Hemingway published *Torrents of Spring* (1926), in which there are obvious parodies of the style of *Dark Laughter,* he had already broken the ties to Anderson, and was "writing off" his obligations both to him and to Gertrude Stein. But Anderson's influence persisted in Hemingway's work; it was the one resource which kept that work linked to its American origins, despite its frequently strange impression of deracination.

It is probably impossible to determine exactly just what Anderson did for Hemingway's writing. The qualities of *Horses and Men* (1923) and *The Triumph of the Egg* (1921) are present clearly enough in Hemingway's *In Our Time* (1925) and in other stories that were to come later. But his principal contribution to Hemingway's work is the point of view of the "American innocent" who endures a too violent education in experience to accommodate himself to it. The sense of isolation is there too: the unsubtle but nevertheless painful loss of innocence, the rude and forceful cutting of the umbilical cord which sends the infant yelling and afraid into a world he can scarcely tolerate and does not understand. Once again, as in Faulkner's case, Hemingway put his own trademark upon the art he made of the feelings, and lost Anderson as he outdistanced him.

Anderson served this role again and again; he shared his concern with style, with the "business of writing," and he shared also the sense of the American experience—of belonging to it and at the same time rebelling against it. The American *isolé* is peculiarly a product of Anderson's imagination, as the European *isolé* is of Conrad's. Anderson's figure comes out of the nineteenth century and into the twentieth: a composite of Lincoln, Huckleberry Finn, and (in at least some versions of it) Henry Ford. Most of all, it is the adolescent's predicament of coming for the first time into adult experience: a vague sense of uneasy curiosity and disappointment, the surprise that there should be more than one world and more than one way of seeing them. Faulkner's more vigorous imagination made it possible for him to embellish the experience, but the pull of innocence and the terror of knowing are also there, as they are in Hemingway's Nick Adams and Frederic Henry, as indeed they are in Thomas Wolfe's Eugene Gant. Over all of these creations Anderson cast an anxious and admonitory eye; they were successes of which Anderson was envious and to the realization of which he had himself made important contributions. His role was the pathetic one of encouraging artists to do better than he seemed able himself to do, and for the most part receiving something less than little thanks for doing so.

3.

The full impression which his speculations about the life of the imagination gives is that of a strange "other world," the world of the fancy more than of the "shaping power." Anderson speaks of the world of the imagination as the "other world," to which one withdraws in order to gather strength for the creative act. It is also the world of dreams, in which the artist is relieved of the world of necessity. It is a world of "lies," of the kind that enlarge the real and grotesquely disfigure the truth. Anderson's reputation in this one of his "voices" comes not from any precision he was able to give the theory of the creative process, but from the peculiar values he was able to give the human situation of loneliness. To this aspect of human life he was able to bring insights of extraordinary power and tenderness. There are many places in his *Notebook* and his autobiographies, in which the solitary retreat is treated affectionately and praised.

There are no Puritans in that life [of the fancy]. The dry sisters
of Philistia do not come in at the door. They cannot breathe the
life of the fancy. The Puritan, the reformer who scolds at the
Puritans, the dry intellectuals, all who desire to uplift, to remake
life on some definite plan conceived within the human brain die
of a disease of the lungs. They would do better to stay in the
world of fact. . . .

There is nothing profound in these remarks, but there is a certain
extravagance in the world of imagined retreat, where "truths" can be
individualized and made precious and protective. This realization is one
of Anderson's great strengths. It is responsible for his best work, in
which his creatures, however ludicrous they may seem to the casual eye,
are endowed with a generous sympathy and permitted their own
secretive worlds.

In an excellent analysis of Anderson, Charles Walcutt offers many
clues to the manner of introducing these speculations into his art. The
most painful, and the most significant, experience is that of the
"awakening," or self-discovery, an intuition of the full meaning a man's
life has for him. This event is usually accompanied as well by a
realization of inhibiting circumstances. The "real world" does not equal
the world of the fancy, which is often preferred. These are the
circumstances of *Winesburg, Ohio*, Anderson's one truly great and
important book. It is not a set of sardonic observations on American
deceit or "Puritanism" or "Philistia," but a study of the variants of what
Walcutt has called "the buried life."

The range of inhibition is great. It often involves simply the matter
of "growing up" (this among other things Anderson demonstrated to
Hemingway as a valid literary experience). But the great inhibition is
the lack of "a tradition of manners": that is, of the means graciously to
communicate and to understand. The creatures of *Winesburg* act
grotesquely at least partly because there is no accepted way of acting
otherwise. The common social *milieu* is harsh, crude, repressive, and
embarrassingly withdrawn and aloof.

The figure of the "grotesque" is a common enough creature in
American literature. There is much to be said for the notion that we
have grown old before we have matured, or that the transition from
childhood to adulthood has been sudden, abrupt, and painful. Anderson's voice speaks in *Winesburg, Ohio* and in the short stories of the
disasters that have resulted in the human personality. It is a fascinating
and an arresting image. It involves us in the nostalgia for a "pastoral

stillness," an Edenic world that we have always thought we had but never actually achieved. It also suggests a kind of aberration of the American personality, who wishes to be loved and respected but is put off from knowing how to assert himself without shock or outrage.

Anderson's great contribution is to define the misery of these eccentricities, which come directly from the extension of American self-consciousness into a world of industrial and commercial crudeness. The major assertion of Anderson's heroes is to "walk out," to protest, and to engage in a journey of self-discovery. But the truth he offers is more profound, as it is more precise, than that. Again in this matter Anderson is a typical psychologist of American manners. The voyage in space does not suffice. The only satisfactory journey is the journey inward, of self-discovery. But circumstances inhibit, and tragedy (or more frequently, melodrama) results.

Winesburg succeeds in ways in which the other books fail. Too often (in *Dark Laughter, Windy McPherson's Son, Many Marriages*) Anderson does not himself know what to do with the truth he has discovered; and he can only write what often amounts to a parody of what he has intended to write. William Phillips has shown us how close in time the sketches of *Winesburg* came to Edgar Lee Masters' *Spoon River Anthology* (1915); but the idea of *Winesburg* is much more shrewdly achieved than that of Masters' poems. Nor is the book either an amateur exercise in abnormal psychology or a book in the tradition of "the revolt from the village." Irving Howe calls it "a fable of American estrangement, its theme the loss of love." As Howe says, the characters of *Winesburg* lack "emotional sustenance." They also lack the means to move gracefully from adolescence to maturity. This is a primary American fable. It is one of Anderson's most authentic voices, and its importance cannot be over-estimated.

Because the "grotesques" of *Winesburg* have not solved their own riddles, they move toward, or are driven toward, the young man who appears "normal," George Willard. He is, or seems, exasperatingly clear-headed, "promising," articulate; since his fellow-villagers cannot communicate with one another, they urge upon him their advice, their pasts, their idiosyncratic inner worlds. As Irving Howe says of them, they are looking for "a ceremony, a social value, a manner of living, a lost ritual that may by some means re-establish a flow and exchange of emotion." The consequence is that *Winesburg* is like no other work of modern American literature. It does not yield to any effort to classify it, but is instead a semi-poetic study of loneliness, of the grotesqueries of lonely spirits seen in a half light. These are symptoms of a desperate sense of loss and of an equally desperate and forceful desire to regain human love and contact.

4.

The remaining voice is the "historical"; or, it is Anderson's attempt to put the *Winesburg* situation within an historical perspective. He is "historical" only in this sense, that having established contact with the figure of the *isolé*, he wants to give cause and reason for his condition. The critical time in Anderson's survey is the period between the Civil War and World War I. Since he was born in 1876, these are also the years when he grew to maturity. They are times of agony, of quick unthinking progress, and of the loss of a sense of leadership.

Anderson's image of American greatness often comprehended two figures: that of Lincoln, lost forever to the American scene in 1865; that of the Mississippi River, as Mark Twain and Huckleberry Finn saw it. As he moved further and further away from the time of his clear triumph, his mind moved back toward that double image. He would wish himself, as writer, to provide that leadership, but he saw "on all sides nothing but cleverness. I am in despair of ever doing anything myself. . . ." In a letter of 1933, he proposes an American hero who would combine, "the future of Henry Ford and Abraham Lincoln."

> Think about the figure of Hugh [McVey] in Poor White, who has something of a Lincoln quality, and then combine him with the figure of Henry Ford. . . .
> All this contrasted with changing life out of agriculture and into industrial America, the splendor or the machines and the factories contrasted with the growing degradation of the life of the people.

These remarks identify Anderson clearly, as a man "educated" in the America of the nineteenth century, still possessing the privilege and mobility of the "Westernizing American," but aware that changes were occurring so rapidly that man's chance of remaining innocent would soon disappear. Anderson tried to recover a lost purity in his fiction, but succeeded only in describing variations of abnormal failure. He was the "man of liberal good will," whose virtues came from an earlier and simpler time, and who did not possess intellectual strength enough to give force to his diagnosis. His heroes and heroines are always victims, with varying degrees of pathos, of an ugly civilization they cannot understand.

Anderson's weakness was in a lack of intellectual force. But it may be said ironically to have been an advantage of a sort. He so felt his own inadequacies as to invest his characters with a strength of sympathy and a rapport that were the result of his sharing them with him. An abundant good will combines with a feeling of distress over its not quite being enough to preserve the world from its own trickery. Despite its manifest faults, *Poor White* (1920) has always seemed to me a remarkable work because of the extraordinary ambition that prompted its creation. More than in any other work, Anderson tried in this novel to create "the myth of America's failure," to write about the decline of the American world from the time when Huckleberry Finn had floated down the middle of it.

In any absolute sense, of course, he does not succeed. In fact, the novel's ingenuity lies always at its surface. But it is an exciting effort and it testifies to Anderson's strenuous sincerity. The novel's hero is compounded of all of the "boy hero" kind of ambition and weakness. He is a latter-day Huckleberry Finn, and he is a "Lincoln type" as well; Anderson intends him to be a representative, mythic figure of the transition to industrial America, a hero but also a victim, and in the end a scapegrace villain who does not understand his own villainy.

Note the progress of his hero. He begins in a lazy town on the Mississippi, "at the point of sinking into the sort of animal-like stupor in which his father [like Huck's "pap"] had lived." The worlds of the Mississippi River and of New England combine, when Sarah Shephard "takes hold of" Hugh, to "make something of him." Sarah is the hard, virtuous New Englander, whose father had learned that the practical necessities of life are closely linked to the religious necessities of the Bible. This type of person was usually harshly treated by Anderson; here he resists the temptation to ridicule him, but rather passes on the significance of his type to his own hero. New England virtue struggles with Missouri complacency; and the two are combined to create a weird, gangling, Lincoln-Ford inventor, who nevertheless somehow remains an Andersonian villager, a "grotesque" but with a legendary influence upon society.

Hugh becomes obsessively interested in "doing good," but cannot go beyond "doing things" with his mind and his hands. This conception of the American hero is a really quite remarkable example of topographic schizophrenia. The wish becomes the skill becomes the deed. On his way from Mudcat Landing to Bidwell, his nervous determination to "do good," or "do something" takes on a characteristically symptomatic form: "Hugh went into one of the residence streets of the town and counted the pickets in the fences before the houses. He returned to the hotel and made a calculation as to the number of pickets in all the fences in town. Then he got a rule at the hardware store and carefully measured the pickets." His nervous calculations continue. Finally, "one Sunday [he] went into the wood back of the town and cut a great armful of twigs, which he carried to his room and later with great patience wove into the form of a basket."

Perhaps a more clever artist (Nathanael West, for example) would have reduced the incident to perverse comedy; Anderson was quite incapable of reducing Hugh to a figure of ridicule. Throughout, he serves the role of an arduous innocent, the metaphor of whose simplicity is brilliantly served by the basket that results from his nervous and empty calculations. The "thing of practical beauty" is an incidental consequence of the exhaustive effort and the ingenuity expended on an abstract problem. When Hugh is allowed to work for "the good of Bidwell, Ohio," his efforts have the same frenetic quality, and they result in the model of a mechanical cabbage planter. His gestures go no further than this: the model. The actual industrializing is undertaken by the Bidwell citizenry.

I make a special point of this because I want to show Hugh McVey as an authentic "folk hero," in the special circumstances of his time and place. He has "something to give," a talent for imitative calculation and design; he has the great sympathetic desire to "be of service." But his brain is spent in calculations. It is not within his power to be a Lincoln as well as a Ford, except on the simplest terms. It is important to see him as the inventor-god, who knows nothing about the evil will of those who will exploit him. The people of Bidwell see him as such a god or hero. Somehow, however, his successes breed disasters. The town of Bidwell becomes an ugly city; the people are not helped, but are actually oppressed. And the great melodramatic culmination is the frantic rebellion of Joe Wainworth [sic], whose craftsmanship has been nullified by mechanical substitutes for his work.

Even the introduction of the sex goddess is appropriate enough, if only to show the pathos of Hugh's life from another perspective. Hugh is a failure as a husband, as he is a failure as a genuine hero. Here as elsewhere, Anderson's idea is brilliant, his execution of it rather less than satisfactory. Except for the strangely melodramatic conclusion (Hugh is attacked by Wainsworth, defended by his wife, realizes his innocence and magically recovers from his impotence), the idea is sustained; and the novel is a creative work of mythic history that deserves more attention than it has received.

As in *Winesburg*, Anderson has tried to point out the psychological improprieties of innocence, even to warn about its dangers. Innocence is presented in *Poor White* in a very different light; it can be said to be a genuine limitation that has widespread and harmful effects. This is not "social realism" or "doctrinal criticism"; it is essentially a poetic metaphor according to which Anderson is attempting a major evaluation of American life. Of course, the results are often ludicrous. The line of thought is not infrequently naive, and the lack of subtlety often gives the novel the appearance of a mock *rites de passage* ceremony.

The most important fact of Anderson's work is its native simplicity. Not that he did not try for sophistication; his worst writing came as a result of his attempts to imitate the sophistications of others. But, in *Poor White* and in *Winesburg*, there is a sense of "simple profundity," which comes from his having attended to his creatures on his level and on theirs. There are more significant things to say about them than Anderson got around to saying. D. H. Lawrence said many of them, as did Freud, in quite another context. Anderson's virtues are most clearly manifest when he tries to be the spokesman of his times. The delicacy of sentiment with which he invests his adolescent narrators in such stories as "I Want to Know Why" cannot be improved on by a superior taste, cultivation, or intellect. The miraculous moments of revelation in "The Egg" and "Death in the Woods" are *sui generis;* Lawrence sometimes comes very close to them in his short stories, but Anderson owes nothing to Lawrence—or to anyone else—for them.

I should say that at his best Anderson succeeds because he is closer to his world than most writers are to theirs. His elaborate attempts to explain the "life of the fantasy" and the "life of dreams" (in *A Story Teller's Story* and other works of autobiography or semi-criticism) are not valuable in themselves; as theory they are vague and meandering discourses. As an explanation of his own "vision," however, they have a considerable merit. Without knowing quite how to discriminate among terms that in philosophical discourse require sharp distinctions, Anderson communicates a state of mind and emotion that is directly responsible for the insights in *Winesburg,* in *Poor White,* and in the best of the short stories.

This work has the virtue of an unpremeditated and a scarcely tutored innocence. It *reveals* an innocence, in himself and in the American world around him. There is nothing holistic in it; Anderson is not a prophet (or at any rate, he is not a good prophet). He possesses instead a great delicacy of sentiment and sympathy, a power of attracting to him (because it is within him) a human substance of the most varied kind. Writing in 1938 to a young man who had sought advice, Anderson spoke of his interest in "common everyday American lives."

> I knew, often quite intensively, Negro swipes about race tracks, small gamblers, prize fighters, common laboring men and women. There was a violent, dangerous man, said to be a killer. One night he walked and talked to me and became suddenly tender. I was forced to realize that all sorts of emotions went on in all sorts of people. A young man who seemed outwardly a very clod suddenly began to run wildly in the moonlight. Once I was walking in a wood and heard the sound of a man weeping. I stopped, looked, and listened. There was a farmer who, because of ill luck, bad weather, and perhaps even poor management, had lost his farm. . . .

5.

This is the very substance of Anderson's writing, his most authentic "voice." He had much that he could teach his contemporaries, but there was little that he could learn from them. When he spoke in the voices of his own creatures and attempted to gesture assent to or rebellion against the world in their ways, his writing had an authentic quality, the quality of simple emotions projected into a world that was becoming too complex to receive them. Much twentieth century American writing is concerned with innocence and manners. The American hero, like Huckleberry Finn, flees the manners of the Protestant world, and searches anxiously for a *milieu* in which moral improvisation is still possible.

Poor White demonstrates how difficult such improvisation has become in American society. That society becomes increasingly to resemble, in its layers of inharmonious manners, a geologist's cross-section. Anderson's characters are especially susceptible to the harmful effects of this confusion; the more because, unlike Lawrence, Anderson does not wish or cannot speak up for them. Like them, he too is lost. His style, when he is not trying to "make it something else," is an expressive condition of the simple agonies and pathos of the human condition on this level.

He was, of course, neither bold nor clever. Ideologies confused him, and he could use them only if he reduced them "to scale"; when he tried to dress them up, the metaphors of his speech became grotesquely inadequate (as in *Many Marriages*). I should regard it as the worst of misunderstandings, however, if I have given the impression that

Anderson was "a valuable writer" simply because he was "a valuable human being." The point I wish to make is far more important than that. He spoke in a genuine "voice" because he *was* that voice, because it had a style that at times closely approached the desperate gaucheries of his clumsy, frenzied creatures, frantic to be heard and understood and loved. Again and again, he avoided sentimentality by making his speech like the hard, twisted, bitter apples of *Winesburg*. He was a master of the speech of the anxious, troubled, naive adolescent, and of the equally troubled and naive old man or woman. At either end of the scale, a precious innocence is preserved at the menacing and hostile center of its enemies. There is something hauntingly pitiful about these "lost souls" who want somehow, anyhow, to prove themselves, and end by proving that they are "queer" or violent or apparently purposelessly mad.

These "voices" are Anderson's, genuinely and even uniquely. That they speak in a language too unsophisticated for our present times does not necessarily discredit them. They are the voices of Hart Crane's hoboes, who "take their liquor slow—and count/—Though they'll confess no rosary nor clue—/ The river's minute by the far brook's year." Their distresses have a history similar to that invented for them in *Poor White*. Anderson's value for us comes down to these facts: that he knew the virtues and the limitations of innocence; that he could plot the history of its decline; and that he could speak of that decline in genuine accents and with genuine feeling.

DAVID D. ANDERSON

wrote this evaluation of the achievement of Sherwood Anderson two decades after the writer's death, when interest in Anderson had never been greater. In his highly sympathetic search for the contribution of Anderson to American letters, David Anderson discusses the ideas that unify all of the writer's work, the misunderstandings that have resulted from too restricted or prejudiced readings of that work, and the permanent values in Sherwood Anderson's writing that assure him an eminent place in the world's literature.

SHERWOOD ANDERSON AFTER 20 YEARS

David D. Anderson

After an active literary career of nearly thirty years, Sherwood Anderson was in critical disfavor when he died on March 8, 1941, a disfavor that has persisted in spite of its paradoxical nature. Critical opinion generally has relegated Anderson to a minor position in American literary history, and yet that history has not only been unable to ignore him but has continued to give him more attention than it accords to many figures considered to be major.

The reason for this is obvious: when he was at his best, he was very good, so good, in fact, that *Winesburg, Ohio* and some of his shorter works have become modern classics, while on the other hand, when he was being most determinedly modern and artistic, as in *Many Marriages* and most of the later novels, he imposed a kind of dating on his work that made it as old fashioned as any other passing fad almost as soon as it was written.

Behind this dichotomy in his work lies another reason for the continuation of critical examination in spite of the absolute pronouncements critics have made. Even while he was still alive, Anderson had taken on the proportions of a mythical figure, one who, perhaps more than any other American, embodied the dream of almost every critic, academic or commercial, who has ever approached him. The myth has maintained that almost alone among people prominent in the history of twentieth century American literature, Anderson had the courage to reject commercial success and devote himself to his art. That this does not correspond closely to the facts of his life has been pointed out by numerous academic critics, but such disagreement is unimportant because it is apparently imbedded as firmly as the George Washington–cherry tree story in American folklore. Incorporating an ideal almost as difficult to realize as absolute truth, the myth seems likely to endure.

The dichotomy in Anderson's work and the myth that has grown up around his life have tended to engender two emotions that dominate Anderson criticism: harshness, stemming from the inability to reconcile the two extremes of his work, and sentimentality resulting from personal identification with the problem behind the myth of his life. These two emotional approaches have become so commonplace that they sometimes exist side by side in the same critical study, resulting in a stereotyped approach that hinders evaluation of Anderson's work, understanding of what he was attempting to do, and recognition of the importance of the close relationship between his work and the unique American experience through which he lived.

Winesburg, Ohio and a number of individual short stories, notably "I Want to Know Why," "I'm a Fool," "The Egg," and "The Man Who Became a Woman," have frequently and justifiably been pointed out as Anderson's permanent contributions to American literature, and *Poor White* has often been added to the list. These works, however, are products of Anderson's earlier active career, when he still received wide critical acceptance, and their worth has never been seriously questioned. At the same time, the list ignores the fact that the short stories have been lifted out of the context of the volumes in which they appeared and have lost much of their meaning and effectiveness in the process. This generally acknowledged list is accurate as far as it goes, but it is incomplete. To these products of his early period must be added the entire volumes *The Triumph of the Egg* and *Horses and Men*, not only because they include such other excellent stories as "Seeds," "Unlighted Lamps," "The Sad Horn Blowers," and "An Ohio Pagan," but because they are collections that are of comparatively even quality. Much of the time they rise to the levels of the usually listed stories, and, most importantly, they are unified collections both structurally and thematically that comment on the nature of men's lives as effectively and as perceptively as does *Winesburg, Ohio*. Stories and sketches are included that are less satisfactory than the best, just as there are in *Winesburg,* but to ignore the subtlety with which Anderson brought unity out of apparent diversity is to ignore one of his most skillful capabilities.

Because the stereotyped approach to Anderson's work states that he had lost his effectiveness at this point, worthwhile contributions of the later periods are unfortunately ignored. To the list must be added parts of *A Story Teller's Story* from the following period, especially Book One and a number of other sections. This volume does contain the same stuff, as many critics are quick to point out, and the book as a whole is uneven in execution, but both structurally and stylistically Anderson is often at his best here, reproducing both the midwestern rhythms and idioms almost flawlessly and incorporating them in the old oral storytelling tradition so that the result elevates that old subject matter to the realm of American mythology.

From the last years of Anderson's career it is necessary to add the complete volumes *Death in the Woods* and *Kit Brandon,* the incomplete *Memoirs,* and numerous essays from *Hello Towns!, Puzzled America,* and other sources. The first is not only his most consistently high-level collection of stories, but it also contains two of his best, "Death in the Woods" and "Brother Death." Most importantly, it is an integrated and mature examination of Anderson's belief that reality must be separated from appearance if it is to be recognized and understood. The collection as a whole is as good as anything he had done in the earlier years.

Kit Brandon is his most objective and most fully realized novel, suffering only from carelessness and inattention, neither of which is sufficient to condemn it. In this novel Anderson comes close to understanding the nature of the American experience as a product of the peculiar circumstances inherent in the growth of the country, an achievement that is matched in his own work only by the incomplete *Memoirs* that was to be his definitive interpretation of the American experience as he had known it.

The best of the essays are parts of this whole, each of them an attempt to come closer to an understanding of an individual, a group, or a set of circumstances. Each of the better essays is dominated by careful attention to craftsmanship as well as by penetrating intuitive understanding of the essence of the material, and in them Anderson focuses attention on the significance of the small, the seemingly unimportant, and the easily ignored in human life.

These are the works that must be included in a convenient list of Anderson's permanent contributions to American literature, a list that, while it is not imposing, is nevertheless not so insignificant as it may seem. But to understand Anderson and what he was trying to do, it is not enough to limit attention to any list of most successful works. Rather Anderson's work can only be regarded as a whole composed of many parts, because the major theme to which he devoted his attention was the meaning of the American experience as he had known and lived it.

Anderson's work in its entirety is an attempt to penetrate appearance and to determine the nature of the reality beneath it. To Anderson, material manifestations were unimportant. He did not deny their existence; on the contrary, as in the case of the twisted apples left to rot in the orchards near Clyde, Ohio, he knew that often appearance was in some odd way related to essential nature, but that the relationship was often ignored or misunderstood. This realization came to him early, certainly by the time he had established himself in business in Elyria, and the literary career that followed resulted from the impact of that discovery upon his mind, a mind that was essentially untrained and uneducated and that found its way to a satisfactory resolution of the dilemma only through a long process of trial and error, acceptance and rejection.

The most obvious discrepancy between appearance and reality was for Anderson the difference between the American ideal as he had learned it and the real that he had seen put into practice during the years that America became increasingly a country dominated by the production and consumption of things at the cost of the values inherent in the ideal. The attempt to separate traditional values from a materialistic ethic that had subverted them led him into literature by way of a back door because the words that he had learned to use effectively as a means of promoting consumption were the only means he had by which to attack this distortion and confusion of values. In actuality, Anderson began his literary career as a propagandist fighting against the corruption of the American ideal by materialism.

Anderson learned, however, by the time he had finished *Marching Men* that there was no easy answer to the problem, and the discovery made him a writer instead of a propagandist. His goal had not changed, but the means he had brought to bear on it were insufficient. Between 1915 and 1918 he began a tentative analysis that would lead him deeply into his subject matter at the same time that he realized the necessity of evolving a stylistic technique that would make his writing effective rather than merely functional.

With the writing of *Winesburg, Ohio* he had not forsaken his purpose to determine the relationship between nature and experience and appearance and reality; he had merely intensified it by closely examining individuals who had been crippled spiritually by the confusion of values inherent in a confused society. Encouraged by the success of his approach, he broadened it in following works, attempting to incorporate more of his experience into his works, only to find that there still were no answers to his problem, a problem that became increasingly personal as he realized that he, too, had been confusing many things for a long time. Once more he shifted his direction and narrowed his scope in order to examine his experience more closely. The introspection that followed enabled him to accept his inability to reconcile the apparent dichotomies in life at the same time that penetration of the surface of his own life gave him a sense of identity and a sense of role, both of which pointed out the values that he had thus far been unable to define in his works.

Out of this crucial period Anderson formulated the concepts that dominated his later work and that remain as his final comments on the meaning of the American experience as it had been reflected in his own life. They were simple enough, so simple that they seem naive at the same time that their simplicity emphasizes the depth that often lies behind the apparently simple. The identity and the place that he determined to be his were those that he had misunderstood and rejected when he had accepted the appearance upon which a material society is constructed; after re-establishing himself as an artist-craftsman who belonged in a town rather than a center of materialism he could go on to formulate his concepts of the nature of the reality behind experience.

Actually they were concepts that he had intuitively recognized from the time that he first realized the existence of the discrepancy between appearance and reality, and they had been reflected in his work from the beginning: man could break down the barriers that separated him from his fellows through compassion and through empathetic understanding. In the process he would recognize the true values in human life, the understanding and love that, mutually achieved, would make human life worth living.

This is the essence of Anderson's philosophy, a solution to the problems inherent in human experience that is both simple and complex. It was easy to say, as he had long known, but at the same time it was, he tentatively concluded, impossible to realize. Close as he was to naturalism and despair at this point, he finally acknowledged that the end itself was an ideal, and like all ideals, beyond the capabilities of human nature. Resulting from this was his ultimate conclusion that the means rather than the end, life itself rather than an impossible perfection, was the only meaning man could know, but it was far from a petty or ignoble meaning.

This is the concept that dominated both his life and works from 1929 to his death: man is his brother's keeper, he declared, whether he would acknowledge the fact or not. It was the realization of this truth that made human life meaningful, and its rejection, brought about by a preoccupation with things, that led to the inevitable dehumanization of American society. The American experience was therefore one that demanded a careful and continuous examination if one would find meaning in it. Its nature, as he pointed out, had been such that from the beginning it demanded that man concern himself with the material appearance of life in spite of its great potential of achieving human fulfillment, and only the individual himself could prevent the material from completely nullifying his potential in his own life.

Anderson's works as a whole record his discovery of this truth, one that a more sophisticated man possessed of more education would have accepted as obvious and then promptly forgotten. Anderson, however, like his nineteenth century predecessors, Emerson, Thoreau, and Whitman, was not interested in discovering the physical laws that govern the universe; instead, he restricted his attention to the obvious problems of human life and tried to find a way to live with them. The entire range of his works from *Windy McPherson's Son* to the *Memoirs* is the record of his attempt to make that possible by finding the meaning inherent in human experience as he had known it.

Anderson belongs properly in the main stream of American idealism that had its inception in the self-evident truths of natural rights, was nurtured in the Transcendentalist realization that somewhere beyond physical appearance lay the ultimate truth of man's fate, and then fell into confused disorder before the combined onslaught of Darwinism and economic determinism. The confusion endured in a world suddenly grown complex, but by the beginning of the twentieth century the disorder had been replaced by a counter-offensive determined to show the evils inherent in a world dominated by materialism. Anderson was temperamentally suited to become a member of this counter-offensive, and he was a member in spirit long before he became one in fact.

The literary movement and atmosphere with which he associated as he found himself as a writer is clear indication of his membership in this idealistic counter-offensive. The keynote of the Chicago Renaissance was Liberation, and it was devoted to freeing the writer from confusion and from the concessions that idealism had made to genteelness. Liberation meant honesty, and honesty meant that the major issues of American life could no longer be ignored. The movement had its superficial aspects, as Anderson learned; at times it seemed to be dominated by superficiality, but its core was a determination to right old wrongs at the same time that it established a new and honest American literary tradition.

Before Anderson joined the Chicago group he had been primarily a propagandist focusing on issues rather than people. His reaction to materialism was instinctive and direct, so that the early novels, *Windy McPherson's Son* and *Marching Men,* are based in protest and rejection while they are expressed in the formidable diction and style of late nineteenth century popular literature. But the literary movement of which the Chicago group was a part taught him that what he was doing was not literature, and it pointed out his new direction.

In the context of the new literary tradition of protest and rejection, Anderson's relationship to his major literary contemporaries is evident in both his attitudes and his techniques. Although he often gave credit to Gertrude Stein for having made him aware of the potential inherent in words and style, nevertheless his affinity to others is much closer. He moved out of Miss Stein's orbit of experimentation after the initial impetus and into a circle that was largely midwestern, so much so that in its view of its birthplace it has been called Russian by D. H. Lawrence.

The two major midwestern novelists with whom Anderson can be compared are Theodore Dreiser and Sinclair Lewis, while among the poets his closest relationship is with Vachel Lindsay and Edgar Lee Masters. Anderson has much in common with all of them, although at the same time there are major differences. Like Dreiser and Lewis, Anderson protested against an environment that made people less than human, and he was aware of this kinship, especially with Dreiser, to the end.

The protests of the three, however, took different directions. For Dreiser there was no way out of the deterministic environment in which his people were caught, while for Lewis there was no need to wrestle with the imponderables as long as one could expose and at the same time secretly understand and sympathize with a society devoted to externals. Anderson could not accept the naturalistic helplessness of Dreiser's people and his own, even while the evidence overwhelmingly indicated that Dreiser was right. Nor could he be satisfied, as was

Lewis, with the indictment of a system. Instead, he sought in his own way to find permanent answers, even after he accepted the impossibility of finding those answers and had to settle for the meaning inherent in the search and in love and compassion for his people.

In spirit Anderson is closer to the poets, Masters and Lindsay. Not only is the basic structural pattern of Masters' *Spoon River Anthology* close to *Winesburg, Ohio,* but both works penetrate below surface appearance to reveal the essence of repressed humanity, an approach that became Anderson's most effective technique. Masters, however, is protesting against the system in the *Anthology;* in *Winesburg* and his other sub-surface examinations Anderson regrets the shortcomings inherent in human nature that prevent deep understanding.

The relationship between Lindsay and Anderson is closest of all because these two, more than any of the others, sought to go beyond protest and condemnation and find new and enduring values upon which to build a humanized society. Both of them sought a faith that was essentially spiritual and idealistic, although Lindsay was primarily concerned with a faith firmly rooted in conventional Christianity, especially in his early years, while Anderson rejected such values in favor of a secular although no less mystic faith. Both of them moved beyond rejection and rebellion and into a final and positive affirmation.

In moving beyond rebellion Anderson became most clearly an idealist and a romantic. He believed firmly that somewhere a life based upon compassion, love, and understanding could be found, and he sought it in the past and in the towns, where man could live communally and close to nature at the same time, finding strength and mutual fulfillment in the process of living.

This is the Sherwood Anderson who is little known and usually misunderstood, and this is the Anderson who did much misunderstanding himself. He was a seeker once he realized that there were no easy answers and put propaganda behind him. In his search for the almost-perfect world (he rejected perfection because it is no longer human) he fused his work and his life, and in so doing moved across both literary and ideological lines so freely that he confused both his contemporaries and himself. Although he considered himself a "modern," he looked back in spirit to a romanticism that freed the individual from his environmental confines. As an artist he attempted to be advanced and experimental, but his most effective style grew out of an old oral tradition.

The confusion and misunderstanding inherent in these contradictions affected both Anderson and his contemporaries to the extent that the idealistic and romantic nature of his work passed almost unnoticed during his lifetime. Instead he was called a realist, a naturalist, a modern, a Freudian, and a Marxist, all of which he was not. To a great extent he must have accepted the titles because he did little or nothing to deny them, and the title of realist that he often applied to himself implies a close adherence to surface phenomena that is merely the point of departure for most of his work.

This misunderstanding has continued to the present. Generally Anderson is still grouped loosely to naturalism and occasionally to the post-World War I decadents, especially Ezra Pound and T. S. Eliot. Anderson's links to these groups, however, are tenuous at best. Not only did he go well beyond naturalism in his search for answers to problems that he saw as essentially spiritual rather than deterministic, but from the beginning of his literary career he rejected the decadence that eventually drove Eliot into the dogmatism of the past in religion and politics as well as literature and Pound into incomprehensibility and authoritarianism. The answers that Anderson sought were no less individual than mystic, and they resolved themselves into a compassion for people rather than for theories or systems of any kind.

On the other hand, Anderson's affinities to D. H. Lawrence and Ernest Hemingway are quite close. Like Lawrence, with whom Anderson identified himself in the twenties, Anderson was concerned with breaking down the artificial barriers isolating men so that mature and lasting love might become possible, and again, like Lawrence, Anderson did not hesitate to use physical love as the outward manifestation of a deeper spiritual love. In spite of Anderson's reputation as a daring and shocking writer, however, he could never bring himself to treat the physical aspects of love with Lawrence's frankness.

The relationship between Anderson and Hemingway is even closer. Not only did Anderson's literary style inspire Hemingway's and through Hemingway an entire generation of American writers, but also the thematic ties between them are quite close. Essentially both of them are idealistic romantics whose people, hurt spiritually by a hostile world, have embarked on a search for meaning in spite of the fact that apparently there is none. Eventually both of them point out in their works that the end of the search is not important; that what matters is the way in which the search is carried out. This is the position that Anderson approaches as early as *Horses and Men,* while Hemingway arrives there much later in *For Whom the Bell Tolls*. For each it comes after a period of flirtation with despair.

After Anderson's idealism had rid itself of anger and indignation when he began his search for permanent values through his association with the Chicago Renaissance, his search for the values that he could adopt and affirm led him to focus on people, on the individual human lives that make up the generality "America" that had been celebrated by others such as Carl Sandburg. In so doing Anderson found himself in the difficult position of trying to find abstract principles through examinations of individual human lives. That he was never able to find those principles not only emphasizes the difficulty of the task, but more importantly, it provides the most enduring of his works—those in which he penetrates for a brief but revealing moment into the heart of another human being.

The durable qualities of Anderson's work lie in the closeness and persistence with which he came to grips with his purpose, and they lie in the subject matter, the techniques, and the spirit that he combined to give form to his theme. The experience he chose for treatment in his work is the record of America as it moved from idealistic youth into cynical and selfish maturity. The loss of innocence concurrent with the rise of industrialism has had no more effective and conscientious chronicler. Furthermore, the people with whom he is always concerned are people still possessed of that innocence who find themselves lost in a society that no longer values either it or them, and Anderson's portrayals are honest, compassionate, and effective as he brings them alive.

The durability of the style that Anderson made his own in *Winesburg, Ohio* and gave freely to the mainstream of American literature is unquestioned. As long as the American idioms are spoken in the easy rhythms radiating out from the midwestern heartland, Anderson's style will be recognized, understood, and appreciated by the people who gave rise to it, no matter what the current critical preference may be. In style more than anywhere else Anderson has come closer to reproducing and interpreting a vital part of the American experience.

The spirit of Anderson's work is the spirit of life, and this, too, will endure. The wonder of human life, a compassionate regard for it, and a compelling sense of discovering significance in the commonplace permeate his works, giving rise to a lyric beauty even in despair. Love, compassion, sympathy, and understanding are the human virtues that raise man above his animal origins and prevent him from being a machine, as Anderson points out at the same time that he shows his acceptance of the concept in his work. Life is not only the great adventure for Anderson; in the final analysis it is the universal value.

In an age that denies the values Anderson believed in even more emphatically than did his own, Anderson's place among the journalists and the sensationalists is small, and his shortcomings as a literary artist will undoubtedly prevent much enlargement of that place in the over-all range of literary history. But as a man who approached life with reverence, who spoke of it with love, and who provided some of the most eloquent expressions of both in his time, his place remains secure.

A CHRONOLOGY OF
SHERWOOD ANDERSON'S LIFE

1876   September 13, Sherwood, third child of Emma Smith Anderson and Irwin Anderson, born in Camden, Ohio.

1884   Anderson family moved to Clyde, Ohio. Father worked in Ervin Brothers' harness shop. Sherwood irregularly attended public school and earned nickname "Jobby" working about town.

1895   Emma Anderson died.

1896   Sherwood worked in Chicago as unskilled laborer in cold-storage warehouse.

1898   April, entered U.S. Army. Stationed briefly in Cuba at close of Spanish-American War.

1899   September, entered Wittenberg Academy, Springfield, Ohio, for last year of formal education.

1900   Worked again in Chicago, this time as writer of advertising copy for Long-Critchfield Company.

1904   Contributed columns to *Agricultural Advertising*. May 16, married Cornelia Lane of Toledo, Ohio.

1906   Fall, became president of United Factories Company in Cleveland, Ohio, a mail-order outlet.

1907   Fall, moved with wife and child to Elyria, Ohio. Headed own company, Anderson Manufacturing Company, to distribute paint.

1912   November 27, suffered nervous breakdown and left company—source of famous legend of rejection of business career.

1913   Returned to Chicago and worked in Taylor-Critchfield Company writing advertising copy.

1914   Associated with leaders of Chicago Renaissance and began publishing in "little magazines."

1915   Wrote parts of *Winesburg, Ohio* and *Mid-American Chants*.

1916   Divorced from Cornelia Lane Anderson and married to Tennessee Mitchell. The John Lane Company published first novel, *Windy McPherson's Son*.

1917   Published second novel, *Marching Men*, and some Winesburg stories.

1918   Lived in New York. Wrote publicity for movie company. Published *Mid-American Chants*, volume of poetry.

1919   Broke with John Lane Company. *Winesburg, Ohio* published by B. W. Huebsch.

1920   Wrote *Poor White* in Alabama.

1921   On first European trip met James Joyce and Gertrude Stein; both influenced his writing. Won first *Dial* award for *The Triumph of the Egg*.

1922   Lived in New Orleans and met William Faulkner. Gave up advertising business and moved to New York.

1923   Published fourth novel, *Many Marriages*, and short stories, *Horses and Men*. Moved to Reno, Nevada, to divorce second wife.

1924   Married Elizabeth Prall. Moved to New Orleans. Published *A Story Teller's Story*, first memoir.

1925   *Dark Laughter*, published by Horace Liveright, a best seller. Bought farm near Troutdale, Virginia.

1926   *Tar*, second memoir, and *Sherwood Anderson's Notebook*. Built country home in Virginia. Began second European tour.

1927   *A New Testament*, prose poems. Bought *Marion Democrat* and *Smyth County News*, county newspapers in Marion, Virginia, which he wrote, edited, and published for two years.

1929   Third marriage broke up. In resulting depression gave newspapers to son Robert, from first marriage. *Hello Towns!*, collected from Marion papers.

1930   Became interested in labor movement through acquaintance with Eleanor Copenhaver of Marion, Virginia.

1931   Traveled to many factories in the South. Committed to cause of proletariat. *Perhaps Women*.

1932   Divorced from Elizabeth Prall Anderson. Attended large communist conference in Europe. *Beyond Desire*, a prolabor novel.

1933   Married Eleanor Copenhaver. Traveled widely in United States. *Death in the Woods,* final collection of short stories.

1935   *Puzzled America,* essays on United States in Great Depression, published by Scribner's after break with Horace Liveright.

1936   *Kit Brandon,* novel of mountain woman's life based on writer's experience with his country newspapers in the late 1920's.

1937   Elected to membership in National Institute of Arts and Letters. Published dramatic versions of *Winesburg, Ohio* and other stories.

1940   *Home Town,* commentary on the passing of small-town America.

1941   March 8, died of peritonitis while on good-will mission to South America, in Panama Canal Zone.

A SELECTED
BIBLIOGRAPHY

BOOKS BY SHERWOOD ANDERSON: 1876–1941

Windy McPherson's Son. New York: John Lane Company, 1916; New
   York: B. W. Huebsch, 1922 (revised).
Marching Men. New York: John Lane Company, 1917.
Mid-American Chants. New York: John Lane Company, 1918.
Winesburg, Ohio. New York: B. W. Huebsch, 1919; New York:
   Modern Library [1919]; New York: New American Library, 1956;
   New York: The Viking Press, 1958.
Poor White. New York: B. W. Huebsch, Inc., 1920.
The Triumph of the Egg. New York: B. W. Huebsch, Inc., 1921.
Horses and Men. New York: B. W. Huebsch, Inc., 1923.
Many Marriages. New York: B. W. Huebsch, Inc., 1923.
A Story Teller's Story. New York: B. W. Huebsch, Inc., 1924; New
   York: Grove Press, 1958.
Dark Laughter. New York: Boni and Liveright, 1925.
The Modern Writer. San Francisco: The Lantern Press, 1925.
Sherwood Anderson's Notebook. New York: Boni and Liveright, 1926.
Tar: A Midwest Childhood. New York: Boni and Liveright, 1926.
A New Testament. New York: Boni and Liveright, 1926.
Alice and the Lost Novel. London: Elkin Mathews and Marrot, 1929.
Hello Towns! New York: Horace Liveright, 1929.
Nearer the Grass Roots. San Francisco: The Westgate Press, 1929.
The American County Fair. New York: Random House, 1930.
Perhaps Women. New York: Horace Liveright, 1931.
Beyond Desire. New York: Liveright, Inc., 1932.

Death in the Woods. New York: Liveright, Inc., Publishers, 1933.

No Swank. Philadelphia: The Centaur Press, 1934.

Puzzled America. New York: Charles Scribner's Sons, 1935.

Kit Brandon. New York: Charles Scribner's Sons, 1936.

Plays, Winesburg and Others. New York: Charles Scribner's Sons, 1937.

A Writer's Conception of Realism. Olivet, Michigan: Olivet College, 1939.

Home Town. New York: Alliance Book Corporation, 1940.

Sherwood Anderson's Memoirs. New York: Harcourt, Brace and Company, 1942.

The Sherwood Anderson Reader, edited by Paul Rosenfeld. New York: Houghton Mifflin Company, 1947.

The Portable Sherwood Anderson, edited by Horace Gregory. New York: The Viking Press, 1949.

Letters of Sherwood Anderson, edited by Howard Mumford Jones and Walter B. Rideout. Boston: Little, Brown and Company, 1953.

Sherwood Anderson: Short Stories, edited by Maxwell Geismar. New York: Hill and Wang, 1962.

WORKS ABOUT SHERWOOD ANDERSON

Burbank, Rex. *Sherwood Anderson.* New York: Twayne Publishers, Inc., 1964.

Chase, Cleveland B. *Sherwood Anderson.* New York: R. M. McBride, 1927.

Fagin, Nathan Bryllion. *The Phenomenon of Sherwood Anderson; A Study in American Life and Letters.* Baltimore: Rossi-Bryn, 1927.

Howe, Irving. *Sherwood Anderson.* New York: W. Sloan, 1951.

The Newberry Library Bulletin, 2d Ser., No. 2 (December, 1948). The Sherwood Anderson Memorial Number.

Phillips, William Louis. "Sherwood Anderson's *Winesburg, Ohio:* Its Origins, Composition, Technique, and Reception." Unpublished Ph.D. dissertation, University of Chicago, 1950.

Shenandoah, XIII (Spring, 1962). The Sherwood Anderson Issue.

Schevill, James. *Sherwood Anderson: His Life and Work.* Denver: The University of Denver Press, 1951.

Sheehy, Eugene P., and Kenneth A. Lohf. *Sherwood Anderson: A Bibliography.* Los Gatos, California: The Talisman Press, 1960.

Story, XXIX (September–October, 1941). The Sherwood Anderson Memorial Number.

Sutton, William Alfred. "Sherwood Anderson's Formative Years (1876–1913)." Unpublished Ph.D. dissertation, Ohio State University, 1943.

Weber, Brom. *Sherwood Anderson*. Minneapolis: University of Minnesota Press, 1964.

INDEX

To prevent this index from becoming too unwieldy to be easily useful, the entries refer only to subjects mentioned by name and only to subjects which the reader of Sherwood Anderson might conceivably need to locate immediately.

[265]